The Greatest ted

940.5421
W4317g

Weingartner, Steven
The Greatest thing we have ever attempted

DATE DUE

B.J. Harrison Library
Marshalltown Community College
Iowa Valley
Community College District
Marshalltown, Iowa 50158

Cantigny Military History Series

Cantigny at Seventy-Five
A Professional Discussion
May 28-29, 1993

No Mission Too Difficult
Old Buddies of the 1st Infantry Division
Tell All About World War II
By Blythe Foote Finke

Blue Spaders
The 26th Infantry Regiment, 1917-1967

A Weekend With the Great War
Proceedings of the Fourth Annual Great War
Interconference Seminar
6-18 September 1995

The Greatest Thing We Have Ever Attempted
Historical Perspectives on the Normandy Campaign

Donated By
Dr. Thomas B. Colbert

Cantigny Military History Series

The Greatest Thing We Have Ever Attempted

HISTORICAL PERSPECTIVES ON THE NORMANDY CAMPAIGN

IVCCD Libraries
MCC B. J. Harrison Library
Marshalltown, Iowa 50158

Contributors:

Stephen E. Ambrose, Joseph M. Balkoski, Clay D. Blair, Martin Blumenson, Vitalii N. Bogdanov, Klaus-Richard Böhme, Thomas B. Buell, D'Ann Campbell, James L. Collins, John A. English, John B. Hattendorf, John W. Huston, Bruce Menning, Geoffrey Perrett, Werner Rahn, Andy Rooney, H. P. Willmott

Proceedings of the conference on "Normandy"
2-3 March 1994

Sponsored by the Cantigny First Division Foundation and the U.S. Naval Institute

Hosted by the Cantigny First Division Foundation and the Robert R. McCormick Tribune Foundation

Edited by Steven Weingartner
Published by the Cantigny First Division Foundation

©1998 by the Cantigny First Division Foundation
All rights reserved
Printed in the United States of America
First Edition

ISBN: 1-890093-06-8
Library of Congress Catalog Card Number: 97-66872

Published by the
Cantigny First Division Foundation
151 S. Winfield Road
Wheaton, IL 60187
708/668-5185

"Eisenhower: Command, Coalition, and Normandy" by Stephen E. Ambrose first appeared in a slightly different version as "Normandy: Why and How" in 1994 May/June issue of *Naval History*. Reprinted from *Naval History* with permission; Copyright © (1994) U.S. Naval Institute.

"Never that Young Again" by Andy Rooney first appeared in the 1994 June issue of *Proceedings*. Reprinted from *Proceedings* with permission; Copyright © (1994) U.S. Naval Institute.

Portions of "The Meaning of D-Day" by Stephen E. Ambrose reprinted with the permission of Simon & Schuster from *D-Day* by Stephen E. Ambrose. Copyright © 1994 by Ambrose-Tubbs, Inc.

"Failure at Falaise" by Martin Blumenson: text and adapted text of pp. 261-273 from *The Battle of the Generals* by Martin Blumenson. Copyright © 1993 by Martin Blumenson. By permission of William Morrow and Co., Inc.

Maps appearing in "Stalin's Response to Overlord: The Belorussian Operation" by Bruce Menning are reprinted with permission from *The West Point Atlas of American Wars*, published by Henry Holt.

Maps used in "The Admirals" by John B. Hattendorf were produced by the Graphics Arts Division of the United States Naval War College.

Views and opinions of the authors are theirs alone. The Robert R. McCormick Tribune Foundation, Cantigny Foundation, and Cantigny First Division Foundation, and their respective directors and officers, disclaim responsibility for statements, of fact or opinion, made by the contributors.

DEDICATED TO:

Captain Joseph T. Dawson
Commander, Company G, 16th Infantry Regiment
1st Infantry Division

His courage and leadership on D-Day, 6 June 1944,

helped to make the Normandy invasion a success

The Greatest Thing We Have Ever Attempted
HISTORICAL PERSPECTIVES ON THE NORMANDY CAMPAIGN

Table of Contents

List of Illustrations, Maps, and Charts .... *pages x-ix*

Foreword
John F. Votaw .... *page 1*

Editor's Preface .... *page 3*

Kickoff Address: Eisenhower: Command, Coalition, and Normandy
                              Stephen E. Ambrose .... *page 5*

Discussion .... *page 13*

Panel 1
Forging the Weapon: Developing the Allied War Machine
                              Moderator: Alan Gropman .... *page 19*

Introduction .... *page 21*

                       Preparing For Overlord: A Battalion Commander's Perspective
                       James L. Collins .... *page 25*

                       Fleet Admiral King and Overlord
                       Thomas B. Buell .... *page 27*

                       Men and Matériel
                       Geoffrey Perret .... *page 31*

Discussion .... *page 37*

Luncheon Address The Road to the Second Front: The Diplomacy of the Invasion
H. P. Willmott . . . . *page 49*

Discussion . . . . *page 59*

Panel 2
Through the Bocage: The Normandy Campaign to the Closing of the Falaise Gap
Moderator: Steve E. Dietrich . . . . *page 63*

Introduction . . . . *page 65*

A National Guard Division in World War II:
Some Thoughts On Military Preparedness
Joseph M. Balkoski . . . . *page 69*

Canada's Contribution and Place in the Allied Order of Battle
John A. English . . . . *page 73*

Failure at Falaise
Martin Blumenson . . . . *page 79*

Discussion . . . . *page 85*

Panel 3
Faces of Command: Evaluating the Generals and Admirals
Moderator: Paul Stillwell . . . . *page 95*

Introduction . . . . *page 97*

Let Us Not Forget Omar Bradley
Clay D. Blair . . . . *page 101*

The Admirals
John B. Hattendorf . . . . *page 107*

Air Leadership and Overlord
John W. Huston . . . . *page 113*

Discussion . . . . *page 119*

Panel 4
International Perspectives: Did Normandy Matter?
Moderator: Kenneth Hagan . . . . *page 125*

Introduction . . . . *page 127*

        Swedish Prognoses Concerning the Outcome of the Second World War
        Klaus-Richard Böhme . . . . *page 131*

        Stalin's Response to Overlord: The Belorussian Operation
        Bruce Menning . . . . *page 137*

        The Impact of the Second Front on German Strategy, 1944
        Werner Rahn . . . . *page 141*

        The Second Front: A Russian Perspective
        Vitalii N. Bogdanov . . . . *page 145*

Discussion . . . . *page 147*

Luncheon Address   Never that Young Again
        Andy Rooney . . . . *page 155*

Discussion . . . . *page 161*

Panel 5
Normandy as History: Have We Learned the Right Lessons?
        Moderator: John W. Mountcastle . . . . *page 163*

Introduction . . . . *page 165*

        The Meaning of D-Day
        Stephen E. Ambrose . . . . *page 169*

        Hilt of the Sword
        D'Ann Campbell . . . . *page 173*

        The Lessons to be Learned: Perspectives and Reflections
        H. P. Willmott . . . . *page 177*

Discussion . . . . *page 185*

Appendix: Chronology of Events . . . . *page 195*

Contributors . . . . *page 205*

Conference Sponsors . . . . *page 209*

Index . . . . *page 211*

List of Illustrations *(Plates 1-14)*

1 Casablanca Conference

2 Eisenhower and Montgomery

3 Bradley

4 King (U.S. Fleet Admiral Ernest J.)

5 King (Candanian Prime Minister Mackenzie) and McNaughton

6 Matériel

7 Rehearsing for Overlord

8 Sergeant in 29th "Blue and Gray" Division

9 Ninth Air Force B-26 bombers

10 Kirk and Bradley

11 U.S. destroyer at Omaha Beach

12 Canadian 9th Infantry Brigade

13 American infantrymen landing on Omaha Beach

14 Bocage country

15 British troops in Caen

16 Canadian 5.5-inch guns

17 M4 Sherman with "tusks"

18 Simonds

19 Tanks of Polish 24th Uhlan Regiment

20 Wreckage of German column

21 German prisoners

22 Soviet infantrymen

23 Casemated gun

24 Swedish frontier patrol

25 "WACs" change tire

Maps & Charts

Chart 1   Naval Command for Operation Neptune 6 June 1944
page 106

Chart 2   Operation Neptune: convoy routes and naval forces
page 109

Chart 3   Operation Neptune: the naval bombardment
page 111

Map 1   Russian summer offensive, 23 June-7 August 1944
page 139

Map 2   Russian summer offensive, 8 August-14 September 1944
page 140

The Greatest Thing We Have Ever Attempted

Foreword

At the start of 1944, the Allies had reason to believe that the defeat of Germany, until fairly recently a doubtful proposition, was now inevitable. But by no means imminent: with the Germans still in control of Western Europe and most of European Russia, it was clear to even the most optimistic observers in the Allied camp that much hard fighting remained before the stated objective of unconditional surrender could be forced upon the enemy. The strategic situation at the beginning of the year practically dictated the Allies' course of action: while the Soviets mounted continual offensives to roll back German gains in the East, the Allies would open the so-called Second Front in Northwest Europe. The fact that there already existed a second front in Italy mattered less than the strenuous and brutal nature of the Italian campaign would indicate: Allied planners recognized that a decision must be reached in the heart of the Continent, first in France and then in Germany itself, or it would not be reached at all.

Thus the stage was set for Operation Overlord. Of course, the Germans no less than the Allies could see where the war was taking them. All the signs pointed north; the writing, as it were, was on the Atlantic Wall, which was duly fortified against the expected invasion. But for all the Germans' preparations, the Allies punched through the barrier within hours, establishing a presence on the Continent that would eventually grow—if at first slowly and at a tremendous cost in lives and equipment—to encompass all of France and Belgium. By early autumn the Allies were pounding on the gates to Germany, serving notice to the Nazi regime that its days were numbered. Not that the Germans needed any reminding on this score: they had already received several such messages from the Soviets, each more emphatic than the one before. The Soviets dubbed 1944 "The Year of Ten Victories," and so it was by their reckoning, beginning with the relief of Leningrad in January, culminating in the great Belorussian operation in July, and concluding with the capture of Petsamo in October. Yet though the battles of 1944, in the East and the West, would seal Germany's fate, final victory would elude the Allies. The war would rage on for more than five months, through the first week of May 1945, before the conflict came to an apocalyptic end in the streets of Berlin.

More than fifty years after they occurred, the momentous events of June 1944 still pose challenges to scholars who would analyze and interpret their impact on the war and world affairs. Our knowledge of that distant time, though vast, is far from complete: accordingly, our understanding of what happened—and, just as significant, what did not happen and why—is also incomplete. It is fortunate that this is the case, otherwise the Normandy conference would have been a dull affair. But it was anything but dull, as this volume demonstrates.

The Normandy conference was held 2-3 March 1994 at the First Division Museum, which is located in Wheaton, Illinois, on the grounds of Cantigny—the estate of the late Colonel Robert R. McCormick, himself a First World War-veteran of the 1st Division. Jointly sponsored by the Cantigny First Division Foundation and the U.S. Naval Institute, it was attended by a diverse group of military historians, academics, and interested individuals from the United States, Canada, Great Britain, Germany, Sweden, and Russia. The conference consisted of five panels whose members presented papers on topics relevant to the established theme of each panel. Also featured were luncheon addresses on succeeding days by, respectively, British historian H. P. Willmott and noted journalist and *60 Minutes* commentator Andy Rooney.

The presentations by panel members were followed by discussions in which the floor was opened to questions and comments from the audience. Edited transcripts of the discussions are included herein. Readers are reminded that in such discussions, what is said in the heat of the moment is not necessarily to be taken as a statement of ultimate belief or immovable position, but rather as an open and uninhibited exploration of the ideas and themes which the conference sought to address. As readers shall see, the opportunity afforded by these sessions to thrash out the issues at hand resulted not only in a number of spirited exchanges but also a worthy contribution to the historiography of the Second World War.

This book of the conference proceedings constitutes the latest addition to the Cantigny Military History Series. The Cantigny First Division Foundation gratefully acknowledges the efforts of all involved, particularly the U.S. Naval Institute and its staff, for its efforts in helping to organize and present the conference. Our thanks as well go to the those who contributed papers to the conference and the attendees whose interest and active participation did so much to make the conference a success.

John F. Votaw
General Editor, Cantigny Military History Series
Executive Director, First Division Museum at Cantigny, Summer 1998

Editor's Preface

Several of the essays in this volume were originally crafted as formal papers with notes included or appended later. Some were derived from the tape transcripts of presentations, without notes; still others represent a combination of the two: pre-written essays interwoven with edited comments from the oral presentations.

Highlights of the panel discussions were edited for clarity and content. In most instances those participating in the discussions, panelists as well as conference attendees, prefaced their remarks by identifying themselves. However, the frequently fast-paced and free-wheeling nature of the discussions sometimes led to lapses in this regard. A review of the session tape recordings usually enabled the unnamed speaker to be identified, but where identification remained elusive the speaker in question is identified in the text as "Conference Participant."

Steven Weingartner
Editor

Kickoff Address

EISENHOWER:
Command, Coalition, and Normandy

Stephen E. Ambrose

The Greatest Thing We Have Ever Attempted

It would be an exaggeration to say the invasion of France could not have happened without Dwight D. Eisenhower, but not much of one. It was Eisenhower who decided that a cross-Channel invasion of the Continent was necessary; in fact, he was committed to such an undertaking at least as early as February 1942, when he was at the War Department: "We've got to go to Europe and fight" he noted in a journal entry at the time. That same month found him discussing the procurement of landing craft and engaging in fierce arguments with the navy's chief of naval operations, Admiral Ernest J. King, over navy priorities for an invasion. He picked the site of the landings, and when he assumed his duties as commander of the Allied Expeditionary Force in January 1944, he immediately insisted on broadening the invasion to a five-division assault front. In the buildup phase he directed the training. He was the funnel through which everything—information, orders, decisions—had to pass. He personally selected the leaders of the American units going ashore on D-Day. He was responsible for the Transportation Plan being adopted over a great deal of protest, a major effort on his part that was the occasion for his voicing a unique threat: either he got command of the Allied air forces or he was going to resign as commander in chief and go home.

Just before the invasion, Eisenhower was sleeping only four hours every night; the rest of the time found him either on the road or working in a conference. He never ate in restaurants and subsisted mostly on coffee, sandwiches, and four packs per day of unfiltered Camel cigarettes. He was often out in the field. When I talk to D-Day veterans, I always ask, "Did you see Eisenhower before D-Day?" Most say yes. He wanted to make sure that as many men as possible who went ashore on D-Day had a chance to at least look at the CO. So he spent a lot of time in the field visiting divisions and various attached units, and a lot of time watching training exercises.

Eisenhower's contributions to Overlord cannot be overstated; he was as intimately involved with it as any human being, more than any other leader.

*

Why was Eisenhower selected to be supreme commander of the Allied Expeditionary Force? There was a negative reason that is well known. President Franklin D. Roosevelt stated the case succinctly in the autumn of 1943 when he told General George C. Marshall, the chairman of the Joint Chiefs of Staff and the man many expected would be appointed to command Overlord, that he couldn't sleep with Marshall out of the country. Had Marshall told Roosevelt that his heart was set on commanding Overlord, that he regarded such command as the culmination of his entire career, who knows how the president would have responded? But the fact is, Marshall never made that request.

But if not Marshall, who? The American Joint Chiefs, whose decision it was to make, had not the slightest intention of bringing Douglas MacArthur from the Pacific to Europe to command Overlord. Nor could they could give command to a British general—not even to Field Marshal Bernard Law Montgomery, much less Field Marshals Harold Alexander and Alan Brooke. So Eisenhower apparently got command of Overlord by default.

But there were several positive reasons for selecting Eisenhower. He had by this time led three successful amphibious assaults: North Africa in November 1942, Sicily in July 1943, Salerno in September 1943. These operations were complex undertakings in which the British and Americans had their own air, naval, and army components; in effect, Eisenhower had had six different commands working under him. In each instance he had demonstrated a remarkable ability to get along with the British.

I've always thought this would have been Marshall's great weakness. Marshall didn't suffer fools gladly, and he would have had an awful time with Montgomery. For that reason if for no other, Eisenhower was the right man for the job of supreme commander of Overlord.

Why were Montgomery and Lieutenant General Omar N. Bradley selected for command of, respectively, British and American forces rather than Alexander and Lieutenant General George S. Patton? As far as the British were concerned, command had to go to Montgomery. Among the top people, Alexander had a reputation for letting Montgomery push him around; he was perceived to have a certain softness and lack of drive. This was the negative reason for selecting Montgomery; the positive reason did not have a whole lot to do with his military abilities, such as they were. The way Montgomery fought the Sicilian campaign and his agonizingly slow progress up the toe of Italy had raised doubts in the minds of many people—and most Americans—about his generalship. But as a result of his victory at El Alamein, the British press and people had built him into the greatest British soldier since Wellington. So the Allies were more or less compelled to give Montgomery command.

Why was Bradley chosen over Patton? The slapping incidents in Sicily were a major reason. But there was a lot more to it than Patton with his big mouth and his too-ready fist. Eisenhower trusted Bradley over Patton. He counted on Bradley to be sensible with the press and to get along with the British; but more than that, he had greater faith in Bradley's military sense. I believe Eisenhower was disturbed by Patton's drive on Palermo. This episode may have seemed to Eisenhower a calculated move by Patton to grab headlines—which it did, but at the expense of an early decisive victory. Moreover, Eisenhower may have felt that Patton was not able to handle the kind of detailed, meticulous planning that had to go into the assault phase of Overlord, and that Patton's personality much better fit the role he ended up playing: exploiting the Allied breakthrough and going for the enemy's jugular. So Eisenhower jumped Bradley over Patton and gave him the choice assignment, even though Bradley was Patton's junior in both age and rank. (Here I must emphasize that all this is purely speculation on my part; Eisenhower never once expressed such views to me either in writing or in conversation.)

Overlord's staff operated on the basic principle of mixing officers from Britain and the United States. If the head of a department or a section was British, then an American would be his deputy, and vice versa all the way down the line. The British and the Americans learned to get along and work well together. Eisenhower insisted that they do so and that they be friends. This was typical of Ike from the time he was a boy in Abilene until the end of his life. It sounds corny, but we all know that with AEFHQ and SHAEF—as with the Eisenhower administration in the White House—this method worked

*

Why Normandy? The major reason for invading there was to achieve surprise. Without surprise there would be no successful invasion. Had the Germans known in advance where and when this battle was going to be fought, there is no question whatsoever that they could have hurled the invaders back into the sea. Had the Germans been able to penetrate the secret of Overlord, the Allies would have to wait until the summer of 1945 to defeat the Germans, and they would have done so not with the Allied Expeditionary Force but with atomic bombs.

To ask the question another way, why did Eisenhower go south when his objective lay to the east? The straight line to the objective—Germany's industrial heartland—ran over Calais through Belgium to the Rhine-Ruhr region, Düsseldorf, Bonn, and Cologne. But instead of crossing the narrowest part of the Channel and then going in an easterly direction over the shortest distance, he picked the widest part of the Channel and went south. He knew that a landing in Normandy would put the major river barriers of the Seine and Somme between the Allies and Germany. But by going south he not only achieved surprise on D-Day, he also kept the German panzers pinned down in the Pas de Calais through June and July waiting for the "real" attack to come. They were still there in September. If it hadn't been for Operation Market-Garden in September, they'd likely be there still.

This was a fabulously successful deception, and the contributions to it came from many quarters, including, but by no means limited to, the British secret services and the American OSS. This story is well known and I won't belabor it here except to point out that the operation could not have worked in reverse; that is, the Allies could not have mounted a dummy operation toward the Calvados Coast that would keep the panzers waiting there while the actual landings took place at Calais. The minute the major Allied force landed east of the mouth of the Seine the Germans planned to pull all their forces then positioned south and west of that river and move them between the Allies and the Rhine-Ruhr region. So the surprise of the Normandy landings constituted a great triumph for the Allies in general and for their intelligence operations in particular.

The great failure on the part of the Allied intelligence community was that it did not anticipate the problems of fighting on the offensive in the hedgerow country. The springtime flooding of the fields behind the Merderet River should have served as a warning of the difficulties in store, had the Allies but known about it. Amazingly, they did not. This, despite the fact that the Normandy countryside was a favorite destination of British tourists before the war. Unfortunately it wasn't the countryside that interested British military leaders when, in 1940, they put out a request to former holiday-goers to France for photographs of the French *coast*. The military received some thirty thousand snapshots in the first week and three million overall. Through the use of these images every single house along the French coast was pinpointed. In the whole of human history this surely represents the most information ever gathered about a specific military objective. Yet the information was limited to the coastal strip. The Allies didn't have any idea what the country was like just two kilometers inland.

I've heard so many American veterans who fought in the hedgerow country say in so many words: "God almighty, yes, we knew there were hedgerows there. We thought they were like English hedgerows the fox hunters jump over. We had no idea there were sunken roads between these hedgerows, that the Germans had this maze of a trench system ready-built for them." Glider pilots have told me they had no idea how high those hedgerows were. They didn't realize they were going to have to stay above them before coming into those little fields around Ste. Mère-Eglise and that they would be running into the hedgerow at the other end. They had no idea that there was this bank of earth that was just going to crush the glider when it hit the hedgerow. Nobody had briefed them on this.

Their ignorance is a mark of how narrow was the focus for the invasion. The Allies were concerned only with the problem of getting ashore because there weren't going to be any problems afterward if they failed to establish a beachhead. But as a result they weren't prepared for the problems they encountered once they got ashore; they hadn't studied the hedgerow country or worked out techniques for fighting in that difficult terrain, and they hadn't been briefed about how the Germans might use it.

One reason that no one studied the hedgerows was that Montgomery promised to take Caen on the first day of the invasion. The capture of Caen would have allowed the Allies to use the city as the base for an attack toward Paris, thus shifting the weight of the Allied offensive to the left and, in doing so, precluding a fight for the hedgerows. While British forces, supported by aircraft operating from airfields around Carpiquet, drove on Paris, the Americans would no doubt have advanced swiftly and without too much effort through the hedgerow country to seal off the Cotentin Peninsula and take Cherbourg.

*

What did Montgomery promise with respect to Caen? At the St. Paul's briefing on May 15, he said he was going to take Caen on the first day. Now, no matter how our British friends twist and turn on this subject, that's what Monty said was going to happen and that's what he intended to do. He even talked about getting to Falaise on the first day. He more or less said, "We're going to knock around and we're going to take advantage of these Germans, who are going to be stunned by what we've done. They're not going to be able to move reinforcements into the battle area. There is no depth to the Atlantic Wall and once we get through it, we're going to drive and drive and drive. And we'll have Caen on the first day and we'll be in Paris soon after that."

As the world now knows, that is not what happened. Instead the Americans broke out on the right after all of that terrible hedgerow fighting. What was so intolerable about Montgomery was his claim afterward that he had planned it that way. He said it had been his plan from the very beginning to hold on the left and break out on the right. And when the Americans disputed his claim, he countered by saying something like, "I can't help it if you Americans are too dumb to understand what I told you." Well, he was a liar.

Nevertheless, one could say that Montgomery's plan for the invasion worked—except that it really never was his plan. Force of circumstance and not Montgomery determined its ultimate character. That brings to mind a favorite saying of Eisenhower's: "In war, before the battle is joined, plans are everything. The minute the shooting starts, plans are worthless." That was absolutely the case on D-Day. The 4th Division, for instance, landed a full kilometer south of where it was supposed to be. The troops on Omaha Beach had been told: "Our planes are going to blast holy hell out of those beaches, and when they're finished there won't be a German alive, there won't be a fortification intact. And anything the air force doesn't get, the navy is going to take care of. You guys just get behind those tanks—we're going to have all kinds of American tanks on the beach—you get behind those tanks and you follow them up the ravines. Your problems are only going to start when you get to the top." But in fact their problems started as soon as they jumped out of their landing craft.

The 4th Division came closest of all the assault divisions to achieving its objectives. But neither the 4th Division nor any other Allied unit got as far inland on D-Day as had been planned. One reason was that the concentration in training had been intensely focused on getting ashore and through the Atlantic Wall, up that bluff at Omaha, over the dunes and flooded area of Utah, and past the little resort villages at Gold, Juno, and Sword. But once the men got a short distance inland, they tended to sit down and brew up some tea and congratulate themselves on having won a great victory. And so, at just the moment they should have been pushing the hardest, they were taking a break instead.

This applies more to the British than it does to the Americans. A British infantry company commander, a captain, once told me how his chaps, after getting ashore and moving inland, were marching along the road to Caen when they came upon a field of ripe strawberries. The men all broke ranks and went out into the field to pick the fruit. In the meantime, the farmer who owned the field came out of his house and approached the captain. Watching as his strawberries disappeared in front of his eyes, the farmer shook his head and said, "The

Germans were here four years and they never took one—not one—strawberry."

The delays before Caen and the frustrations of fighting in the hedgerow country combined with the increasing impatience of the Allied high command, governments, press, and peoples of the Allied world to put a tremendous strain on the alliance. There was a growing fear that a stalemate was developing and that the fighting in France was going to be a replay of the Western Front in the First World War. Montgomery was the target of much criticism in this regard. The anti-Montgomery sentiment built up among the Americans, even among those broad-minded individuals who were serving in SHAEF and associated on a daily basis with their British opposite numbers. Before long, many Americans were calling for Montgomery to be relieved of his command.

And it wasn't just the Americans who were demanding that Monty be sacked; a number of British commanders also wanted him removed. Every day toward the end of June, members of the British contingent at SHAEF urged Eisenhower to get rid of him. Eisenhower was the only man capable of standing up to these men, and I think it was one of his greatest contributions to the Allied victory that he resisted them. He understood that you simply had to work with Montgomery; that, whatever the military considerations, the political considerations made it impossible to fire him. And he knew that it was more important to keep the alliance together than to get a more aggressive commander for the British forces in Normandy.

The miracle was that Eisenhower was able to keep Patton and Montgomery fighting on the same side instead of fighting each other. I know of no one else who could have done this. From beginning to end, the name of Dwight D. Eisenhower is forever going to be linked to Operation Overlord, the beginning going way back to 1940 and the end coming at Reims on May 7, 1945. The Supreme Commander was Dwight David Eisenhower the whole way through, and he did a magnificent job.

The Greatest Thing We Have Ever Attempted

Discussion

Scott Belliveau: What about Eisenhower's development as the American "proconsul" in his relations with Churchill and the rest of the British political establishment? That seemed to be a role that grew as the war progressed.

Stephen Ambrose: You said it right. Eisenhower became, as it were, ambassador to Winston Churchill for Franklin Roosevelt. Obviously, there are many political difficulties when two nations are fighting a war together. Several come immediately to mind. First, Churchill was very much opposed to the Transportation Plan because of his fear of inflicting French civilian casualties, which he said would smear the good name of the RAF all over the world. Eisenhower persuaded the British that the plan had to be implemented. Second, Eisenhower wanted to keep visitors out of southern England—not just Slapton Sands, but the whole of southern England. Churchill was much opposed to imposing such a ban on travel and thus interfering so drastically with people's lives. But, again, Eisenhower was able to convince him that it had to be done. Third, Churchill was present when de Gaulle came to Eisenhower on the first day of January 1945 and protested Eisenhower's plan to pull out of Strasbourg to shorten the Allied line. Eisenhower was dealing with de Gaulle and Churchill almost as though he were a head of government. He bowed to de Gaulle's arguments and Churchill supported him, saying "I think you've done the right thing."

Eisenhower's position was always as much about politics as it was about military matters. It was inevitable that this would be the case and would remain so right on through to the end of the war, when there were bitter disagreements over whether or not to make Berlin the objective of the Western Allies' final offensive. So, yes, a great deal of politics went into Eisenhower's job.

James Collins: I don't think Montgomery and Patton were rivals in Normandy. They were operating on different echelons of command and there was no rivalry whatsoever. The rivalry in Normandy was between Montgomery and Bradley. The rivalry between Patton and Montgomery occurred in Sicily, where they stood on the same command echelon, but it was finished by the time Normandy came about. Patton didn't particularly care for Montgomery, Montgomery didn't particularly care for Patton—but I don't think their dislike for each other mattered a single bit in Normandy.

Stephen Ambrose: I'm going to argue with you on that. Patton wasn't in Normandy, he was sitting back in England impatiently waiting to get going. While he was there he certainly had a lot of cutting things to say about Monty. Things flared up again between the two men in December of '44, and their competition became an important element of the whole Allied command story.

James Collins: It seems to me that the Normandy campaign goes up to the end of August, when Patton was involved. We can argue about that, but I want to consider this business of Bradley having been selected as commander of the U.S. First Army for D-Day. One of the most important reasons for Eisenhower's selection of Bradley is that they were classmates and knew each other very well. Now, Patton and Eisenhower had been good friends since 1919. But Patton was senior to Eisenhower, and that must have embarrassed him from time to time.

Stephen Ambrose: Embarrassed who, Patton or Ike?

James Collins: It embarrassed Eisenhower to be dealing with a man so senior to him—Eisenhower was of West Point class of '15, whereas Patton was of the class of '09. But there would be no such problem with Bradley. And consider Bradley's status when he was selected for command in Normandy. He was a rather obscure corps commander in Sicily. Nobody really knew anything about him. He had no experience in amphibious operations. Patton, on the other hand, had engineered two amphibious operations, one in French Morocco and the other in Sicily. He was capable of this meticulous planning you suggested he was not capable of.

Douglas Porch: Steve, can you speculate on the chances for success of an invasion in 1943 and the possible consequences?

Stephen Ambrose: Sure. A couple of years ago I was at a conference similar to this at the University of Texas, except half of the audience were senior scholars from Britain. They could not believe they heard me say that Eisenhower always felt that the 1943 invasion, "Roundup," would have worked. But Eisenhower never backed down from the recommendation he made in the summer of 1942 that the right way to fight was to go across the Channel in the spring of 1943.

The arguments for and against a 1943 invasion are many. In 1943 the Atlantic Wall didn't exist. In 1943 the Germans were fighting a lot deeper in the Soviet Union than they were in 1944 and they had less ability to transfer forces from the Eastern Front to the West. German tank production did not peak until 1944, which meant that German strength in France in 1943 was nothing like what it was going to be in 1944. Of course, one reason for this is that in 1942 we had gone into North Africa and consequently weren't in England building up a threat against the French coast. But we put more men ashore on the first day of the invasion of Sicily than on the first day of the invasion of Normandy, so it's not right to say that we didn't have the landing craft available in 1943 to mount an operation on the scale of Overlord.

On the other hand, the air supremacy that was so critical to success in June 1944 had not been won in 1943. The Luftwaffe had not yet been driven out of France. The Allied bomber forces were not as large as they were going to become. Also, the American army thought itself well-trained by 1943, but the battle of Kasserine Pass in February of that year proved they weren't so well-trained, or as tough, or in as good condition as they had thought. Kasserine also showed the Americans that they had yet to find the right commanders.

An ultimate argument against a 1943 invasion is that the commander—the Bradley of the operation—would have been Lloyd Fredendall. That almost closes the case, it seems to me. But it's a question that is not only intriguing because of the many "what-ifs" involved but also because it is of such momentous importance politically. A successful 1943 invasion followed by a drive to the Rhine and the Ruhr would have saved the world the worst year in human history, 1945. It would have crushed the Nazis without having to pay the price of bringing the Red Army into Central Europe. At least that's one of the possible scenarios that one could imagine for a successful 1943 invasion.

Alan Gropman: If you say that, you've got to turn the coin over and look at what would have been the result if a 1943 invasion had failed—and it would have failed without air supremacy. What would Europe look like today?

Stephen Ambrose: That's right. The opposite side of

the coin is that a failure in 1943 might well have led to the Red Army liberating not just Poland and eastern Germany but western Germany and France. So the Continent was at stake.

Conference Participant: You mentioned that one of Eisenhower's great strengths was that he was able to resist the temptation to sack Monty. Why do you think he was less willing to resist that temptation in late 1944 than in early 1945?

Stephen Ambrose: You mean why didn't he fire Monty at the time of the Bulge?

Conference Participant: Yes. It seemed he was more willing to consider doing that in 1945 than he was in the summer of '44.

Stephen Ambrose: Montgomery had gone further in provoking him. Montgomery was past insufferable. At SHAEF in late December or early January, at the time of the Battle of the Bulge, there were discussions over morning coffee that Monty had screwed up everything and that we had lost our chance to pinch off enemy armor in the Bulge. Monty, they said, had passed on opportunity after opportunity. He had done everything wrong and then he had had the gall to tell the reporters what great soldiers the Americans make when they're given good leadership. He had provoked Eisenhower, and he was he was also provocative to an extraordinary degree in his demands for a single command. It wasn't so much that he was demanding a single thrust, which was by this time no longer really a point of contention, but that he was demanding a single command, which was just absurd in light of the numbers of men involved and given the current political and military situations. But he kept demanding a single command, and it was just a miracle that Eisenhower remained patient. Eisenhower did a couple times threaten, "Either shut up and withdraw this demand, or I'll take the matter to the CCS."

There's a wonderful scene with Major General Francis "Freddie" De Guingand, Montgomery's chief of staff. Freddie came back to Montgomery with this letter and said, "Listen, they're about to sack you. You've got to realize how serious this is." "They couldn't do that," said Monty; "who would replace me?" Freddie said, "Alex [Field Marshall Harold Alexander]. They've got it all laid out." "Oh, my God," said Monty, "I forgot about Alex. Freddie, what do I do, what do I do?" "Sign this," said Freddie. That's the letter that ended with "Your loyal and devoted servant, Bernard Law Montgomery."

Lewis Sorley: You mentioned the hedgerows and the flooded plains in Normandy. Recently I was talking to "Red" Reeder, who took a regiment ashore on Utah Beach on D-Day, and he told me they had known about the flooded plains. He said they'd also been told that the Germans had plowed furrows across the plains. So they knew they could be wading through water at waist or chest level, depending on how tall you were, only to come to a furrow where you might sink in over your head. To prepare for that they paired up the swimmers with the non-swimmers and they told the soldiers going in, "No matter what happens, you must hang on to your weapon." They waded in and came to the first furrows. Red said, "When I saw the non-swimmers sink and still hang on to their weapons, I knew we were going to win the war."

Richard Zeitlin: Did the Germans have contingency plans for when they realized that the attack on Normandy was the main attack? I mean, not long after D-Day came the buildup on the beaches. There were lots and lots of people on the beach. And, in contrast to the Allies, the Germans very well knew what the hedgerow country was about. Why didn't they do more to contain Allied troops on the beachhead?

Stephen Ambrose: I think the German performance in the battle on June 6, 1944, and their preparations for it were just miserable. The reason for this was what Hitler regarded as Germany's greatest asset: unquestioning discipline, from the führer right down to the lowest private, unquestioning obedience. And it did them in.

It seems to me that the story of D-Day is a story of the victory of democracy over totalitarianism. Hitler thought that he would always out-produce us, that the totalitarian state is inherently more efficient than these democracies with their squabbling parliaments, their labor unions and their strikes, and all the rest of it. He turned out to be badly wrong about that. He also thought that young Germans brought up as Nazi youth in the fanatical and totalitarian state that was Nazi Germany would always out-fight kids brought up as Boy Scouts, soft and effeminate in the democracies. He was as badly wrong about that as he was about being able to out-produce the democracies. Man-for-man the American soldier in the campaign in Northwest Europe was way better than his German counterpart. And I'm not talking just about battalion troops here either, I'm talking about even Waffen SS. The American best, the rangers and the airborne, were way better than the German best. The ordinary National Guard divisions like the 29th were way, way better than the German divisions. The reason was precisely that the junior officers and the noncoms in the American army had been brought up as Boy Scouts in a democracy and they weren't afraid to take the initiative. If German officers had been in command of the 4th Division when it came ashore—if instead of Teddy Roosevelt and General Collins it had been Guderian and Rommel at the earlier stages of their careers—what would they have done? If the Germans had been assaulting at Omaha Beach and they had come ashore and had found that the invasion plan was useless, that all the pre-invasion briefing had been wasted, that the situation didn't remotely resemble what they had anticipated, what would the German officers have done? I guarantee you they'd have gotten on the radio and called headquarters and said, "What the hell do we do now?"

I offer in evidence here the words of Colonel Hans von Luck. Hans, who is a very dear personal friend of mine, commanded the 123rd Regiment of the 21st Panzer Division. He had more than one hundred tanks under his command. He was awakened at midnight on June 5-6; reports came in of paratroop landings, and then reports of glider landings, and then reports that the German garrison at the bridge at Bénouville had been driven off. Hans had anticipated that the Bénouville bridge would be the first objective the Allies would try to take by air assault because it's the only link between the two sides of the Orne waterways. He knew the attack routes that he wanted to take to get there. He would have been attacking a glider-borne company that had for its antitank weaponry those little hand-held PIAT guns. If he had been an American officer, I just can't help but believe he would have been off and running. What did Hans do? He sat there through the night, he sat there through the morning. He lost the cover of darkness and he lost the cloud cover of the morning. When Hitler finally woke up and released the 21st Panzer Division, Hans went into action and within minutes his tanks had to scatter off into the woods when naval gunfire was called down on them by Allied spotter planes.

That really doesn't deal with your question about why the Germans didn't respond more effectively to the invasion. Hitler wanted to pour concrete. In the first place, the problem facing the Germans was that they had conquered way more land than they could defend. And they hated being on the defensive—they weren't trained for it. Hitler especially had a psychological hatred of fighting on the defensive. But he had to change the Wehrmacht to make it more amenable to defensive operations.

The Wehrmacht of 1944 was very different from the Wehrmacht of 1941. It was equipped with big, heavy, slow tanks that were practically fortresses and nearly as immobile; they got a third of a mile to the gallon. Its collective mindset was to pour more concrete and put in more and more mines—just the opposite of what a blitzkrieg army would do—because Hitler insisted on defending every inch of conquered territory.

Of course, he had a lot of unreliable troops. By 1944 about a third of the Wehrmacht battalions in Normandy was comprised of Russians, Poles, and other non-German troops. Put them into trenches and put a German NCO behind them with a pistol in his hand and they would pull the trigger on a machine gun. But you wouldn't dare get them out of the trenches and start maneuvering with them for fear they would disappear. You couldn't rely on such people to execute counterattacks. Rundstedt, the old man who was there for window dressing, was the one who in a lot of ways had it right: fall back, he advised, get out of the range of that naval gunfire, let the Allies commit themselves, then hit them with a counteroffensive—not just a counterattack—at some key point inland, when you've negated their naval gunfire strength.

Rommel said the problem with that is you're assuming we can move tanks by daylight, and we're not going to be able to do that. It's not just the naval superiority, they've got air superiority. So we have to stop them at the beach or we're not going to stop them at all.

But to stop them at the beach you had to know where they were coming. You couldn't defend four thousand kilometers of coastline. It was ridiculous, the Atlantic Wall. It was the greatest building feat in human history and it was the biggest blunder in all of military history—bigger even than the Maginot Line. It took four years to build and millions of miles of barbed wire, millions of land mines, millions of tons of concrete poured. At Utah it held up the 4th Division for about an hour. At Gold, Juno, and Sword Beaches, British and Canadian troops were through the wall before noon, and at Omaha, by 3:00 in the afternoon it had been cracked.

The truth is, the Germans never had a chance either way. Rundstedt's way wasn't going to work and Rommel's way didn't work. The Germans should have quit the war even before this attack came. They didn't have any contingency plans because none were possible.

The Greatest Thing We Have Ever Attempted

Panel 1

FORGING THE WEAPON:
Developing the Allied War Machine

Contributors

James L. Collins, Thomas B. Buell, Geoffrey Perret
Moderated by Alan Gropman

The Greatest Thing We Have Ever Attempted

Introduction

"War machine" is a curious term, associating armed conflict with heavy industry, armies with the tools of manufacture. In the age of the silicon computer chip it is something of an archaism, derived from a bygone era when sprawling factories and clattering assembly lines provided nations with the measure of their economic might and technological advancement. To say that a war machine is a weapon that can be "forged" has a similarly outdated ring, bringing to mind images of roaring blast furnaces, soot-billowing smokestacks, and molten steel pouring out of giant Bessemer convertors.

Outdated, yes: but still appropriate, especially in reference to the Normandy invasion. The Allied forces—ground, sea, and air—involved in Operation Overlord constituted an enormous and immensely complex mechanism with myriad component parts, both human and inorganic, each with an application or task to perform, all employed to the same end or working toward the same goal. Much of its equipment was literally forged in fire; so too, in a different but very real sense, were the men. It was a machine made for war and geared for battle, a multifarious, many-barreled weapon designed for use on the beaches of Normandy and the Continent's interior. Fighting was its function; victory was its product.

James Collins, the panel's first contributor, was one of the machine's million-plus human components, an artillery officer who arrived in England in late 1943 as part of the great troop buildup for Overlord. Collins discusses the training effort that preceded D-Day, focusing on the difficulties involved in attempting to conduct realistic exercises in the increasingly crowded English countryside. As he points out, creating circumstances in training that might at the very least simulate actual combat was critical to preparing the Allied soldiers, especially the untried ones, for their assault on Hitler's *Festung Europa*; it meant, among other things, shooting live ammunition whenever it was possible to do so and practicing as often as they could the intricate and exacting art of storming an enemy-held beach. Collins also touches on other aspects and episodes of the pre-invasion phase, such as Operation Tiger, the practice landing at Slapton Sands that turned into real combat—and a bloody fiasco—when German E-boats attacked the Allied flotilla; and the successful effort to deceive the Germans into thinking that the Allies, when they finally invaded, would land at the Pas de Calais instead of Normandy.

*

Transporting the Allied ground forces to Normandy was the navy's job, and in June 1944 the United States Navy was headed by Admiral Ernest J. King. The man was aptly named: as both commander in chief of the U.S. Fleet and chief of naval operations, he possessed what seemed near-sovereign powers over American naval forces and affairs, and conducted himself in a suitably imperious manner. As a result he exercised tremendous influence in matters of strategy and resource allocation. But he answered to Marshall and the president, and like any good soldier he followed their orders, if sometimes less than gracefully: a man of blunt speech, irascible temper, and strong opinions, he could and often did clash with his peers and superiors. In particular, he opposed the Allies' "Europe First" policy, arguing often and adamantly for the primacy of the Pacific war in America's strategic formulations. Although overruled—the defeat of Germany would remain at the top of the list of Allied objectives, with first claim on resources—his exertions on behalf of the struggle against Japan rightly earned him regard as the architect of victory in the Pacific. But, as Thomas

Buell explains, King also played a key role in the development and success of Allied naval operations in the war against Germany. After a flawed effort against German U-boats in the early stages of the Battle of the Atlantic, he went on to preside over the great amphibious operations in North Africa, Sicily, and mainland Europe, all of which established lodgements that the Germans, for all their experience and battlecraft, could neither destroy nor contain.

*

The American troops that assaulted the Normandy coast were members of a powerful army that had committed forces to numerous battlefronts worldwide, fighting in varying conditions and in a range of circumstances against enemies who often differed greatly in their war-waging methodologies. As recently as 1939 that same army had comprised a mere six divisions, all understrength and ill-equipped—a negligible force in the reckoning of military analysts everywhere, incapable of initiating and sustaining large-scale combined-arms operations of the type that had already been undertaken in Spain, China, and Manchuria, and that would soon be launched in Europe and North Africa. American equipment was, in several key areas, pitifully inadequate for what was then considered modern warfare: fighter aircraft were undergunned and underpowered; tanks were thinly armored and poorly armed; too many artillery pieces were obsolete holdovers from 1918. The troops also looked like holdovers from 1918, with their "doughboy" helmets unchanged from the battlefields of the Meuse-Argonne and bolt-action rifles still standard issue, even though the army had officially adopted the M1 Garand semiautomatic rifle as early as January 1936. Overcoming these and a host of other shortcomings, the United States Army in World War II was, says conference contributor Geoffrey Perret in his book *There's A War To Be Won* (1991), "so good [that] it never lost a campaign"; moreover, it "lost only one battle out of more than a hundred fought around the world, at Sid-bou-Zid. . . . [a]nd suffered only one other major check, the Rapido River crossing."

In his contribution, Perret portrays the evolution of the U.S. Army from weakling to powerhouse as a two-track process of developing capable leaders and quality equipment. Perret shows how the army's small size and matériel deficiencies in the interwar period actually worked to its advantage by forcing the men in uniform to emphasize education, which was available, over good equipment, which was not, at least not in quantity.

The influence of such education on subsequent performance is not easy to quantify. In some instances it is not at all apparent. Like armies everywhere in every era, the U.S. Army had commanders who were mediocre or worse. Lloyd Fredendall and John Lucas are two of several who come to mind. They, too, were educated in army schools. But they were not typical. In the Second World War, American generals were mostly competent, often excellent, and in some cases brilliant. Notwithstanding the Fredendalls and Lucases, it is certain that the prevalence of command proficiency was attributable in large part to the schooling officers received in the 1920s and '30s. Arthur Wellesley, the Duke of Wellington, leader of an earlier allied coalition that ended Napoleon Bonaparte's martial career in the Hundred Days Campaign of 1815, supposedly remarked that "the Battle of Waterloo was won in the playing fields of Eton." The aphorism's authorship is uncertain, and probably not attributable to the Iron Duke. But no matter: whoever uttered it spoke for the British upper class, which believed—or wanted to believe—that Eton and its sister colleges in general, and the game of football (soccer) in particular, played a formative role in molding character and inculcating the leadership skills and strategic thinking displayed by so many British officers, from subaltern to general, in the Napoleonic Wars. Understanding that this claim is not meant to be taken literally—the Battle of Waterloo was, after all, won after much carnage on the muddy, blood-soaked ground in front of Mont-St. Jean in Belgium—one may make a similar claim for the U.S. Army in World War II: that the foundation for its victories was established in the classrooms and study halls of institutions such as the Infantry School at Fort Benning, the Command and General Staff School at Fort Leavenworth, Kansas, the Air Corps Tactical School at Maxwell Field, and the Army War College and the Army Industrial College in Washington, D.C.

But even the best military education is of little value without the means to apply it. Soldiers can be intelligent and they can be brave, but without adequate matériel their efforts against a well-equipped foe are likely to prove unavailing. The lesson being, that victory in war usually requires good (and up-to-date) matériel as well as good men.

In general, the U.S. Army got such equipment. But not right away, of course, and in some areas not at all. In 1941, for example, the army's armored forces were saddled with the M3 Lee/Grant medium tank, a hastily conceived and poorly designed hybrid of earlier models and new features that included a bigger gun and thicker armor. Inspired by the well-armed and armored German mediums (PzKpfws III and IV), the M3 achieved important successes in the hands of British crews during the Western Desert battles of 1942. But it quickly outlived its usefulness: handicapped by a high profile and a hull-mounted 75mm main gun with limited (30 degrees) traverse, it was outmoded from the start of its operational career and, as result, soon disappeared from Western battlefields. It was supplanted by the M4 Sherman, which was certainly an improvement but, as Perret observes, still not the superlative main battle tank the Allies needed to fight on equal terms with later German models, notably the Panther V and Tiger VI. However, the United States produced other items of matériel that were not only superlative but decisive factors in the army's success. Perret singles out five items for discussion, reviewing their development history and explaining the nature and significance of their contributions to the functioning of that most complex of inventions, the Allied war machine.

The Greatest Thing We Have Ever Attempted

Preparing For Overlord: A Battalion Commander's Perspective

James L. Collins

You have already heard about the preparations for Overlord at the highest level of command. I propose to give the worm's eye view. I was the commander of a field artillery battalion that arrived in England just before Christmas of 1943. I spent about six months in England, and it was all training.

As commander of a corps artillery battalion, I was not scheduled to go ashore on D-Day and I wasn't sure exactly how many days after the invasion my unit would land in France. As a result, I had a fairly low priority for getting training areas in which to exercise our guns. No training areas were available in the South Downs because they were all plugged up with 4th Division units and the like. But we did manage to get some rather strange training areas that I'm sure would never be authorized in the U.S. For example, we would put our guns in the field of a small farm and shoot across inhabited areas into the impact area, with the shells going over towns, farms, whatever. Fortunately, there were no serious mishaps. However, I was usually at the far end of the impact area with a number of my officers—we were simulating firing close-in to the infantry in front of us—and I found it rather unnerving to have a salvo land to our rear, as sometimes happened.

Providing close-in artillery fire entailed big changes from our training in the United States. Instead of establishing an observation post up on a mountain or in a spot overlooking the battlefield from afar, we positioned a forward observer right up alongside the company commanders, near the impact area.

We also devoted much time and effort to learning the techniques of amphibious landings. Since we had received no amphibious training back home, we had to start almost from scratch in England. A training area was set up on the southwest coast of Devon, near Dartmouth, and we made simulated landings there, pulling our guns off LSTs, LCVPs, and LCIs. Several large-scale exercises were run on the Devon coast, among them "Operation Beaver" involving the 4th Division. Beaver was an unmitigated disaster, and it was decided to repeat the exercise under the name "Operation Tiger."

Held at Slapton Sands between 26 and 28 April, 1944, Operation Tiger was more buggered up than Beaver. There was a lack of communication between the navy and the army because the two services were operating on different radio frequencies and thus unable to talk to each other. The navy commander postponed H-Hour by sixty minutes, but because word of the postponement didn't get through to everybody a lot of people in the second echelon landed before the first echelon. During the night of April 27-28 about seven German E-boats slipped past the British escort ships and got in among the LSTs, sinking two with torpedoes and badly damaging a third. Some seven hundred U.S. soldiers and sailors were killed and wounded, mostly men of the 1st Engineer Special Brigade. In fact, casualties for Operation Tiger were greater than the casualties on D-Day at Utah Beach, where this group was preparing to land.

In the late 1980s a great fuss was made in this country about this so-called Slapton Sands incident. There were allegations that the military had engineered a cover-up and lied to the press about it. Several books were written on the subject and one of them, by Edwin Hoyt, was pretty good. But there was no cover-up. At the time, certainly, the incident was not publicized because the Allies were greatly concerned about the ability of the Germans to find out where and when our landings would be. It was feared by many that some of those who were missing in the operation had been captured and would divulge this information to the Germans. Of course, the exact site of the landings was not known to the people involved in Tiger, but a sharp intelligence officer could deduce from the nature of the operation and from the terrain at Slapton Sands about where the landings in France would have to occur.

Operation Tiger was not the only exercise at Slapton Sands that experienced problems. But rather than talk about other operations, I will conclude by mentioning that the deception plan for D-Day depended a great deal on the ground troops. For example, the radio operators in my battalion were responsible for sending canned messages back and forth between various units and from different locations. We were also responsible for seeing to it that some of the inflatable tanks and guns were kept operational, and we'd move them around from time to time near Dover to try and convince the Germans that we were going to land at the Pas de Calais.

Fleet Admiral King and Overlord

Thomas B. Buell

My role this morning is to discuss how Fleet Admiral Ernest J. King contributed to the Normandy campaign. During the Second World War, King was the most powerful man in the United States Navy by virtue of his wearing two hats: that of commander in chief of the United States Fleet and chief of naval operations. But his dominance transcended naval matters. As a member of the Joint Chiefs of Staff (JCS), he was one of the two most influential planners of American grand strategy, commensurate in authority and prestige with General of the Army George C. Marshall. As the American naval representative on the Combined Chiefs of Staff (CCS), he exerted enormous leverage in the formulation of Allied grand strategy. His greatest source of power was vested in his control of American naval forces. Without King's ships there could be no invasion of the European mainland, whether across the Channel as Marshall wanted, or in the Mediterranean as the British advocated. Whatever strategy would eventually prevail, American sea power was supreme, the Royal Navy was second best, and King never let the British forget that cold fact.

King agreed with and supported the Allied policy of defeating Germany before Japan. Even so, he was firm about the need to apply unrelenting pressure on the Japanese, who would dig in and consolidate their defensive positions if left alone. The two objectives were not mutually exclusive, but they did require that decisions be made about the allocation of resources between the European and Pacific theaters. Nominally it was to be 85:15 in favor of Europe; King wanted something closer to 70:30, a goal that was eventually achieved in principle. In the event, as long as Marshall agreed to give him a free hand in the Pacific and to support him against the British, King in return would support Marshall's bid for a cross-Channel invasion.

A cross-Channel invasion was Marshall's passionate dream. He had wanted to land in Europe as early as 1942. His plan for doing so, however, was vigorously opposed by the British, who preferred to take the so-called indirect approach in the Mediterranean. As it happened, the Allies lacked the means to invade France in 1942, and landed in North Africa instead—an undertaking that was well within their capabilities, as the success of Operation Torch demonstrated. But once the decision to take the indirect approach was made, the Allies were committed to continuous warfare in Africa and Italy well through 1943. Not until 1944 could they amass the resources needed for a cross-Channel invasion.

King's thinking about a cross-Channel invasion was shaped in large part by concerns about Russia. He wanted Russia to do most of the fighting and thereby tie down a significant proportion of Axis forces on the Eastern Front—a strategy that, not incidentally, would result in less risk and fewer losses to the Western Allies. To keep the Russians going, he was willing to send them supplies to the extent possible. But he worried that, regardless of the aid they received, they might negotiate a separate peace with Germany once they had regained their borders, after which the Germans could send the bulk of their forces west as they had done after the Russian collapse in the First World War. Confronted by a German army vastly augmented by reinforcements from the Eastern Front, the United States and Great Britain would, King believed, find it all but impossible to mount a cross-Channel operation. For that reason, King advocated an invasion of France no later than the spring of 1944, thus providing the Allies with a foothold on the Continent even if Russia quit the war.

King and Marshall wanted to get CCS agreement on a 1944 invasion at the Quadrant Conference, held in Quebec in August 1943. The two men leaned hard on Roosevelt beforehand to insist on a cross-Channel invasion—Operation Overlord—and to resist any British arguments for further delay. In the first day's meeting the British, as expected, demanded that the Allies press forward in Italy in 1944 and postpone an invasion of France. King bluntly told the British that not a single American warship would be used to support any British offensive in the Mediterranean. If the ships were not used for Overlord, King said, he would send them to the Pacific, where they were badly needed. According to Admiral Leahy's diary, "British insistence on expanding the Italian operations provoked King to very undiplomatic language, to use a mild term."

The wrangling resumed the next day. The British were willing to give provisional acceptance to a landing in France, on condition that Germany first be weakened by offensive operations in Italy. But King and Marshall kept pressing the British until, finally, the latter agreed in principle that Overlord would be a reality in 1944. In doing so, however, the British voiced many reservations about the operation, causing King to doubt the depth of their commitment. (His doubt was well-founded: the British hedged for another two months, until Soviet dictator Josef Stalin weighed in on the subject.)

With Overlord now a likelihood, an enormous logistical effort had to be undertaken if the Allies were to be ready by the following spring. The most important requirement was landing craft. King and his staff grossly miscalculated the requirements for amphibious assault shipping, creating shortages that hampered Allied operations worldwide. These shortages were already apparent in the summer of 1943; Marshall had warned about them at Quebec.

The problem began in mid-1942. With the invasion of North Africa pending in November, and an invasion of France projected for 1943, the navy had embarked on an emergency building program to produce the landing ships and small craft needed for those operations. But production fell short of demand, and by September it was obvious there could be no cross-Channel invasion in 1943. King was thus able to convince the JCS that construction of amphibious shipping could be substantially reduced, and he reoriented the shipyards to building warships. By mid-1943, priority of construction had shifted to other ship types such as destroyer escorts, which were desperately needed for the Battle of the Atlantic, and battleships, which were hardly needed at all. The continued construction of battleships was wasteful, for they contributed nothing of substance to winning the war while consuming resources that should have been allocated to amphibious shipping.

Uncertainty about future operations—when and where they would take place, what they would entail—made it difficult to establish production quotas for amphibious shipping. But such quotas were of critical importance because the shipyards could turn out only so many ships each year. King was not helpful in this regard. On the one hand, he advocated formulation of a master plan that would clarify future ship requirements; on the other hand, he often deferred long-range decisions to "think things over" while the shipbuilders waited impatiently for production figures. (In any case, ship requirements were never established because conference reports issued on the subject by the combined chiefs were so riddled with compromise and often so vaguely worded that no one could figure out how many ships were needed or what they were needed for.)

There was yet another problem. Influenced by King's penchant for secrecy, his operational planners were reluctant to disclose information about future undertakings to naval procurement planners. And the civilian secretaries—Secretary of the Navy Frank Knox, his under secretary James Forrestal, and their principal assistant—were even less well informed, even though it fell to them to purchase the matériel King needed.

It didn't help that Vice Admiral Frederick J. Horne, the deputy chief of naval operations, was responsible for the navy's logistics. Logistics had never been popular in the prewar navy—aspiring career officers sought command at sea and operational assignments instead—and Horne was a product of that tradition. Accordingly, he had neither the interest nor the expertise to lead and direct the massive and unprecedented logistical effort required for the 1944 campaigns in both the Pacific and Atlantic Oceans.

Small wonder, then, that shortages existed. Fortunately for the navy, Horne had on his staff a proponent of logistics, Captain Paul Pihl, who was also a friend of King's and had access to the navy chief. Pihl headed an extraordinary effort to improve the navy's logistics, though he had no direct impact on amphibious shipping procurement. Due in no small measure to the work of Pihl and men like him, the navy somehow muddled through. By June 1944, it had assembled enough amphibious shipping to allow concurrent amphibious assaults at Normandy and half a world away at Saipan. In the early years of the war no one would have dreamed that such enormous sea power could have been brought to bear simultaneously against Germany and Japan.

*

King's contributions to Overlord were not limited to naval matters. He was also influential in choosing its overall commander. Early on in the planning for Overlord, Roosevelt had wanted Marshall and Eisenhower to switch jobs, Marshall to command in Europe and Eisenhower to return to the United States as army chief of staff. Marshall was more than agreeable to such a move. He wanted command of Overlord and did not pretend otherwise. But although King sympathized with Marshall's aspirations, he felt that Marshall could not be spared from the JCS and told him so. King discussed the issue with his JCS colleagues Leahy and Arnold, and they concurred with his view. The three men also met individually with Roosevelt to urge the president to keep Marshall in Washington. In the meantime, however, Churchill (as well as influential civilian advisors) were telling Roosevelt that Marshall had earned the privilege of personally leading the campaign he had so long championed.

When the press began speculating on Marshall's next assignment, King contacted journalists with whom he had been meeting privately. The admiral asked them to write stories favorable to his point of view, and several cooperated. The media succeeded in focusing public attention on Marshall, creating a stir over how he might best serve the country. Feeling the heat, Roosevelt stalled for time.

Stalin finally forced the issue at the Teheran Conference in November 1943. The equivocation must end, he declared, and a second front had to be established in France and nowhere else. He utterly rejected the British alterative of pouring more forces into Italy as a prelude to Overlord. With Stalin holding the conference hostage, the CCS agreed on a date for the Normandy assault, one that was largely governed by the availability of King's landing craft. Still Stalin was not satisfied. Who would command Overlord? he asked. Roosevelt and Churchill told him that it had not been decided. Stalin's reply was ominous: "Then nothing will come of these proceedings." Roosevelt promised a decision presently.

The CCS, together with Roosevelt and Churchill, returned to Cairo to resolve the final details of both

Overlord and operations in the Far East. Field Marshal Alan Brooke and King often clashed at such meetings, and Cairo was no exception. General Joseph Stilwell recorded one such encounter in his diary. "Brooke got nasty and King got good and sore," he wrote. "King almost climbed over the table at Brooke. God, he was mad. I wish he had socked him." Eventually agreement was reached. Before they adjourned, Roosevelt made his decision on the European supreme command. It would be Eisenhower.

Overlord was successful, and the liberation of Europe began. The British gave it their best effort once they realized there could be no turning back. It was coalition warfare at its finest, and King was instrumental in making it happen.

Men and Matériel
Geoffrey Perret

One of the first actions General George C. Marshall took after becoming army chief of staff on September 1, 1939, was to organize a maneuver that was unusual for the army: an amphibious assault. Making an attack against a defended shore was considered the business of the navy and the marine corps. But Germany had invaded Poland the same day, and Marshall realized that, if the United States was drawn into the war, the army might have to fight to establish a presence on the Continent. In the maneuver, held in January 1940, the 3rd Infantry Division landed at Monterey Bay, defeated the National Guard division opposing it and, theoretically at least, moved on to take San Francisco. (The chief umpire for the maneuver was Lieutenant Colonel Dwight D. Eisenhower.)

However, any notion that the army had mastered the techniques of the amphibious assault was dispelled in June 1941 when a more demanding operation was mounted near Cape Hatteras, North Carolina. Nothing went right for the attacking force. The General Staff observer who reported on the operation concluded, "The whole experience convinced me that a successful landing is impossible unless all resistance is previously neutralized." How then did an army that was so deficient in technique turn itself in only three years into a force capable of playing such a brilliant role in the greatest combined arms operation in history? The short answer is, it didn't. It didn't take three years, that is. The U.S. Army and the Army Air Forces had been preparing in one way and another to undertake such an operation for twenty years before D-Day.

This is a story of men and matériel. I'll begin with the men. In 1929 President Herbert Hoover ordered the General Staff to conduct a policy review. The Kellogg-Briand Pact had just been signed and Hoover was, in effect, demanding that the army justify its existence. The General Staff reported back that war was unlikely as things then stood. That was the good news. The bad news was that if the army continued to dwindle in effectiveness, the prospects of a war involving the United States would rise appreciably.

At this time the army was half the size authorized by the 1920 National Defense Act. Instead of having the 300,000 men the law anticipated, the army was down to 150,000 and falling. In the course of its review the General Staff spelled out the principle that should guide the army in these parsimonious times. The army could spend its shrinking budget mainly on men or mainly on matériel. The General Staff argued strongly that the emphasis should be on men.

Douglas MacArthur inherited this policy when he became chief of staff in November 1930, and no one agreed with it more strongly than he. MacArthur believed that men won wars, not machines. Throughout his five-year tenure as army chief (he left that post in October 1935), he defended that position before a Congress that was deeply skeptical of the military. It was a huge gamble on his part. On the one hand, he understood that if and when the United States was plunged into war, it would have to fight immediately and more or less with what it had; on the other hand, he knew that the army didn't have the matériel to fight a war and wouldn't get it for some time to come. But he couldn't risk drawing attention to this fact. In order to win approval for his program he had to go before Congress and tell it that the army was ready to fight and could make do with the weapons at hand.

The emphasis on finding and training the right men to lead the army in what MacArthur openly referred to as "the next war" was concentrated on the army's graduate schools, especially the Infantry School at Fort Benning, Georgia, the Command and General Staff School at Fort Leavenworth, Kansas, the Air Corps Tactical School at Maxwell Field, Alabama, the Army War College in Washington, D.C., and the Army Industrial College in Washington, D.C.

The U.S. Army that stood poised to land in Normandy in early June 1944 was in large part the realization of a dream nurtured at Fort Benning. It was organized and trained according to ideas the Infantry School had developed, and it was led from the battalion level to army command by Infantry School graduates. Of the sixteen American divisions deployed to Normandy in June 1944, nine were commanded by Benning graduates. Three of the four American corps commanders in the Normandy campaign had been at Benning. Bradley had been an instructor there and his deputy, Courtney Hodges, was one of the school's first students.

The Infantry School in effect remade the army. It simplified tactics to the point where it taught only one tactic, the holding attack, and it decided how the army should be reorganized, from the squad up through the division. Leavenworth, meanwhile, took able young captains and majors—most of them Benning graduates—and taught them how to think about handling divisions and corps, with an emphasis on making decisions quickly under pressure. The whole point of the Leavenworth course, in fact, was decision-making, because that had been the army's major weakness during World War I.

Leavenworth also taught one tactic, the wide envelopment; and D-Day is a perfect example of that maneuver. At the shortened Leavenworth course during World War II, officers studied only two problems. The big problem was the landing in France, and the maps from that course show that it was solved using almost the same plan as the one subsequently used for Overlord: five divisions were to be put ashore while airborne drops were made on both flanks. Of course, the graduates of Leavenworth took their maps with them to Europe, where to their amazement they landed on the very beaches they had been studying in Kansas the previous year.

Every division and corps commander in the D-Day assault was a Leavenworth graduate. Eisenhower had been the honor graduate in the class of 1926. Many senior army air force officers were also Leavenworth graduates. These included air force chief Henry H. Arnold; Carl Spaatz, commander of U.S. Strategic Air Forces in Europe; Lewis Brereton, commander of the Ninth Air Force; Hoyt Vandenberg, Spaatz's protégé and the deputy commander of Allied Expeditionary Air Forces; William Kepner, commander of VIII Fighter Command; and Elwood Quesada, commander of IX Tactical Command.

Although some of the ablest air corps officers attended Leavenworth, and several—including Brereton—became instructors there, most airmen much preferred their own Tactical School at Maxwell. Even so, there was a deliberate effort to pattern the Maxwell school on Leavenworth.

The Army Industrial College was *sui generis* among military schools. The Wilson administration had completely botched war production in 1917-1918. It was an experience the army had no intention of reliving, and in 1924 it took money it could ill afford to spare from its meager budget to create the Army Industrial College. (It also persuaded President Calvin Coolidge to establish the office of Assistant Secretary of War, which would be responsible for overseeing army procurement and guiding the mobilization of the economy for war.) The college maintained a regular survey of American industry so that at any time the army knew who could produce what and when, and to what standard. And when the army got money for educational orders in the late 1930s, it taught manufacturers how to make weapons. The college's graduates included Arnold, Eisenhower, and J. Lawton Collins.

The Army War College in the 1920s was a somnolent place where most students were senior officers who were kindly allowed to spend a pleasant year in Washington before shuffling off into retirement. MacArthur transformed the War College by allowing younger officers to be assigned there. Although the problems they worked on were usually at the level of grand strategy and weren't particularly relevant to the coming war, the curriculum enabled the college to identify dozens of majors who were thinking like major generals.

In civilian life, manners maketh the man. In the interwar army, it was the schools that made the officer. The pattern of an officer's assignments between the wars was supposed to be staff, school, troops—and the most important of these was school. In World War II there were nearly 150 men who commanded divisions. Unlike what had happened in the AEF in the First World War, comparatively few got fired. Roughly half the division commanders in World War II were West Point graduates. Most of those who did not wear the academy's black ring—including superb division commanders such as Clarence Huebner, who led the 1st Division in the assault on Omaha Beach—had risen through the army school system.

Only by finding the right men and developing their abilities was the army able to create the right tools, to forge the weapons for D-Day. It was Mark Clark—a graduate of Benning, Leavenworth, and the War College—who designed the division-making machinery that allowed the army to grow from six understrength divisions in the spring of 1940 to a force of nearly eighty powerful, well-armed divisions at close to full strength in the spring of 1944. It was Albert C. Wedemeyer, graduate of both Benning and Leavenworth, who in the summer of 1941 drew up the Victory Program, a statement that provided estimates of the manpower and production requirements for America's participation in the war. Two of the four authors of AWPD-1, the AAF's plan for fighting the war, were Haywood S. Hansell and Laurence Kuter; both were Leavenworth graduates. Brehon Somervell, the young and dynamic head of Army Service Forces, was the Leavenworth honor graduate of 1923 and graduated from the War College three years later. It was such people who forged the weapon.

*

As for the matériel that made a crucial difference on D-Day, I would single out five items. First, the basic weapon of the American infantryman in the assault: the M1 semiautomatic rifle. The development of the M1 was a twenty-year saga that had as many twists and turns as any movie thriller. At the end of World War I the U.S. Army—like every army, I think—wanted a semiautomatic rifle. There had been attempts during World War I to create such weapons, but nothing had come of them. Producing a semiautomatic rifle was the army's biggest research and development effort of the interwar period. Ordinance specifications called for a weapon that weighed no more than 8.5 pounds, fired a bullet of about .276 caliber, and was accurate to eight hundred yards. By 1929 the army had two semiautomatic rifles offered to it for consideration: one from John Garand that fired a .30-caliber round, and one from John Pederson that fired a .276-caliber round.

The army organized the so-called Pig Board to test these weapons. Twenty pigs were rounded up, anesthetized, and shot with both kinds of bullets. It turned out that the small bullets did more damage than the big ones. The reason: when a bullet hits something, it becomes unstable and starts to tumble. Light bullets are more unstable than heavy ones; as a result, more internal damage was done to the pigs by Pederson's .276-caliber round than by Garand's .30-

caliber round, which tended to go straight through the animal. The army told Garand to write off several years of work on the .30-caliber rifle and develop a rifle that fired a smaller bullet. And so, for the next three years, Garand strove to develop a .276-caliber rifle.

In the meantime another board had met. Some ordnance experts felt that the Pig Board's results were illusory because pigs are softer and fleshier than human beings. Goats, on the other hand, are lean and hard, with a high proportion of muscle to fat—much like a healthy young man. So a "Goat Board" was convened, and twenty goats were anesthetized and shot. The results were the same as with the Pig Board, but only at ranges under two hundred yards. At longer ranges the .30-caliber bullet did more damage because it was still traveling fast at the same distance, while the .276 was quickly slowing down. Nevertheless, the Ordnance Department unanimously recommended the smaller bullet to Army Chief of Staff Douglas MacArthur.

Now, MacArthur was not a hunter and he was not really interested in firearms; but he had been to war. And his experience of war caused him to look askance at the idea of a small bullet. He rejected the .276-caliber weapon and made the army come up with a semiautomatic rifle that fired a bigger bullet.

John Garand's M1 semiautomatic rifle with the .30-caliber bore was adopted in 1936, just after MacArthur stepped down as chief of staff. There were a lot of army NCOs who didn't want the rifle because it involved a much tougher marksmanship test and thus jeopardized their five dollar-per-month marksmanship pay. But they had no choice in the matter: they got the M1 and they got used to it. The marines, who were equally dismissive of the Garand, did have a choice and exercised it in favor of their trusty old bolt-action Springfields, a 1903-vintage weapon. The Springfield remained standard issue in the marine corps until mid-war. The marines were thus late in discovering what the army knew early on, that it had found the best rifle of the war. More to the point, the army hadn't found the Garand; rather, it had *created* the Garand.

At the other end of the scale, literally, was another crucial item: the LST, or Landing Ship, Tank. At first the navy had no interest in the LST. Admiral King wanted to build carriers and submarines first, other ship types second, and LSTs not at all. The British, however, pushed the idea and Marshall took little or no persuading. He had the first LST built out of wood a long way from salt water at Fort Knox, Kentucky, so that the design could be developed while he got after King to adopt the vessel. In due course the wooden model engendered the real thing, a four-thousand-ton ship that could carry up to twenty tanks and a dozen two-and-a-half-ton trucks.

Then there was the Republic P-47 Thunderbolt. The P-47 came into existence in part because the two aircraft the army was developing in the late 1930s as its next generation of fighters, the Lockheed P-38 Lightning and the North American P-51 Mustang, were to have in-line glycol-cooled Allison engines. When Republic Aviation came along with a third fighter powered by an Allison engine, the air force thought it would be even better than the P-38 and the P-51 and designated it the P-44. Then one day in the spring of 1940 General Henry H. "Hap" Arnold, head of what was then called the U.S. Army Air Corps, had an idea. Concerned that the air corps was betting everything on the liquid-cooled engine, he paid a visit to Republic Aviation at Farmington, Long Island, and called on the company's top designer, Alexander Carvelli. By then the P-44 had been redesignated P-47, and Arnold told Carvelli to remove the Allison engine from the plane and replace it with a radial engine.

Many people involved with military aviation thought this a stupid idea. Conventional wisdom held that a fighter should be no wider than the pilot's shoulders, which was not possible with a radial engine. This was particularly true of the power plant Arnold wanted for the P-47, a big engine designed for bombers. Putting that engine into the P-47 would significantly increase its girth, to the detriment of performance. Or so the experts believed. Arnold ignored them. He insisted on a radial engine and it was duly installed.

In the event, the P-47 was a brilliant plane. It was the P-47 that broke the back of the German fighter arm: American pilots flying P-47s shot down huge numbers of experienced German pilots in the autumn of 1943 and in the winter of 1943-44, forcing the Luftwaffe to replace their veterans with downy-cheeked youths who had at best one hundred hours in the air. Opposing them were American pilots with four hundred hours or more of training. By March 1944 the Allies had achieved air superiority in the skies over Europe, and it was the P-47 that did the job. This was a precondition to D-Day: without control of the skies, there could be no invasion. By the time of Overlord, the air superiority legacy had been handed on to the P-51 Mustang, which turned superiority into something close to supremacy most of the time. The Thunderbolt, however, subsequently proved invaluable in the tactical support role, becoming the best ground attack aircraft of the war.

The fourth item is the jeep. The army had been trying to develop a tracked vehicle like Britain's diminutive Bren gun carrier when it got wind of the American Bantam Car Company in Butler, Pennsylvania, and its rather abrasive owner, Harry Payne. And Payne had come up with something better than the Bren carrier. He had been working on a small truck that four men could manhandle out of potholes. At the army's invitation he quickly produced seventy hand-built prototypes. They performed well in tests, but still the army wouldn't buy them. Payne persevered, eventually wangling and introduction to the secretary of the General Staff, Major General Walter Bedell Smith. Payne showed Smith one of his prototypes, and the general was won over. Exercising his right to interrupt Marshall on any important matter, Smith walked into a meeting of generals in the chief of staff's office and asked his boss for five minutes. He made a pitch for Payne's vehicle and when he was finished Marshall asked him, "What do you think?" Smith replied, "I think it's good." On that basis, Harry Payne got an order for fifteen hundred prototype vehicles.

But the army was concerned that American Bantam lacked the capability to mass-produce the vehicle. And so Willys Overland and Ford were persuaded to build prototypes of their own design. These were pitted in a three-way competition against the American Bantam vehicle. The Willys design won out, Ford was subcontracted to produce it—and American Bantam went out of business. What came to be popularly known as the jeep—the name given to it by Willys engineers—was soon pouring off the assembly lines, bound for a distinguished combat career in which it would prove vital to the mobility of the wartime army.

The fifth and final item is the DUKW, nicknamed the "Duck." This strange, hybrid vehicle made over-the-beach supply possible. The artificial "Mulberry" harbors that were towed across the Channel were ingenious but overrated. After the American artificial harbor was wrecked in the ferocious Channel storm of June 19-22, the tonnage brought across Omaha Beach exceeded anything brought in through the Mulberries. On D-Day and in the days and weeks immediately following the Normandy landings, hundreds of DUKWs took men, artillery, ammunition, and other supplies from the LSTs to the beach, and brought the wounded back to the ships.

I'm not suggesting that the army got everything right in its efforts to forge the weapon it wielded in Overlord. There were, inevitably, embarrassments and failures. The M1 carbine that was issued to officers was virtually useless. Tank design was absurd: the M4 Sherman, which was the mainstay of American armored units, was developed by committees that never met. The result was an undergunned and inadequately armored machine with a propensity for catching fire when hit by enemy antitank rounds. The Allies did not get a first-class tank until the end of the war, when the British Centurion was introduced.

Arnold and Robert Patterson, the assistant secretary of war responsible for procurement, tried to stop the development of new transport aircraft, despite excellent, fervently given advice to the contrary. When the two men finally became aware of their mistake, too much time had been lost to get a first-class transport aircraft into the war by 1944. The Douglas C-47 Skytrain (or Dakota or Gooney Bird, as it was variously known) was too small, too vulnerable to light flak, and had a range too short to provide a truly satisfactory solution to the problem of air transport. Hence the piecemeal introduction of the airborne divisions into Normandy. A proper transport aircraft program would have put fleets of four-engine aircraft over Normandy on D-Day dropping entire airborne divisions in a single lift and eliminating the need for hundreds of gliders to come in on D-plus-one.

The army air forces also lacked first-class photo reconnaissance aircraft. The Signal Corps botched radar development by trying to reinvent everything the British had done. The Ordnance Corps persistently failed to provide the AAF with modern bombs. It isn't surprising that the air weapon that would have done the most to help in the battle of the hedgerows, napalm, arrived at the end of the campaign; nor is it surprising that napalm was developed by the AAF, not the Ordnance Corps.

In final analysis, however, the American forces that were committed to Overlord were well-led, well-trained, and well-equipped for the most difficult of all offensive operations, combined airborne and amphibious assault against a defended shore.

Discussion

Kenneth Hagan: Mr. Perret's comments went a long way toward explaining why it was Ike and may have had to be Ike, as Steve [Ambrose] said. But I wondered as I heard [Geoffrey Perret] talking about the contrast between the army and the navy in terms of their emphasis on education; I was wondering whether Mr. Buell would pick up on that. How did it come to be King? You said that in the navy there was not an emphasis on logistics; but what about the educational system? All that comes to mind in this regard is Nimitz's comment that "they study gentlemen at the War College."

Thomas Buell: The navy never put the emphasis on education that the army did. It was true then and I think it's true today that officers make flag rank who have never seen the inside of the Naval War College or anything else, whereas you've got to punch your tickets in the army and in the air force to move up. Prior to the Second World War, the Naval War College was really the only school that mattered. Although navy officers could go for post-graduate education, it was always in a technical subject, engineering and so forth, and really had nothing to do with war-making. There were good people who went to the Naval War College. I think virtually every officer who had a major command in the Second World War, with the exception of Leahy, was a graduate of the college. What did they study there? War Plan Orange.

But the way they studied war was not the way the war was actually fought. So when after the war Admiral Nimitz said that everything we did against the Japanese had been done at the Naval War College, I think he was trying to get support to salvage the college at a time when the navy was down in the dumps.

What they did do is, they learned how to plan, they learned what an operation order was about, they learned what the estimated situation was, and they got to know each other. And they certainly got to know the geography of the Pacific—they knew it as well as the backs of their hands. But, to summarize, the way the navy educated its officers before the Second World War was entirely different from the way the army educated its officers.

Judy Litoff: Developing the Allied war machine also included developing a plan for caring for the many anticipated casualties. We know there were thousands of American Red Cross workers and army nurses stationed in the U.K. in the spring of 1944 who were as anxious to get across the Channel as was Patton. I just wondered if any of the panelists could talk about Allied preparations for caring for the Normandy casualties.

James Collins: The army had a rather detailed plan, and in the early stages of the actual landing we had a goodly number of medical units and people who were designated as stretcher-bearers and so forth. There was a plan where small boats brought supplies and individuals ashore, unloaded, and then picked up casualties and took them out. Of course, there were many foul-ups in that people would get wounded and put along the beach or, preferably, in a sheltered area; and some of those casualties didn't get evacuated for several days. However, all in all, the medical plan, the evacuation plan, worked out quite well.

John Huston: Air evac was going on as early as 13 June. By that date C-47s that had originally taken gliders in and dropped paratroopers on the night of June 5-6 were landing on carve-notch strips. They probably took out only a handful of casualties, but at least air evac was going on within a week after the invasion.

James Collins: Yes, that's right. I was really referring to the first few days. But after airfields were established on the far shore, aircraft became the primary way of evacuation to England.

Stephen Ambrose: When did the first nurses get in?

Judy Litoff: D-plus-four.

Stephen Ambrose: No nurses went in on D-Day as far as I'm aware of.

Judy Litoff: The first American woman who went ashore was Martha Gellhorn, on D-plus-one. She stowed away on a British hospital carrier that was docked off of Easy Red Beach and went ashore on a water ambulance. She got into a lot of trouble for doing that.

Alan Gropman: Steve, when did the first black units go ashore?

Stephen Ambrose: The 320th Barrage Balloon Battalion (Colored) was the first unit of black troops to go ashore in France. They went in on D-Day at about 1100 hours at both Utah and Omaha and they tied up barrage balloons.

General Collins, I was fascinated by what you were talking about with regard to Slapton Sands, and how a good intelligence officer would have been able to pick up even from troops that hadn't been briefed where they were going. There's an amazing story: Hitler got the report on those E-boats knocking off those LSTs in Operation Tiger. Hitler had never been in Normandy and he had never been in England, but he had the most amazing ability to store topographical information in his mind. And he took one look at that report on Slapton Sands and said that the only place in France that resembles it is what became Utah Beach–which was the reason they were practicing at Slapton Sands, because it so closely resembled Utah Beach. That's when Hitler started to move some reinforcements–not enough, obviously–into the Cotentin.

Orwin Talbott: I'd just like to reinforce that comment about Slapton Sands. At the time I was a rifle company commander in a regiment that was attached to the 4th Division. A bunch of our people were with the 4th Division for Operation Tiger. They saw this marsh area behind the beaches and they looked on maps for a comparable place in France. The only place they could find was what became Utah Beach. About the end of May I was asked by a briefer, "Where are we going to invade?" And I put my finger right on it. The briefer asked, "How the hell do you know?" And I had to tell him how.

Joseph Balkoski: When I was working on my book about the 29th Division and interviewing veterans of that division who fought in the bocage, one of the things that was frequently pressed on me and that has been pretty much forgotten is the failure of the army to develop smokeless and flashless gunpowder. These veterans complained that their gunpowder really put the platoons and companies at a disadvantage in the hedgerow fighting because the Germans did have smokeless and flashless powder. So I was going to ask Geoffrey Perret if he had heard anything about that. If it's true, it seems that it should be a major issue. It seems that 50 percent of the riflemen I interviewed brought this is up spontaneously.

Geoffrey Perret: This is a complaint that had been heard in the army ever since the Spanish-American War, when the defenders in Cuba had smokeless ammunition and the Americans were firing weapons that created huge black clouds of smoke. The Ordnance Corps didn't get everything right, and this is one of the things. It couldn't concentrate on everything.

I think most troops learned to live with the smokeless powder. It wasn't an issue in most places. But you see why in the bocage it was an issue, because people were fighting in fields that were the size of this room. As a rule the battlefield was empty. You'd look at a World War II battlefield and you wouldn't see anything move. It took a very good eye to see who and what was out there. And a lot of the fighting was done at night; most attacks were executed at night. So smokeless powder really wasn't a problem. But if you had to fire your weapon in a field this size and there's somebody on the other side, in effect, of the room, and he can see you, then it is an issue.

Richard Behrenhausen: I'd like to ask General Collins and General Talbot about the impact on the chain of command of training failures--that is, training incidents, training accidents, poor results in training. Were the command teams set and allowed to train or was there a lot of turmoil, officers moved in and out of positions, commanders relieved? How did the command structure deal with that prior to the invasion?

James Collins: There was always a debriefing shortly after the "event" at which the commanders, down to platoon leaders at times, were assembled. The difficulties were gone over, corrective measures were taken. For example, it was proved that the navy and the army were unable to communicate because they were on different radio frequencies, and that the Americans and the British were unable to communicate in many cases. So the frequencies were reallocated. Sometimes it was necessary for one side to give radios to the other to enable communication.

Not everything was corrected, not necessarily because of a failure in plans but because of human failures. You'd have a small group on the beach that was supposed to go from A to B, and they'd be pinned down and just never get there. So the local commander had to change things. But all in all, the two principal exercises, Beaver and Tiger, were able to pinpoint problems and identify corrective measures. Then the men were briefed and went back and practiced in their home areas on dry land.

Orwin Talbott: My own battalion, from the six months immediately preceding D-Day, had very good stability–but it just happened that way, I suppose. We had a lot of turnover before that. We had one rifle company commander in the battalion who didn't go with us because he couldn't pass the physical; he never did get overseas. But in my own company, we had the same people all the way through until we hit the beaches. Then, of course, there was tremendous turnover for the rest of the war.

As far as the matter of training and safety: we didn't realize it at the time, but looking back, I don't think there's any doubt that there was too much emphasis on safety and not enough on realism, particularly in regard to live-fire exercises. This is always a problem, of course, because as soon as somebody gets shot, not only the mothers, but Congress and everybody else gets into the act. That makes it very difficult. But nevertheless there was more emphasis on safety than on realism.

Alan Gropman: Let me see if we can get Clay Blair to address that, because in his paper he's going to talk about how Bradley fired people. The question is, as things came up in training for Overlord, was there turmoil in the chain of command as people revealed their inadequacies?

Clay Blair: I don't think so, no. On a higher level, yes, but not on that level.

Alan Gropman: Were there changes at even the highest level in Bradley's army because of failures in the period up to D-Day? Did Bradley have to sack people?

Clair Blair: No, I don't think so, not to that point, not to D-Day. People were sacked when they were put to the real test, and when political considerations had to be put aside in favor of action and doing things, particularly when they got into trouble in the bocage. My impression of Bradley's staff work first in First Army Group and then in First Army was that it was a well-oiled machine. There may be some exceptions that I've forgotten, but both those staffs were outstanding.

Stephen Ambrose: There was one company of the 506th that had a mutiny by the sergeants and got rid of the CO in that fashion. That was probably unique. Generally, men didn't fail in training. There is one failure, I heard about it around six months ago. The reason that Lieutenant Colonel James E. Rudder went ashore at Pointe du Hoe—they didn't want him to go ashore, and the story has always been that he went because he said he wanted to be there. Actually, the night before they loaded up, the exec who was supposed to lead the rangers in at Point Du Hoe got roaring drunk. And Rudder had him put under arrest. And Rudder took over.

Clay Blair: In another area of study which I carried out on American airborne forces in Normandy and elsewhere, I discovered that several regimental commanders in the 82nd and 101st Airborne Divisions were relieved very promptly for incompetence or lack of aggressiveness or, in some cases, stupidity. That was at the colonel level. I've forgotten their names now, but one was a glider regiment commander who failed at the bridge over the Merderet River. Another was a 101st Airborne regimental commander named Moseley, son of the famous political figure. He was relieved almost immediately, too. And another colonel was relieved after him.

Geoffrey Perret: I think the Joint Planning Staff knew there would be training failures and accepted that this would be the case. I think the plan for Overlord contains an acceptance of failures in training. The solution to this problem was to yoke experience with inexperience, to have well-tried and tested units fighting alongside absolutely green units. So you find the inexperienced 101st Division is involved, but also the 29th Division, which had been trained almost to death–every possible training technique that was available was tried out on the 29th.

Now, people knew that Britain was a small country. It had only so many training areas. We had to shove millions of people in there, and we couldn't give them all realistic training or train them to a high standard. Only some units got anything resembling realistic training, and the 29th was one of them. They yoked the two airborne divisions together, the 82nd, a very experienced airborne division, with the 101st, which had never made a combat jump in its life.

They did the same thing with the corps commanders. They had two experienced corps commanders, Collins and Corlett, and two guys who had never done this before, Middleton and Gerow. You could even say they had done the same thing higher up, with Bradley and Hodges. Bradley had fought in World War II, Hodges hadn't. So it seems to me that when the joint planners looked at this issue, they knew that some of these units would not be well-trained; but they tried to make sure that they'd be in the vicinity of units that were not only well-trained but also knew how to fight their way out of trouble.

Paul Stillwell: I want to respond to Tom Buell's negative comment about battleships. Tom talks about resource allocation and putting money into battleship construction rather than landing craft or antisubmarine warfare vessels. I think that's a view born of hindsight, which shows us that there were few great battleship duels in World War II and therefore we didn't need those ships. But that's not something we knew going into those battles. Admiral King, as Tom Buell mentioned, was very big on the importance of the Pacific War while at the same time recognizing that the defeat of Germany was our first priority. The battleships were potentially available for a duel with their Japanese counterparts at the Marianas in June 1944 and in the Philippines in October of that year. Ironically, part of the reason they did not get involved in surface actions was that they were considered too valuable in their role of providing antiaircraft screens for the carriers. Had circumstances worked out differently, had Halsey not lived up to his nickname of "Bull" and charged after some empty Japanese carriers, we might well have had the battle that Tom says we didn't need the battleships for.

Thomas Buell: I agree with Paul that my view of battleships is hindsight. At the time, obviously, the navy felt there was a need for these ships. Certainly, everyone else did. The British kept building battleships, the Japanese kept building battleships, and it wasn't until after the war that we realized that the surface engagements they were built for would rarely occur. And it turned out that the fast battleships never got involved in the support of amphibious landings; they were always mobile and it was the pre-World War II battleships that provided most of the naval gunfire support.

Lewis Sorley: I'd like to offer a comment that supplements what Geoffrey Perret had to say about the importance of the army school system, which I agree with completely. But I think it's also true that the nature of service in the army in the period between the wars was in itself an important training ground and developmental process for the people who rose many levels in World War II. The army was then in the grip of what General Prescott once called "serious austerity." The units were scattered, the communications were less robust than today; therefore, local commanders had a certain degree of autonomy they may not have today. They learned to make do. They had many opportunities to innovate. In the units there was a lot of stability so that people in command of troops really got to know their soldiers and, therefore, in contrast to the post-World War II period, you couldn't stay a short time, get a good fitness report, and move and escape revealing deficiencies that only became apparent later.

Because of the austerity, there was a weeding-out process. People for whom money and luxury were important didn't last in that army; they left voluntarily. In fact, in the Depression we were even urging people to leave because we were having a hard time paying those that were there. The people being paid rather poorly and living in austere conditions had to make their own fun, and there was a camaraderie that developed among the young officers and their wives. They made their own fun, and a lot of it revolved around the horse–the horse show, the fox hunt, the hunt breakfast, and so on. This helped these people get to know each other and develop the mutual trust and confidence that were extremely important when, later, they went to war together.

Kenneth Hagan: I want to ask Tom Buell to flesh out the command relationships that King may or may not have had on the Atlantic side. I'm not referring to ASW [antisubmarine warfare] or the earlier landings, but primarily, or maybe exclusively, Normandy. What comes to my mind is Simms in World War I, who was obviously Wilson's man and who was more important in many respects than Benson, the chief of naval operations. Ghormley and Stark, and later Hewlett–had King worked with these guys? Did he have favorites in the European theater, like he had Nimitz in the Pacific, or did he just work through the Joint Chiefs of Staff?

Thomas Buell: Stark was the senior naval officer overseas. But he was essentially stashed over there because it was awkward having him in Washington as CNO and King as Commander in Chief, U.S. Fleet. King went to Roosevelt and said, "One or the other of us has to go." And so Stark went to the U.K. He had a huge staff, but I've never really been able to figure out what he did over there. In my study of King, I found that he really had no communications with Stark. In general, King worked through his chief of naval personnel, and they simply assigned the best officers they could get to go there. I don't think he gave anywhere near the amount of time to thinking about what was going to happen in Europe as he did to the Pacific.

Alan Gropman: Could you kill this question on training by talking about any changes that occurred in the 29th Division during this particular phase? Were there essential changes in the division's training?

Joseph Balkoski: Yes, there were a number of changes that took place in the training period, mostly due to the eccentricity of the division commander, who would relieve people if he found a dirty garbage can in a kitchen or some such incident. But frequently these people were brought back into the same positions of command they had had in England--they were brought back once the shooting started. There was a tremendous turnover at all levels in the 29th Division, for incompetence, cowardice, and other reasons. But I was going to ask Geoff [Perret] another question. He mentioned General Corlett, who commanded the corps in which the 29th Division served when it took St.-Lô. I looked into Corlett's papers at the Military History Institute. I found a really good memoir of his, and I was surprised to discover that he had commanded the 7th Division when it assaulted Kwajalein in February 1944. When he was brought over to England he sat in on the planning for D-Day. And in his memoir he's very angry about the fact that the Pacific amphibious technology was not brought over to Europe and a lot of his expertise was ignored. He specifically mentioned the tracked assault vehicle the army and marine corps used in the Pacific. It was called the Alligator. Why was it not used in Normandy? It was available, and apparently there were senior commanders asking Bradley and Eisenhower why it wasn't brought to the ETO.

Geoffrey Perret: No coral in Normandy. They didn't need the Alligators in Normandy, but they needed them for those Pacific atolls where you usually had to get across a coral reef just to get to the beach. Also, the beaches at Normandy are not that steep. Some of the Pacific islands, they just stick up out of the water; the beach goes straight down. You could not have a gentle run up that kind of beach with an LSM or LSI or LCT; you have to land right on the island. They really didn't need the Alligators in Normandy; the troops in the Pacific needed them a lot more, and that's why they were out there.

Corlett was in Europe because he'd impressed the hell out of Marshall. The way he took Kwajalein was to take the island next door instead of going straight for Kwajalein. He put his 155 and 105 millimeter guns on it and then pounded the defenses on Kwajalein from a mile and a half away. Then he made the assault on Kwajalein.

Well, this was such a neat idea that, when Marshall heard about it, he said, "Send this guy to

Europe." He also sent Collins, who begged for a role in Europe. Collins was another Marshall protégé. This provided the army with two corps commanders who had experience. The original corps commanders were men who had risen essentially through the schools and as staff planners. I think it was a good idea to pull them out and replace them with people who had experience, although the two were very bitter about this.

Now, because Corlett and Collins were from the Pacific, they were treated as if they were from the bush leagues. Nobody wanted to hear what they had to say. It's absolutely true. But that didn't really matter. The fact is, they had the experience. Now, maybe their experience was ignored in the planning and training phases, but it was certainly going to be valuable once the troops got ashore.

Stephen Ambrose: There was a lot of resentment from the commanders in the Pacific that nobody asked them for their advice. They knew they were experts at amphibious operations, but the SHAEF staff didn't feel that way at all. The men at SHAEF had run three amphibious operations and didn't think they had to go to the Pacific to learn about them. In the Pacific there was a different enemy and different terrain conditions which, it was thought, were not relevant to Normandy.

Geoffrey Perret: The air force also sent somebody out from the Pacific to tell SHAEF how to run the air side of Overlord. Again, this was Marshall's idea. Marshall said to Arnold, "I want somebody from the Pacific that's had a lot of these kind of assaults." So they sent Frederick Smith, a very bright young man who was Admiral King's son-in-law. He had a letter from Arnold that tells Spaatz, "This is your air expert. You do what he says." Smith was embarrassed to show it to anybody. He went to Arnold and he begged him, saying, "Please, they'll kill me if I show them a letter like this." He said, "Please, don't proclaim that I'm some great expert." And even though he had the letter rewritten, when he went to Europe he was still embarrassed to show it to Spaatz. He said, "Now, you understand, this letter was written over my objections. I'm not the great expert. You don't really need me here. Maybe you can find something for me to do much farther down the chain of command."

Stephen Ambrose: This is a good place to make this point: There was a lot of criticism later, with regard to the heavy casualties at Omaha, to the effect that, "God Almighty, you had control of the sea; why didn't you pound and pound and pound for three or four days the way you did out in those Japanese islands, and just obliterate that damn beach? Then we wouldn't have taken those casualties." But Admiral Morrison a long time ago pointed out that if they had done that, they would have given away the invasion site. And the Germans have got land lines of communications. Out in the Pacific, once you start hitting an island, the Japanese can't get any reinforcements into it.

Lewis Sorley: There's one exception to treating the people from the Pacific like bush leaguers. It resulted from General Marshall sending Lieutenant Colonel Red Reeder out to Guadalcanal to look into the nature of the fighting there and come back and report to him. Colonel Reeder wrote his report, sent it to Marshall, waited two weeks–and didn't hear anything. He was really afraid that he had disappointed General Marshall. Then he was called in, and Marshall said, "Red, I hope you don't mind. I've written an introduction to your report and I've had it published in fifty thousand copies. I'm sending it all over the army." And that report, which was called "Fighting on Guadalcanal" was, in fact, distributed as widely as possible by Marshall. It's a very interesting report because it is, in essence, what we would today call an oral history. It is almost entirely composed of what sergeants, lieutenants, and captains told Red about the fighting and how they'd learned to deal with what they had encountered.

Conference Participant: It should be pointed out that the classic success story of a Pacific general who made out okay in the ETO was Joseph Collins, who commanded the 25th division in the Southwest Pacific and then VII Corps in the ETO. So they weren't all ignored. Of course, Collins had an inside track with Marshall and Bradley through his service on the Secretariat and at Fort Benning in the early '30s.

Alan Gropman: We can't forget that both wars were heating up almost simultaneously. There was never any 90:10 split, any 80:20 split, even a 70:30 split. Almost simultaneous with Normandy is Saipan. You've got Nimitz moving across the Central Pacific, MacArthur and Halsey moving up from the Southwest Pacific. These operations are going on simultaneously. Are you going to take your good corps commanders out of the Pacific and put them in Europe when you've got combat operations going on in both theaters? I think it's a lot to ask.

Richard Zeitlin: I'd like to ask Tom Buell: Was the naval gunfire support at Normandy successful; was there ever an attempt to analyze and determine whether it had been successful?

Thomas Buell: I could not cite a specific report. But just to comment on how long naval gunfire support should be scheduled for--in addition to the Germans being able to get forces to Normandy very quickly, there was also the problem of weather. Eisenhower had, what, a forty-eight-hour window to get ashore? That was the situation. As far as I know, the navy did what it was supposed to do. It had the old battleships, and they used their heavy guns effectively. The destroyers went in at close range when they had to, when they were called in to go right after the German tanks. And the British, of course, had their warships there too. So, to the best of my knowledge, there's never been any criticism; there's nothing I've ever read that said that the naval gunfire support was anything other than thoroughly satisfactory. That's always been my understanding.

John Hattendorf: In October of 1944, immediately after the invasion, Captain Charles Cook of Admiral King's staff circulated to all major commands the compilation of reports about the D-Day landing. A significant part of that compilation addressed naval gunfire support. There had been major criticisms of it. It had not lived up to what the navy thought it would do. One of the things that was learned in Normandy was that naval gunfire was not effective unless it made a direct hit on the heavy casemated defenses. There were also problems with coordinating naval gunfire support and the air bombardment, and problems of communications involving how far the support should extend and the timing of it. I think, on reflection, the commanders of the gunfire support felt immediately after the operation that the naval gunfire should have begun earlier and lasted longer in relation to the activities of the other services.

Thomas Buell: But you know, John, that has been said about every amphibious landing: it should have started earlier, it should have lasted longer. So I don't think that was anything all that different. Those are probably the toughest defenses that NGS had to go against. There were heavy concrete emplacements and they were awfully tough to knock out.

Alan Gropman: There were six thousand ships of various types out there–battleships, destroyers in front of the battleships, cruisers in between the battleships and the destroyers. And of all the specialists who went ashore in the first wave, the highest casualties were among the people who were providing liaison for the naval gunfire support, because they had to be up where they could see what was going on. Having worked with the army for years–I was in C-130s in Vietnam, involved in air strikes–I learned that you can never do enough. I don't care what it is. That's just the nature of the business. You just can't ever do enough and, therefore, the navy couldn't do enough. But everything I've read indicates that the navy's performance was nothing short of outstanding. Before you criticize the navy, consider the fact that we had one hundred thousand people going ashore into the teeth of about fourteen divisions, and the fact it all worked.

Scott Belliveau: I have a question about training, and maybe General Talbott and General Collins can address it. With regard to the training you received before the landing and the type of war you had to fight after the landing, did you find the training deficient, did you find problems with it, do you wish you had known more about certain things and less about certain things? What was the general experience insofar as what we were taught and what we actually learned?

James Collins: Well, actually, I think our training was a good preparation, but I'll tell you that there were a hell of a lot of minor snafus. As an example, when we went down to the "hard," as it was called, to board the LST, I had been previously told not to worry about loading the LST, that we had plenty of "experts" to do this. Well, I got there, and instead of an American LST, I had a British LST. And the crew on that LST didn't know how to load artillery or how to organize it inside. I had not studied this problem because I was told that experts would be there. So on the spur of the moment I had to organize a loading plan for this LST. But the LST wouldn't take all of our vehicles, so we had to leave behind a small party of my ammunition-train service battery. What I'm saying is that the training that was received before the landing was fine, but there were a lot of loopholes left there.

Now, going to the far shore, things went quite well, things went much according to plan. I was not there on D-Day; I got there on D-plus-6. The beach was still getting shelled, but it was unobserved fire and no there was no great problem getting ashore.

Orwin Talbott: My outfit was the 90th Infantry Division, which was a rather infamous outfit in Normandy. Two division commanders and some regimental commanders and battalion commanders were relieved. But I have to say in all fairness that by February of '45 Ike listed the 90th as one of the five best divisions in the theater, and Patton listed it as the best by the end of the war. With the kind of fighting we had in Normandy–the bocage was a surprise to all of us, and we did a lot of fumbling around and took a lot of unnecessary casualties trying to figure out what to do about it. It was not until we got some new blood in that we began to straighten things out and take charge, and initiate on our own ways to solve the problem of that machine gun buried in the far corner of that next plot of the hedgerow with the three feet of earth and roots protecting it. These were tricky jobs and we'd had no training for them at all. At the platoon leader level of leadership, technical training–though not personal bravery–was particularly lacking, I thought.

Geoffrey Perret: I'd like to say something about the 90th Division. William DePuy was in that division and he said, "Everything we needed to know was in the manuals, but we never read the manuals." And so I appreciate General Talbott's comment. It's the division's fault, really. In that case it wasn't the army's fault. If they wanted the answers to those problems, they could have looked in the manuals, but they just didn't do it. But getting back to air and naval cooperation or lack of it, D-Day was only another example in a long line of unhappy examples of the army and the navy literally failing to converse, the air force and the navy literally failing to communicate. I don't know about the navy side of this, but the airmen felt that it was impossible to communicate with the navy–that if you told them something, they wouldn't listen to you, and if you suggested something, they wouldn't even listen to that because the navy was this mysterious organization that had its own way of doing things that nobody else could possibly comprehend.

One of the things the navy did that the air force found extremely irritating was that the navy would shoot at anything that flew near a warship. In the end the air force decided, "It's impossible. We've tried to work out a way of cooperating with them. On D-Day we will avoid their warships unless its absolutely essential to do otherwise." William Kepner and Elwood Quesada, the commanders respectively of VIII and IX Fighter Commands, said, "We will not put anything over a U.S. Navy warship except a P-38, because the Germans don't have anything that looks like a P-38." And the navy still shot two of them down.

Stephen Ambrose: On this general theme: the air-ground coordination that was so outstanding in December of 1944 and such a critical factor when the skies finally cleared hadn't been established in June of '44. They didn't have the techniques yet.

Let me just throw out a couple of things here. If I were given the opportunity to make a critique afterwards, the first thing I would say is, "Don't drop the airborne at night." There was a debriefing of the 82nd battalion commanders in July when they got back to England, and that was generally their conclusion. And of course it was the last time we had a major night drop. Dropping them at the dawn would have been much better; they would have gotten together a lot quicker and they would have been more effective, it seems to me.

On this naval gunfire support issue, which is what prompted this comment, I would suggest in a critique what the navy itself said beforehand: "Why do you guys have to go in at first light or very quickly thereafter?" The army said, "We need a whole day to get established." Some army people–Corlett, I believe, was one of them–said, "Go in at night. The confusion will be terrific, but it's not going to be any greater than the confusion you're going to encounter anyway. Make a night landing without any pre-bombardment at all, or wait until 1000 or 1100 hours." The navy said, "Give us six, seven hours to hit those targets," instead of the half hour to forty-five minutes they were actually given. That, in retrospect, seems like it would have been a good idea.

Paul Stillwell: Again, on the naval gunfire, I've heard consistently high praise for the ships of Destroyer Squadron 18 going in virtually on the beach. This was not part of the softening-up process, but direct support of the troops that were under fire on Omaha during that terrible period when they were pinned down. The destroyers *Frankford*, *Emmons*, and *Doyle* were really instrumental.

A much more controversial point to be made on naval gunfire was the necessity of the bombardment of Cherbourg on the 25th of June. General Collins and his troops were moving up the peninsula to capture Cherbourg. This was really Admiral Kirk's baby because he was trying to feel his oats under Admiral Ramsey, the overall Allied naval commander, and he was sort of saying, "Well, we don't need the army's permission to do things." Admiral Morrison sort of said that the bombardment provided effective help to the ground forces, but Admiral Carlton Bryant, who was one of the flag officers there, on the battleship *Texas*, said in the aftermath that he didn't believe the naval bombardment of Cherbourg hastened its capture even by one hour.

Conference Participant: I can add one point to Stephen Ambrose's comment. The senior American naval commander, Admiral Kirk, had recommended in his after-action report that future operations should be done in midday, in broad daylight, in order to get the best timing. He said the early dawn landings or night landings were unnecessary and too dangerous. Daylight gave the best conditions for visibility for both air and naval operations.

Thomas Buell: The thing that hasn't been said and perhaps is implicit here is that an amphibious assault is just about the most dangerous military operation you're ever going to pull off. I suppose an air drop behind enemy lines is also dangerous. But it's scary–from everything I've ever read about it, you're so vulnerable with those troops and those bouncing boats, and they can't defend themselves. So many things can and do go wrong despite your best planning. I know that, from the navy's standpoint, to make an amphibious assault work was probably the greatest challenge they had. They looked upon it as the most dangerous thing they ever had to do.

Alan Gropman: Let me sum up on that point. One of the reasons Hitler didn't invade England in 1940 is that he didn't have anything like we were going to have–Torch in 1942, Husky in 1943, Overlord in 1944. We had those things because the marine corps had developed the doctrine in the 1920s that the navy built upon. In the beginning was the word, in the beginning is doctrine, something we haven't talked an awful lot about here. What we did talk about was the value of training and rehearsal. I heard a cabbie answer a tourist the other day in Washington, D.C.–the tourist asked how to get to the Kennedy Center, and the cabbie said, "Rehearse, man, rehearse." I can tell you that during Desert Storm, during the time that Schwarzkopf had with the enemy's eyes blinded, there was a great deal of rehearsal that was going on south of the Kuwait border.

We also learned a lot about the development of mundane systems, like the jeep and the M1–that they mean a lot. Eisenhower said there were five systems that struck him as being most important during the war: the bulldozer, the DUKW, the C-47, the two-and-half-ton Dodge truck, and the jeep. None were warfighting systems. But these were the systems that were most important to him.

From Geoffrey Perret we learned about the value of schools such as the Army Industrial College that was founded in '24. It went joint in 1925 and it even had non-army commandants in the 1930s and the early 1940s. This is very important for what happened during the war in terms of building a joint structure. We learned from Geoff the value of pairing experience with inexperience. We also learned from Geoff and almost everybody in this room about the weaknesses between the services and among the services in terms of joint cooperation. The navy shot down a lot of air force C-47s in Husky, and mostly it was the air force's fault. In any case, we haven't straightened out that mess yet. The air force and the navy were not able to communicate during Desert Storm. Ladies and gentlemen, it is time that the services be able to communicate.

The Greatest Thing We Have Ever Attempted

Luncheon Address

THE ROAD TO THE SECOND FRONT:
The Diplomacy of the Invasion

H. P. Willmott

The Greatest Thing We Have Ever Attempted

One wonders which was worse: Anglo-American wartime military diplomacy that, amidst mutual incomprehension and exasperation, fashioned the strategic policy of the two Western Allies; or the manner in which American and British commentators and historians have picked over the pieces in the postwar period. There is, of course, a ready answer: the arrangement of an historical program that scheduled me as your lunchtime speaker on the subject of diplomacy, for which I am not noted. But with respect to the matter in hand, it is hard to avoid the conclusion that historical portrayal and interpretation have largely followed national lines and, in so doing, for the most part have generated more heat than light. Indeed, if I may be permitted to provide an example, some eighteen months ago I attended a lecture on this very subject given by perhaps the most preeminent military historian in the United States. I walked away from this lecture thinking that if the French vice is lechery then the British vice is treachery. I also took away two self-evident conclusions: that, on the basis of the lecture, American national mythology was alive and well; and that, in terms of American national demonology, for some Americans my country, Britain, was, is, and seemingly always will be the real "evil empire."

For a Britisher to address a largely American audience on these issues represents a task fraught with obvious dangers. One is reminded of the Irish verse: "The strangers came and tried to teach us their ways and despised us for what we are: they might as well have been chasing moonbeams." One notes the ever-present danger of a British presentation on this subject is the appearance of talking down to an American audience. Most certainly it is not my intention to be thus misinterpreted, and therefore I would open my remarks with two comments on which we might all agree.

First, the events of June 1994 seem fated to be discussed in a veritable flood of publications, most of which, being of dubious taste and even less value, will serve only to prove that too many trees died in vain. Second, it seems likely that not a few of these publications will cling to that notion that has gained much ground in recent years even among allegedly respectable academic opinion in the United States, namely that the invasion of Northwest Europe could and should have been attempted before June 1944—if not in 1942, then most certainly in 1943.

To these comments I would add a third, and one that is both timeless and related directly to the events about which I am tasked to speak: allies are not necessarily friends, and alliances are seldom if ever struck between equals. Allies share an all-important common single interest of such importance that those divergent interests are held in check; nevertheless, the latter remain, only to grow in importance with the approach of victory or defeat. One is always amazed by histories that appear to be surprised by the differences and points of detail that separated the Americans and British; and, indeed, one is equally amazed, and not a little irritated, by the lack of care and attention paid to those factors that shaped British policy.

British policy has been the subject of stereotype. One is told that British policy traditionally has been peripheral, and that in the Second World War Britain sought to use naval supremacy to wear down a continental enemy by time and distance. One has also been told, usually by American historians, that political considerations shaped British determination to prosecute a Mediterranean strategy. Certainly, political considerations and the desire to use naval supremacy to wear down a Continental enemy by time and distance by imposing costly but marginal obligations was paraded by the British high command in its defense of the Mediterranean commitment: the same factors underpinned British deliberations in the examination of Operation Jupiter, the proposed invasion of Norway.

But the general comment lends itself to three observations. First, what was called "the British way of war" by that self-advertising charlatan Liddell Hart does not bear serious scrutiny, as even the most cursory examination of British army battle honors would reveal. One can hardly find a less peripheral battlefield than Blenheim, and that plus the battles of Ramillies, Oudenarde, Malplaquet, Dettingen, Fontenoy, Waterloo, Ypres, the Somme, and Amiens, as well as Minden, the 1794 campaign, and Walcheren in 1809 share the common characteristic of being fought in the strategic heartland of Europe, or at least Western Europe. Throughout Britain's many wars between 1649 and 1918, and not least in the First World War, a British field army of very respectable size and capability invariably went to the Low Countries or western Germany to make the largest single British military contribution to the war in which Britain found herself.

Second, in those wars in which Britain did not commit an expeditionary army to the main theater of operations in Western Europe, the reason was simple. In the War of American Independence there was no theater of operations on the Continental mainland. In the Napoleonic Wars the British involvement in Portugal and Spain stemmed from the defeat of her allies and Britain's patent inability to challenge French primacy in Western Europe. If Britain did indeed adopt peripheral strategies in the Peninsular and the Second World Wars, she did so not by choice but because they were imposed upon her by circumstances and weakness.

Third, there has been precious little attempt to define the alleged political considerations that the American high command suspected at the time to be so important in shaping Britain's Mediterranean strategy in the Second World War. In preparing for this conference paper one read through the first hundred pages of Carlo d'Este's *Fatal Decision: Anzio and the Fall of Rome,* and there one noted no fewer than five references in the first sixteen pages of text to such considerations. Leaving aside one rather strange observation—"the inevitable fiasco that results whenever political aims take precedence over [sound] military practice"—never once in these sixteen pages were such British aims and considerations defined, as if a contemporaneous suspicion on the part of the American high command of British motives was in itself proof of fact. But British aims in the Mediterranean were defined in a British chiefs of staff paper that seems to have been most carefully omitted from the book. That paper reads as follows:

> Our final conclusion is that the Mediterranean offers us opportunities for action in the coming autumn and winter [1943-1944] which may be decisive, and at the least will do far more to prepare the way for a cross-Channel operation in 1944 than we should achieve by attempting to transfer back to the United Kingdom some of the forces now in the Mediterranean theater. If we take these opportunities, we shall have every chance of breaking the Axis and of bringing the war to a successful conclusion in 1944.

What is so often missed in any discussion of the Mediterranean strategy is the simple fact that as often as not strategic choice is illusory: one fights where one can rather than where one would. The corollary is obvious: that 1942 and 1943 commitments stemmed directly from the 1940 commitment when Britain had no choice but to fight in the only theater in which she was in contact by land with her enemies.

If Operation Torch is justified in terms of the need for American troops to enter the German war in 1942, then it was equally true of Britain vis-à-vis the

Mediterranean theater in the years 1940-1942. The alternative, and specifically the alternative to mount an invasion of Northwest Europe either in 1942 or 1943, would have been to abandon Egypt and with it the whole of the British position in the Middle East. Clearly this never presented itself as a practical proposition. But even this consideration is of little account when compared to the one matter that critics of British calculations and considerations never explain. War is political in nature, and war serves political aims. General George C. Marshall might have claimed that he would never send a soldier to die for a political purpose, but that would seem to be Marshall's problem and not a comment on those who would. If British strategic policy was shaped by political considerations, then that was only right and proper.

For one's own part one would note three matters that were critical in shaping British policy toward the Mediterranean and Overlord. The first, obviously, was the events of 1940-1941. Attention naturally concentrates upon the defeat of 1940. It is vitally important to remember that in the space of eleven months British forces suffered the ignominy of not one but three defeats on, and three evacuations from, the European mainland. These defeats undoubtedly made the British high command very cautious, and rightly so. If the British chiefs of staff were to be accused of not wishing to undertake an invasion of Northwest Europe until such time that success was all but assured, then that would be a charge to which Alan Brooke and his colleagues would cheerfully plead guilty.

Second, less obviously, was the grave concern with which the British high command viewed Britain's import and reserve positions throughout the war. In committing itself to Overlord, Britain accepted that this operation would have to proceed despite estimates that stockpiles of food and raw materials would be reduced to a two-months' supply by mid-year. The winter of 1944-1945 saw the first cases of serious undernourishment in Britain, even though by this time there existed shipping resources on a scale never previously available to the Allies, and the United States was involved in directly supporting forces in Northwest Europe. An invasion of Northwest Europe in 1942 or 1943 would have required Britain to provide the main logistical support at a time when her import and reserve positions varied between the worrying and potentially precarious. A measure of the potential seriousness of the British import/reserves position is indicated by the fact that Operation Torch, which was smaller than Overlord and supported in part directly from the United States, reduced the Royal Navy to one month's oil reserve by March 1943.

Furthermore, an invasion of Northwest Europe in either 1942 or 1943 would have involved a lengthening or slowing of the convoy cycle on which Britain was totally dependent for imports. In this context, it is worth recalling that in 1938 Britain was dependent upon 60 million tons of imports (plus oil) per year. By 1944 Britain was surviving on 27 million tons, and had less than three months' reserves to hand. At the rate of 1944 deliveries, Britain could not have survived until 1946. Had Operation Jupiter been conducted in 1942 or 1943, the result would have been the loss of five hundred thousand tons of imports, a total equivalent to one-eighth of Britain's reserves in mid-1944. If so small an undertaking as Operation Jupiter could have such an effect, it is somewhat difficult to resist the perverse conclusion that, had an invasion of Northwest Europe been attempted before 1944, the only country that would have been brought to surrender would have been Britain.

Third, one knows from one's own research that at least from the middle of 1943 perhaps the most important single factor shaping the thinking of the British chiefs of staff was the awareness that the entire class of 1946 available to the armed forces would not be sufficient to meet the minimum needs of the Royal Navy, which was the least demanding of the three services on manpower. In 1943 certainly, and one suspects that throughout 1942 as a cloud on the horizon, the British chiefs of staff knew that if the war dragged into 1946 the national manpower position would become impossible. This was perhaps the main reason for the decision to send a carrier force to the Pacific rather than accept an expanded military and air commitment in Southeast Asia: the carrier force would be less costly in manpower than an increase of ground and air forces in Southeast Asia. But given the accusation of a British dragging of feet on Overlord, it needs to be noted that the British chiefs of staff had every reason to agree to an early Overlord and that they refused to consider either a 1942 or a 1943 option despite an incentive of seemingly overwhelming importance. In reality, of course, it was this manpower situation that underpinned the British resistance to any premature effort that might result in the loss of Britain's last manpower reserves: for Britain, and for both Britain and the United States, there could be no second Overlord if the first failed.

In terms of the decisions that led to Overlord two matters would seem to command immediate attention. The first is the popular view that the American high command in 1942 and 1943 was obliged to make a series of concessions to the British on questions of the strategic policy for the European war. My view is that the American high command made no concessions to the British but to reality: the American concessions were to immutable factors such as time, numbers, and distance rather than to her ally. If in these years the British had a better grasp on reality than the Americans, then so be it. The reality of the American position in 1942 was that a nation coming to a war cannot determine its terms of reference but must take them as they are and, to borrow a saying, not to seek to make them something they are not and cannot be. Perhaps the American high command in 1942 can be excused for not recognizing this. There is no excuse for alleged historians making the same mistake fifty years later.

The second matter I mentioned is to question the effect of Marshall's insistence upon a cross-Channel invasion in 1942. It is difficult to resist the thought that the meetings of April and July 1942, when Marshall tried to force Sledgehammer on the British, cost the U.S. Army's chief of staff any respect in terms of his strategic judgement the British service chiefs had for him. Certainly, Brooke seems never to have recovered fully from the experience, thereafter regarding Marshall as an all but impossible individual with whom to deal in terms of argument and the devising of common policy. Of course, to state this risks raising American hackles: Marshall has been raised to a position in the pantheon of American heroes that permits no questioning of judgement, and no censure or reproach. Inevitably, therefore, the issue for American historians has been Britain's alleged bad faith over Sledgehammer in 1942 and Roundup in 1943.

The real questions that should command attention are the two that American historians seemingly never ask. The first is obvious: if Marshall's views in the spring of 1942 on the critical importance of an invasion of Northwest Europe in that year were correct, why had so little been done in the way of American planning for such an operation over the previous twenty months—it being remembered that almost two years had elapsed since the fall of France and forty-two months had passed since Marshall had taken up his appointment as chief of staff? The second question is no less obvious: why in April and July 1942 did Marshall and Admiral Ernest J. King press for a landing in Northwest Europe for that year when King most certainly knew that the lack of amphibious shipping would preclude such an operation?

One could add a third question: how could the Americans service chiefs contemplate an autumn invasion—which would have to be supplied over open beaches—despite the bad weather the Allies were certain to encounter? Between 1 October and 28 February in any given year, the eastern Atlantic and Channel approaches average seventy-six days of Force 7 weather conditions and another ten days of more severe conditions. With the Great Storm of 19-22 June 1944—when thirteen merchantman and over eight hundred minor craft were driven ashore—to serve by way of example, if only in terms of timing and meteorological factors, Marshall's insistence on a 1942 operation was hopelessly flawed. And it should be noted that the winter of 1942-1943 proved worse than usual: Force 7 weather was encountered on 105 days with another 15 days of even worse conditions.

Even more importantly, Marshall's insistence on a 1942 endeavor came at a time when the Allies did not possess air superiority over northern France, had not established command of the sea and, critically, did not have either the manpower or the logistical infrastructure necessary for the conduct of a sustained campaign on the European mainland. The self-evident point about a cross-Channel attack seems often to be forgotten: that a landing was but the means and not an end in itself, and that the aim of such an operation was not to land in northern France but to conduct a major campaign in Northwest Europe. Given the fact that the major burden of such a campaign had to be borne by the United States, a 1942 endeavor was clearly out of the question. Whether the position would have been any different in 1943 is doubtful.

Consideration of these matters lead naturally to an examination of the question of when, if at all, a cross-Channel operation could have been executed before June 1944. Put another way, discounting 1942 from serious consideration, could an invasion of Northwest Europe have been conducted in 1943? Given lead-times for planning and the concentration of formations, it is hard to resist the conclusion that the Symbol conference at Casablanca in January 1943 represented a "go-now-or-never-in-1943" choice; and, one would note, it is quite possible that the 1943 slot had closed even before this conference. Even if one does not accept either of these two propositions, there is no doubting that by the time of the Trident conference in Washington in May the 1943 cross-Channel deadline had passed. The difficulty herein is that in examining Anglo-American military diplomacy, there are four quite distinct phases: the April-July 1942 exchanges; Symbol; the Trident-Quadrant conferences (which I prefer to consider as one); and the subsequent exchanges on Overlord and a host of related matters that occupied so much of the autumn and winter of 1943-1944. The problem that emerges from these exchanges is presented by the Trident-Quadrant combination. It is not that there were occasions when the British argument was correct and other times when the American contention was correct, but rather at these conferences there were occasions and arguments when both the Americans and British were correct at one and the same time. Hence the difficulty of an agreement.

The basis of all American dealings with the British was contained in a four-part thesis: that the defeat of Germany could only be accomplished by the defeat and destruction of the Wehrmacht on the North European Plain; that the road northward through the Italian peninsula was one that in strategic terms led nowhere; that Italy threatened only to be a liability to whichever side occupied her; and that a Mediterranean commitment, once embraced, could not be limited but would serve to divert resources and attention from the main theater of war.

There is little doubting the essential correctness of these individual points. The Torch commitment led inexorably to a wider undertaking in the central Mediterranean that in itself was sufficient to destroy any American hope for a cross-Channel invasion in 1943, and the Italian theater could never be more than a secondary, perhaps tertiary, sideshow. Moreover, the American high command grasped the brutally vulgar fact that only through main-force action could the Wehrmacht be defeated.

A very careful reading of the 1943 conferences reveals that the British high command never disputed the accuracy of the first two American points. But the British high command sought a German defeat, not the defeat of Germany, in the Mediterranean theater; and, with regard to victory on the North European Plain, it saw the invasion of and subsequent campaign in Northwest Europe as the means of completing, not accomplishing, the defeat of Germany. The British adherence to the Mediterranean strategy sprang from the realization that in 1942 the Allied terms of reference had not been altered by the American entry into the war and that existing commitments had to be pursued. The element of choice that in 1942 the American military assumed was its to exercise did not exist, and closing down the Mediterranean theater either in 1942 or 1943 in order to concentrate resources for an invasion of northwest France would merely have eased German commitments and enabled the Wehrmacht to concentrate its resources for such an eventuality.

One point that is seldom considered by those critical of the Mediterranean commitment is the question of the likely German reaction to the appearance of American inactivity in the second half of 1942. It beggars belief that if there had been no American commitment in the Solomon Islands and North Africa, there would have been no corresponding strengthening of the Wehrmacht in Western Europe. The British high command was surely correct in its argument that the clearing of North Africa was an essential and unavoidable commitment; and if one accepts a minimum lead-time of eight months between the end of a campaign in North Africa and the start of a campaign in Northwest Europe there could be no cross-Channel operation in 1943 unless Tunis had been taken in November 1942. As it was, there can be no serious questioning of the British insistence that the defeat of Italy possessed major political and psychological significance. If matters Italian possessed no major value, why did Mark Clark's Fifth U.S. Army make such efforts to capture of Rome ahead of the British?

The major problem that confounded Anglo-American military diplomacy with respect to Overlord lay not in the operation itself but in the question of timing for 1943 and, with reference to the exact relationship between the European and Mediterranean theaters, between Overlord and the conflicting demands of the Italian and southern France alternatives. The arguments of February-March 1944 over the relative claims of these alternatives reflected little credit on either the American or the British high commands, and the final American insistence on an August 1944 Anvil makes little sense in light of the fact that Anvil's proclaimed *raison d'etre* lay in its synchronization with Overlord. The fact that the American high command insisted upon Anvil despite its not coinciding with Overlord and at a time when its military value was at best dubious would suggest that considerations other than military underpinned American calculations. Moreover, the attempt to justify Anvil in terms of the importance of the ports of southern France in ensuring the supply of American divisions in Northwest Europe is dishonest: the justification of Anvil was not logistic but strategic, and, that being the case, it is difficult to resist the conclusion that American insistence on Anvil was prompted by determination to demonstrate the power of decision.

Here one is in uncharted waters because even at a distance of fifty years it is difficult to produce a statement of account for either Italy or Anvil/Dragoon. There were many aspects and episodes of the Italian campaign that were unsatisfactory. One thinks immediately of the lack of any clear objective when Allied forces first landed on peninsular Italy, and then of the pursuit phase from the Winter Line in early June 1944, when the German Tenth Army slipped through Allied fingers and thus escaped annihilation. One thinks too of Churchill's nonsensical attempt to move beyond Italy with the Istria-Vienna operation, which the British chiefs of staff opposed because the twenty-four divisions needed for it were simply not available.

The Italian campaign certainly tied down many Allied divisions, but in 1943 these divisions could not have been employed elsewhere to any useful purpose. Furthermore, in 1944 and 1945 the number of Allied divisions in Northwest Europe were sufficient to requirements; therefore, Italy cannot be said to have been a drain on Allied military resources. Likewise, and for much the same reasons, the Mediterranean was not a drain on Allied naval and amphibious resources, most certainly not after the invasion of Sicily—though it could be argued that Torch involved unnecessary losses in the North Atlantic for at least six months. The Mediterranean commitment undoubtedly slowed the pace of the U.S. Army Air Force's buildup in Britain and the start of its strategic bombing effort, but to what effect is impossible to say with any certainty.

Against these considerations, there is the fact that the Italian campaign imposed upon the German high command a commitment of between twenty and twenty-seven divisions—including a minimum of a dozen first-grade divisions—for the better part of two years. It also forced the diversion of five divisions from Western Europe and Germany in the ten days immediately preceding Overlord. But Harold Alexander's claim that his command tied down fifty-five German divisions in Italy and neighboring theaters is special pleading, as the majority of divisions in southern Europe were often as not involved either in reforming or assigned an occupational role rather than detailed to anti-invasion duties.

But the Italian campaign does present a number of issues that those who argue the Sledgehammer case should consider most carefully. The first is the example of Operation Shingle and the fact that it was only by the most narrow of margins that the Allies avoided defeat at Anzio. Would an Allied landing in northern France in 1943 have necessarily fared any better, and indeed would such a landing not have resulted in a victory that so narrowly eluded the Wehrmacht in front of Anzio? That the Allies were not defeated at Anzio can be attributed in major part to overwhelming air and naval supremacy, neither of which would necessarily have been available at Normandy and in the Cotentin peninsula in 1943.

The second matter that should be considered is the implicit assumption that underpins the 1942-1943 assertion, namely that the forces that would have come ashore in 1942 or 1943 possessed the Allied capability of 1944. Most definitely this was not the case. The U.S. Army did not have its 1944 numbers available until 1944, and in 1942 and 1943 most certainly did not have the technique it displayed in 1944. As Bradley noted in so many words, the technique of 1944, specifically the combat experience of the army, corps, and divisional staffs, as well as the logistical capability, could not have been acquired except in North Africa and Italy.

No less importantly, one wonders what might have happened if an invasion of Northwest Europe had been attempted in either 1942 or 1943 without there having been eighteen months of remarkably harmonious relations between American and British field commanders. The differences and unpleasant-nesses are always stressed, and in 1944 relations were often strained and sometimes extremely heated and bad tempered, but on the basis of past confidences ruffled feathers and fur could be and were smoothed. Could such harmony—uneasy harmony, perhaps, but harmony nonetheless—have been achieved in the course of a 1942 or 1943 invasion of northern France; could it have been improvised on the hoof? Could such episodes as the Coningham-Patton exchanges have been negotiated in the midst of a Kasserine Pass-type battle fought around St.-Lô in mid-1943?

One suspects that these questions point to the most important aspect of Overlord and the whole of the Mediterranean enterprise. The North Atlantic was much wider fifty years ago than it is today. The existence of a standing alliance for more than four decades and modern means of communications tends to blind us to the fact that when first they met in August 1941 the British and U.S. high commands were strangers: there was no common basis of organization, no familiarity with one another's problems, no permanent consultative system. One tends to forget that wary suspicion and distrust (if not worse) characterized Anglo-American relations throughout the interwar period, and time—1942 and 1943—was needed to establish trust and understanding. When one considers what was at stake in the issues that at one and the same time divided and united Britain and the United States in this war, it is perhaps not altogether surprising that the path the two countries trod was often broken and difficult.

Again, at a distance of half a century it is too easy to lose sight of the fact that here was one nation involved in a struggle for her very survival and another entering into her inheritance. Wartime Anglo-American military diplomacy was characterized by trust and understanding: the Americans did not trust the British, and the British did not understand the Americans. And rightly so, but in a war in which perhaps for the only time in history possession of the trident changed hands without conflict between predecessor and successor, the Americans and British forged a relationship and common strategy that worked, and, one would submit, worked rather well. Most certainly there were areas of disagreement, about Overlord but more seriously over the Mediterranean and Burma. But whatever the many failings of the Americans and British in their dealings with one another, these pale into insignificance when set alongside the decision-making process of Germany and her relations with her associates (which barely merit the label "diplomatic" still less "successful"), and even of the Imperial Japanese Army and Navy in their dealings with one another. Perhaps things could have been arranged to better effect, but in the greatest war in history in which victory could not be won quickly and by short cuts, the strategy that was forged would seem to pass scrutiny, errors and omissions excepted.

Discussion

Alan Gropman: You make a good point about parochial and chauvinistic history, which isn't history at all; it's an oxymoron. Chauvinistic history is propaganda, and there's been too much written on both sides—by Max Hastings on the British side and many historians on our side—about the infallibility of George Marshall. Let me tell you, when you get around to publishing this piece, what I think needs to be added to it. You're right, an invasion in '42 would have been a tragedy; '43 would have been a mistake and probably wouldn't have worked. However, what's left out of your argument is the pressures on Marshall. Why is Marshall pulling for an invasion at this particular time? When he's calling for it, the Russians are in deep trouble and the American strategy is to put few people in the field, become the arsenal of democracy, strategic bomb the hell out of the bad guys, use the Russians to kill Germans, and use the Russians to invade Japan. Remember, we didn't know the A-bomb was going to work, and the project to build one was just getting started anyway. There were enormous pressures on Marshall to help relieve what was happening to the Russians at this particular time.

H. P. Willmott: I would agree with you. The other point concerning American policy that one wonders about is how much of this was a sort of an instinctual "let's guard ourselves against the navy and the Pacific lobby." How much of this in '42 was really geared to bureaucratic problems as well? I don't know the answer to that one. I think the point I would really pick up is this one about Stalin and the Soviet argument. One of my great dislikes is this chauvinistic, ethnocentric, "let's-point-the-finger-at-other-people" history, which I think diverts us from consideration of real issues. I try not to be British here, although I find myself instinctively arguing certain of their arguments for them. But I do think with regard to the Soviet Union there is a point to be made along these lines. It was said this morning that if a 1943 invasion had been conducted, one of the great benefits would have been that the Soviet Union would have been kept out of Central Europe. But who on our side in 1942 or '43 gave that any serious consideration? The point is that nobody on our side really thought the defeat of Germany could be accomplished without the Soviet Union playing a full part in that victory. I defy anybody to say otherwise, and the consequence of the Soviet Union playing a full part in the defeat of Germany was that there was going to be a postwar Soviet military presence in Central Europe. You can't turn around and say we should have gone ahead in 1943 with this invasion to preempt the Soviets when in fact it was intended to complement their efforts. You just can't read history backwards in this respect.

Thomas Buell: You asked, "Why did King back Marshall in his quest for a '42 invasion?" King realized that Marshall's staff was emotionally involved in the '42 invasion because that's what the boss wanted, and one way or the other they were going to find a way to do it. I think King knew it would never happen, and he knew that when you looked at the logistics of a '42 invasion you could see that it was an impossible undertaking. I think it was purely politics that King wanted to have a united front; he wanted to do a favor for Marshall so that Marshall would do a favor for him. But I don't think he ever believed you could have had a cross-Channel invasion in '42.

H. P. Willmott: It sounds almost as if King were acting in a very British way here, doesn't it?

Thomas Buell: There was also a lot of diplomacy on the Joint Chiefs of Staff to get what they wanted. A real point of contention between the British and American combined chiefs as to whether we could pull off a '44 invasion seemed to be a British insistence that conditions had to be right, that the Germans had to be weakened to the extent that there would be a good probability that Overlord would be successful. To do that, the British said, you had to keep pumping more and more resources into Italy. That was what drove the American frustration, and they finally said, "At what point is Germany sufficiently weakened that you feel we can land?"

H. P. Willmott: The problem here is that for every American solution there is an insoluble British problem. It's a genuine problem because there were genuine issues. Now, I know what the conventional histories and explanations say, and the basic argument is that it is always November 1943 when the final British objections are overridden. It's always a problem to decide on these issues. I've worked all the way through the British Joint Planning Staff files, right through '43 and '44, and they're very, very interesting, because it's quite clear from the files that at least mentally the Planning Staff, as early as June 1943, had penciled in May 1944 as the month when the invasion could be undertaken. The decision to do this was really taken at the Trident Conference. There were still many roadblocks to the invasion and many of the British objections, some of them by Churchill, were legitimate. Nevertheless, in the planning files for August and September 1943, the decision to invade in May 1944 is definitely there. Even three months before the final Sextant Conferences, British plans are being prepared on the basis that May 1944 cannot be shifted; all their planning is built around that date.

Conference Participant: The problem was, they were not conveying that to the Americans.

H. P. Willmott: Danchev's account about Marshall indicates that the Americans had adopted a very realistic approach in dealing with the British which the British never understood. The British also have certain recourses which they always use. One is to "consent and evade," which you means you agree while you're there, and when you get back to London you repudiate. The other standard issue in the British diplomatic kick-back is to send a light-weighted irrelevance from the Royal Family on a tour.

But the real point is, and this comes across when you look at the Central Planning Staff files as well—particularly the files that were being prepared by the navy for the British presence in the Pacific—is that the invasion was going to happen. It is there, and there's a disjuncture. The loose ends don't tie up presumably because there is a problem of cross-Atlantic negotiation. We tend to forget how new this all was at this stage. But also as you go up the chain of command there is definitely the occurrence of the "filter up/filter out" phenomenon. I think attitudes were struck by certain people with regard to their opposite numbers; they didn't like each other and there's no two ways about that.

Cole Kingseed: Earlier today we talked a little bit about Roosevelt's decision to select Ike instead of Marshall to command the invasion force. Would you mind commenting on the reaction of the British high command to that decision?

H. P. Willmott: The British were delighted. It's as simple as that. In April 1945, of eighty-nine divisions in Northwest Europe, the Americans had sixty-one and the British had twelve. So there was no question of who would provide the commander for the war in Northwest Europe: it was going to be an American. Alan Brooke might have wanted to command the invasion; who wouldn't, for professional reasons, have wanted to command that operation? But there was a realization by the British that by 1943 Britain was almost totally dependent upon the United States. There's only one area of the war in which the British weren't dependent upon the United States, and that was RAF Bomber Command. In every other respect, the Americans hold the power of decision. The British grasped that, and, let's be quite clear, it must have been very, very difficult for certain people, particularly Churchill.

Now, one of the things about Churchill's behavior in '44 which is appalling at virtually every level is that he's in the grip of the de Gaulle syndrome, the penchant for increasingly divisive action as the power of decision diminishes. But there was no doubt about it, the war was going to be an American-dominated show. And the point is, by autumn of 1943 Eisenhower had earned the trust of the British. The whole point about the Mediterranean commitment which I think is so important, because it was so critical to the subsequent conduct of the war, is that the command relationships between the British and the Americans were established. By the time Eisenhower was named supreme commander virtually everybody in the British and American command structures knew everybody else. Ramsay and Cunningham had both served with the Americans in the Mediterranean. The air forces presented a different situation and it caused problems. The line commanders had worked together and occasionally against one another, but, hell, what do you expect? Why do you get generals? After all, they fall into one of two groups: maladjusted sociopaths or paranoid schizophrenics. What else do you expect from them other than to behave just as they did? Of course they quarrel, of course they're bad-tempered, and of course they're egotistical and want to see themselves having the main role. They're all prima donnas.

But seriously—I was being serious about generals—the real point is that, yes, the British were delighted by the choice of Eisenhower. There's always sniping, but it's not the finger-pointing that should be considered important, it's the fact of how much agreement there was. We can all point fingers and say, "The American performance wasn't that good" or "The British performance was not good." It leads us nowhere, really. We should be looking at far more fundamental issues, which perhaps I might be able to do tomorrow if you can take a second dose of me.

Geoffrey Perret: You rubbished Anvil/Dragoon as being totally pointless, but I was curious to know how the twenty U.S. divisions that were waiting to deploy to the ETO and couldn't get in through northern Europe because Cherbourg turned out to be a pretty small port—how were they going to get into France without first taking Marseilles?

H. P. Willmott: I didn't rubbish Anvil/Dragoon. I said that the justification for the invasion of southern France when it was proposed in November '43 was that it should be synchronized with Overlord. Synchronization was the only justification, really, that one can see—it would have to be conducted at the same time as Overlord, and what I said was that it slipped two months. Were the ports of southern France so essential to the United States?

Geoffrey Perret: Absolutely. In '44 they were absolutely essential.

H. P. Willmott: Do you mean to say that the sixty-one American divisions that were in northern Europe...

Geoffrey Perret: About forty-one divisions . . .

H. P. Willmott: . . . could not have been supported?

Geoffrey Perret: That's right. Just take a look at the capacity of the ports in northern France. They expected Cherbourg would be able to handle five times as much as it actually handled. They couldn't get Antwerp open, so how were the troops going to get in? Not only the troops, but their equipment as well.

H. P. Willmott: Yes, agreed. The ports in northern France proved remarkably resistant and they could not be reduced quickly. Okay, I will buy into what you're saying quite willingly. But the arguments of April, May, and June of '44 are on a very different level.

Geoffrey Perret: Yes, but you see, Marshall was the one who saw the need for taking Marseilles, not Eisenhower. Eisenhower was arguing for Anvil on the basis that you described. It was Marshall who said to him, "Look, you have to take Marseilles."

H. P. Willmott: Right.

Geoffrey Perret: And Eisenhower, once he was persuaded, said "yes" and then he stuck to having a second invasion because he recognized the merit of the case that Marshall had made to him.

H. P. Willmott: Yes. Fair enough. Perhaps there's more to Anvil than I had thought. On the other hand the argument about Italy is once again the complicating factor. The British argument, of course, is that Anvil is far too distant from Normandy to complement the invasion. So they want to carry out the operation in southern Italy which is even farther away. This is the sort of logical absurdity which the British did get themselves into over this argument. But the obvious question is why argue in favor of an operation on strategic grounds and then, when the strategic argument was abandoned, insist upon the operation on the basis of logistics?

Geoffrey Perret: But sometimes the way you take an objective is not by the straightest route.

H. P. Willmott: Agreed: the old comment that the longest way around is the shortest way there.

Panel 2

THROUGH THE BOCAGE:
The Normandy Campaign to
the Closing of the Falaise Gap

Contributors
Joseph M. Balkoski, Martin Blumenson, John A. English
Moderated by Steve E. Dietrich

The Greatest Thing We Have Ever Attempted

Introduction

Immediately following the D-Day landings, the Normandy campaign began predictably with the Allies striving to enlarge their lodgment and the Germans struggling to contain it. There was no mystery as to ultimate intentions: the Allies were aiming for a breakout; the Germans, to drive the invaders into the sea. But the two sides proved more or less evenly matched insofar as the Allies could make but little headway against the Germans, while the Germans could not budge the Allies much less push them off the Continent. Their strategies having canceled each other out, the combatants went at each other with all the lack of finesse of heavyweight boxers slugging it out in center ring. Standing as if toe to toe and trading mighty punches in the relatively close confines of the Normandy countryside, they bashed and battered their way to a standstill, fulfilling the worst fears of Allied leaders, civilian and military alike, who had already trod this path of simultaneous carnage and futility in the attrition battles of the Great War. At the end of June the capture of the Cotentin Peninsula with the port of Cherbourg, although an important triumph for American arms, was followed by the fighting in the hedgerows, a bloody, yard-by-yard grind for the units involved.

The 29th Division, a National Guard outfit from Maryland and Virginia, was one of those units. By then it was no stranger to combat, having received its baptism of fire on 6 June when its 115th and 116th Regimental Combat Teams assaulted Omaha Beach while temporarily attached to the 1st Division; and, after the Allies broke out of the bocage country, it would stay more or less involved in the war right up to the German surrender. As a charter member of the Allied Expeditionary Force and an active participant in the struggle to liberate Europe, the 29th provides panelist Joseph Balkoski with a textbook case for analyzing the role played and contributions made by National Guard divisions in a regular army often given to doubting the worth of such formations.

Balkoski discusses the 29th's makeup, training, and performance, and in doing so he addresses the larger issue of the National Guard's mission and effectiveness as a source of combat-capable units in time of war. Panel moderator Steve Dietrich, in his introductory remarks, observes that this is an issue that remains relevant to the army because of what happened when the National Guard and Army Reserve were excluded from participation in the Vietnam War. The failure to mobilize guard and reserve units for duty in Southeast Asia, said Dietrich, guaranteed that a majority of Americans would have no direct stake in the war's outcome, thus eroding and finally obviating popular support for the war effort and, ultimately, America's foreign policy goals in that region. Therefore, in the early 1970s army commanders, led by Chief of Staff General Creighton Abrams, undertook a reorganization of the U.S. Army aimed at ensuring the employment of guard and reserve units in any major conflict to which the regular army was committed. Henceforth a number of army divisions would have only two active brigades; the third brigade would be a National Guard "roundout" brigade that would be called to active duty to bring the division up to full strength in the event of war. But the mobilization of guard brigades takes time, which in war has an inconvenient habit of speeding precipitously ahead of the plans that men would harness to it. Such was the case in Operations Desert Shield and Desert Storm, when the necessarily rapid deployment of the U.S. armed forces to the Persian Gulf theater forced the substitution of other active army brigades for the National Guard roundout brigades (though dozens of reserve component support units did deploy.)

The attempt was made, however, to use the roundout brigades as envisioned; indeed, they were activated in full expectation that they could be deployed in time for battle. But it was not to be. "Regular army evaluators found the National Guard brigades to be unfit for combat and entered them into extended training programs," Dietrich reports. As a result,

> The roundout brigades were not declared combat-ready in time for battle, and never deployed. The incident sparked an ongoing, often acrimonious, debate between the guard and [the] regular army as to why the units were not used, the army claiming that [the] part-time units were not up to standard, and the guard charging that the army did not want to give the guard units an opportunity to prove themselves, and that they were, in fact, more combat-ready than some of the army units that did deploy.

The experience, Dietrich said, has been the subject of countless articles, impassioned letters to editors, and investigations by the Army Inspector General, the General Accounting Office, the Rand Corporation, and other organizations with links to the armed forces. "To help better prepare for future employment of reserve component forces," said Dietrich, "the army and the guard are keenly interested in historical examples of large guard combat units in action." Joseph Balkoski provides such an assessment, one that indicates at least the possibility of a satisfactory resolution to the issue for all concerned.

*

The next contributor, Lieutenant Colonel John English (Canadian Army), discusses Canada's contributions to the Allied effort in Normandy. This too is a topic that Steve Dietrich finds worthy of study because of the circumstances likely to confront America in the 1990s and beyond when military action is contemplated and undertaken. "As the new order of the world evolves," Dietrich remarked in his introduction for English,

> The United States armed forces are finding themselves less involved in unilateral actions and more frequently a member of a multinational team, and often not the nation in charge. The Canadian army in Normandy offers examples of the challenges of one nation's armed forces operating in cooperation with and . . . under the control, as well as in control of, the armed forces of other nations. Differences of experiences, equipment, logistical requirements, organization, doctrine, training and perceptions of one nation's soldiers about the other's . . . [as well as] other thorny issues open themselves to analysis.

Dietrich observes that these multinational forces are often impromptu in nature, organized rapidly in response to fast-developing crises around the globe. To achieve success, he says, it is imperative that they learn how to cooperate. Dietrich cites the disastrous U.S. Army Ranger operation in Somalia and "the latent emergence of NATO leadership in the face of American indecisiveness in Bosnia" as examples of what a lack of cooperation can entail. "Analysis of historical examples such as the cooperation of Canadians, British, and Polish forces in Normandy," asserts Dietrich, "can help lead to smoother coalition operations today."

*

The panel's final speaker, Martin Blumenson, examines the climactic episode of the Normandy campaign, the effort at Falaise to trap and destroy the bulk of two German armies in a Cannae-like battle of annihilation. In any consideration of this battle and its outcome, the proverbial "what-ifs" accumulate thickly and clamorously around the inevitable question of what should have been accomplished versus what was accomplished. One thing is certain: Falaise was no Cannae. But it almost was, and it is that element of near-success that both maddens and perplexes students of the operational art, and excites historians to frenzies of controversy over what happened and why, and who was to blame. What, after all, can one say about a victory that was at once a vast achievement and a huge disappointment? Blumenson calls it a failure: as stated in the subtitle of his book *The Battle of the Generals,* on which his paper is based, Falaise was "The Campaign That Should Have Won World War II."

The achievement of victory that results in something more like failure is certainly not new to warfare; that standard was set as long ago as 279 B.C. when Pyrrhus of Epirus won the battle of Asculum against the Romans but saw the best contingents in his army terribly reduced in the process. "Another such victory and I am lost," he famously remarked after counting the casualties among his elite troops. Of course, the victory at Falaise was neither catastrophic in the Pyrrhic sense, nor was it fatal to the Allied war effort: the Allies were not going to lose the war by allowing a sizeable number of enemy troops to escape the pocket. But, according to Blumenson, the consequences of the failure that occurred at Falaise were nonetheless severe: instead of bringing the war to an end in the closing months of 1944, the fighting was prolonged through the winter of that year and into the spring of 1945, thus inflicting untold, and perhaps avoidable, death and destruction on a continent that had already suffered far too much of both. Steve Dietrich comments that what Blumenson and many other Second World War historians regard as the true harvest of Falaise—reaping failure from victory—has a latter-day parallel in Operation Desert Storm. Nor is he alone in this belief. It is, he says, "the subject of a debate that has raged monthly in the Naval Institute's *Proceedings* since [the spring of 1993]":

> In the July issue, a retired air force colonel accused U.S. Army ground force commanders of failing to encircle the Iraqi Army and then pushing them out the back door to safety instead of destroying them. The Allied execution, he alleges, was flawed. As a result . . . the Republican Guard escaped in sufficient strength to harass its own countrymen, Kurds in the north [and Shiites in the south], and remains a threat to its neighbors. The air force colonel's assessment so outraged the army that officers and analysts, including myself, have published rebuttals in every issue of *Proceedings* since. Is it not possible, then, that an earlier publication of Professor Blumenson's recent book, *The Battle of the Generals* . . . could have aided Desert Storm planners and commanders in bringing a more decisive ending to the Persian Gulf War?

Desert Storm, says Dietrich, offers another object lesson on the consequences of failing to crush an enemy army in the field when the opportunity to do so presents itself. But according to Blumenson, the modern text on this subject was written at Falaise in August 1944.

The Greatest Thing We Have Ever Attempted

A National Guard Division in World War II: Some Thoughts on Military Preparedness

Joseph M. Balkoski

On October 14, 1941, General George C. Marshall, the chief of staff of the U.S. Army, received a letter from Lieutenant General Lesley J. McNair. "The National Guard is built on an unsound foundation in that its officers have had little or no training as such," McNair wrote. "The Guard is now or soon will be occupying space and facilities which could be used to better advantage for new units, organized soundly and led adequately." McNair suggested a simple solution to Marshall: "It would be better to ease Guard units out of the picture as fast as others can be created in their places." Marshall filed the letter away and took no action.

The status of part-time state military forces in the American defense establishment has been a contentious issue since the birth of the republic. Today the National Guard is recognized as the nation's primary military reserve, a role dating back to the National Militia Law of 1903. When Congress first passed this law, it issued an ultimatum to the states: all National Guard units must be good enough to be fully interchangeable with units of the regular army. This early twentieth-century version of the "Total Army" posed a daunting challenge to the National Guard, for part-time soldiers could devote but little time to realistic training for modern war. Nearly a century later, the National Guard's ability to perform its role in the Total Army of the 1990s came into question during Operations Desert Shield and Desert Storm, when several guard "roundout" brigades did not deploy overseas with the active army division to which they belonged.

World War II history may shed some light on the current debate concerning National Guard readiness. While researching a recently published World War II history of a National Guard outfit, the 29th "Blue and Gray" Division from Maryland and Virginia, I discovered some relevant facts relating to the division's mobilization, training, and combat record. These facts demonstrate how the realities of war profoundly changed the army's original idea of how National Guard units would be used in the conflict.

The U.S. Army in World War II is frequently categorized as a homogenous force of nearly identical and interchangeable units constituting a vast melting pot of draftees. Although this view is in large measure accurate, most historians do not realize that the American army contained many unique fighting units. For example, the 1st and 29th Infantry Divisions, the two outfits paired in V Corps for the Omaha Beach landing on D-Day, could hardly have been more different. One division had regular army origins and still had a core of crusty professionals; the other was a National Guard division made up of citizen-soldiers with distinctive regional roots. One division possessed plenty of combat veterans who were hardened realists about war; the other was filled with green troops who had a tinge of idealism. One division had twenty-seven years of continuous history; the other had only three years of active service and something to prove.

As early as the summer of 1940–more than a year before Pearl Harbor–guardsmen and their civilian employers across the nation were warned that mobilization was imminent. The 29th Division was federalized on February 3, 1941, allowing the "29ers" to train for more than ten months before America entered the war. Eventually the division trained for almost three and a half years before it heard its first shot fired in anger. During this period the 29th participated in two series of important maneuvers in the Carolinas; reorganized from the "square" to the "triangular" format; embarked for Great Britain; and trained in amphibious warfare techniques at the U.S. Army Assault Training Center on the north coast of Devon—the first U.S. Army division to utilize this key facility.

Although historians commonly refer to the 29th as a "National Guard" division, its militia flavor was considerably diluted during its forty-month period of active service before Operation Overlord. The thinning process began almost immediately upon the division's mobilization in February 1941. At the time almost all of its units were at less than 50 percent of their prescribed TO&E strengths. By spring of that year, the division's manpower was more than doubled by a huge influx of draftees. Thus, only a few months into active service, 29th Division guardsmen were already a minority in their own companies and batteries. However, as most conscripts hailed from Pennsylvania, Maryland, and Virginia, the division retained its regional flavor.

Later, transfers, sickness, and other infusions of draftees further reduced the percentage of guardsmen in the 29th. One of the most notable reductions occurred when an entire battalion of the 175th Infantry (a guard unit from Baltimore, Maryland) and a battery of the 110th Field Artillery were transferred out of the division to form the "Army War Show," which toured the country to promote the sale of war bonds. (The units were subsequently used as cadre for the 100th Infantry Division.) When the 29th triangularized in March 1942, it lost an entire infantry regiment (the 176th from Richmond, Virginia, which subsequently performed guard duty in Washington, D.C.), two battalions of engineers from the District of Columbia (one of which was shipped to the 37th Division in the Pacific), and several support units. Shortly thereafter, one battery of the 224th Field Artillery Battalion was transferred to Bermuda, where it performed coastal defense duties for more than a year. Clearly the 29th Division did not go to war as the guardsmen had envisioned in February 1941. When trained companies, batteries, and battalions were needed elsewhere, the army did not hesitate to take them from the division.

The extent to which the 29th's National Guard roots had withered by the spring of 1944 can be determined by examining the serial numbers of the men listed on company rosters on the eve of D-Day. I did this for many companies of the 116th Infantry ("The Stonewall Brigade" of the Virginia National Guard), the regiment that formed the 29th's first wave on Omaha Beach. This study showed that the 116th's prewar guardsmen amounted to about 20 percent of the unit. This percentage was probably a little higher in the 116th's two sister regiments (115th and 175th) because more than five hundred fresh troops—euphemistically designated "over-strength men"—were assigned to the 116th on the eve of D-Day in anticipation of high casualties on the beach.

Significantly, guardsmen constituted a much higher percentage of senior NCOs in six of the companies I examined. In four of those companies—the ones that landed at Omaha Beach at H-Hour—some 71 out of 123 NCOs (58 percent) at the rank of staff sergeant or higher were guardsmen. Furthermore, 23 out of 31 NCOs (74 percent) at the rank of technical sergeant or higher were guardsmen. In light of the fact that staff sergeant was the prescribed rank of a squad leader and technical sergeant was the rank held by a platoon sergeant (the senior NCO in a rifle platoon), it is clear that prewar Virginia guardsmen held most of the key enlisted positions in the 116th's rifle squads and platoons on D-Day. One of these NCOs, Technical Sergeant Frank Peregory of Company K, would win the Medal of Honor on June 8. During World War II army trainers used to say, "This is a sergeant'swar." If so, guardsmen in the 29th Division shouldered a great responsibility.

In the six months of active service before D-Day, the 29th Division's National guardsmen suffered a far higher rate of attrition among their officers than among their enlisted men. Background information on the division's officers as of D-Day is sketchy, but a figure of 25 guard officers out of a prescribed 140 officers per infantry regiment (about 18 percent) is a reasonably accurate guess. Such a figure works out to roughly one guard officer in each of a regiment's twelve rifle/heavy weapons companies, plus several others in support of companies and in staff positions at the battalion and regiment levels. As a rule of thumb, young first and second lieutenants from prewar guard days had risen to the rank of captain by 1944 and commanded companies. Platoon leaders were generally OCS men who had no military experience before Pearl Harbor.

The 29th was commanded by Charles Gerhardt, a crusty West Pointer of the class of 1917. It would be stating the facts mildly to say that, before D-Day, Gerhardt scrutinized the division's National Guard field-grade officers who aspired to battalion and regimental command. Although he was tough on all officers regardless of their backgrounds, his actions before and during the Normandy campaign clearly indicate that he was a little quicker to find fault with guardsmen. Gerhardt felt that good discipline was a function of strong leadership; and, like many regular army officers, he believed that discipline of the "old army" school was not strictly enforced by guard officers because they had been trained as part-time soldiers in the prewar years to standards that were not as stringent as those of the regulars.

It is therefore no coincidence that none of the 29th Division's three infantry regiments on the eve of D-Day were led by guardsmen, although several capable guard officers no doubt deserved such a command. (At the close of the Normandy campaign, when casualties and the strain of battle had severely reduced Gerhardt's pool of suitable field-grade officers, he finally assigned guardsmen to regimental command. They performed as effectively—if not more so—than their predecessors.) Mention must be made of the 29th's G-3 throughout the war, Lieutenant Colonel William J. Witte, a brilliant electrical engineer out of Johns Hopkins University and a long-time member of the Maryland National Guard. So important was Witte to the planning of divisional operations that Gerhardt was once moved to declare that "Witte has got it all figured out. He's my Napoleon." And the division's third-in-command, divisional artillery chief Brigadier General William Sands of the Virginia National Guard, was one of Gerhardt's most trusted subordinates throughout the war.

On the eve of D-Day about three-quarters of the 29th's battalion COs were Maryland and Virginia guardsmen. Many held their jobs and performed brilliantly for the rest of the war; many more became casualties; a few were hastily relieved. The 29th's most legendary soldier, Major Thomas Howie (the famed "Major of St.-Lô"), was a highly esteemed Virginia guardsman who was much beloved by his men.

Although many senior regular army officers during the war lacked confidence in officers with National Guard backgrounds, the example of the 29th Division proves conclusively that this attitude did not result in systematic discrimination against guardsmen. True, the 29th Division of 1944 did not resemble the 29th Division of 1941; whole units were summarily transferred out of the 29th with little thought given to divisional integrity; older officers were swept away without ceremony; qualified guard officers languished in positions beneath their levels of skill. However, at the "point of the spear," tough enlisted guardsmen who understood army ways and knew how to fight led the way at squad, platoon, and company levels. Moreover, once the shooting started in Normandy, even old army traditionalists like Gerhardt allowed the cream to rise to the top regardless of a soldier's background. As a result many brave and capable guard officers flourished. The simple fact that SHAEF rated the 29th Division highly enough to assign it a critical role in Operation Overlord is proof that National Guard units had overcome most of the stigmas that had plagued them since mobilization.

A note on casualties in Normandy. Losses in the 29th Division were so high that the character of the division had changed completely only a few weeks after entering combat on June 6. Upon the fall of St.-Lô on July 18, the 116th Infantry had suffered an astounding loss of 3,150 men—almost exactly the regiment's strength when it embarked at Weymouth, England for Normandy. It had undergone a near-total turnover of personnel in six weeks! In March 1945, when the 29th Division was in reserve, the 115th Infantry was scheduled to receive a Distinguished Unit Citation. It is said that General Gerhardt wanted each company guidon to be carried by a member of that company who had served with the outfit on D-Day. Half of the regiment's companies could produce a few men with that distinction; the others—mostly rifle companies—could find none. Every GI in the rifle companies had joined the regiment as a replacement

In my opinion the 29th Division was one of the U.S. Army's most accomplished combat outfits of the European theater in World War II. One of the reasons why this was so is that men with prewar military training survived the army's tough weeding-out processes and imparted their military skills to the draftees at all levels of command, from squad leader to regimental commander. The division's casualty figures confirm that a great many of these men gave their lives while performing this role; almost all of the rest were wounded. Perhaps that is the price that had to be paid to produce a unit that could overcome the formidable enemy defenses on Omaha Beach on June 6, 1944. Perhaps that is the price that any military unit must be prepared to pay to achieve greatness.

Canada's Contribution and Place in the Allied Order of Battle
John A. English

Surprising as it now may seem, Canada's Prime Minister W. L. Mackenzie King was among the last of the Allied government leaders to learn of the landing in Normandy. This occurred when he was roused from sleep in the early hours of June 6, 1944, by a Royal Canadian Mounted Police duty constable, who informed him that D-Day was in progress. By this time King should have been conditioned to such developments because previously he had virtually ensured Canada's exclusion from the higher direction of the war. The Dominion had received no advance warning of the Anglo-American landings in North Africa nor any indication that a decision had been taken at the Casablanca Conference to invade Sicily (an operation that saw a Canadian division in action for the first time). Although Canada ultimately gave Britain threefold as much financial assistance as America on a per capita basis and finished the war with a small but powerful army, as well as the Allies' fourth-largest air force and the third-largest navy, she had from the start attempted to fight a war of limited liability.

What I would like to do is briefly review Canada's rather anomalous approach to the war and explain how her higher war machinery worked, often to the detriment of Canadian military deployments and Canadian military representation on the staff of Allied headquarters.

Fielding Canada's Second World War Army

Canada deployed army elements overseas early in the war in response to a tactful and extremely subtle British request for a "small fighting unit." The first Canadian troops arrived in Britain in December 1939. In keeping with the plans of the Canadian general staff, the 1st Canadian Division was dispatched with a sizeable number of ancillary troops, particularly artillery, the presence of which all but guaranteed the continued growth of the Canadian army in Britain. Between October 1940 and the summer of 1942 two additional infantry divisions, two armored divisions, two artillery brigades or AGRA (Army Group Royal Artillery), and two armored brigades were also dispatched.

Notwithstanding this commitment, the King government would clearly have preferred to concentrate on industrial production and providing air, naval, and garrison forces rather than fielding a large expeditionary force almost certain to require conscription for sustainment. A later attempt to reduce the risk of casualties by giving priority to the British Commonwealth Air Training Plan backfired badly as it condemned the Royal Canadian Air Force to colonial status and saw ten thousand Canadian airmen perish in the RAF's Bomber Command.

In contrast the army was left to become the most national of Canada's services, although there could never have been a First Canadian Army without British support. The blatantly political decision of the Canadian government to dispatch I Canadian Corps to Italy, however, effectively split the Canadian army overseas and relegated First Canadian Army to a follow-up role in the then-projected invasion of Northwest Europe. This created a situation wherein Number 83 RAF Group, with fifteen of its twenty-nine squadrons Canadian (i.e., RCAF) in origin, operated in support of Second British Army while Number 84 Group, which was bereft of Canadian squadrons, ended up supporting First Canadian Army. The Italy decision additionally led to the 3rd Canadian Division being placed under the command of General Sir John Crocker, GOC of British I Corps, for the D-Day assault.

Training and Doctrinal Development of the Canadian Army

The training of the Canadian army overseas reflected the piecemeal nature of its formation, the inadequacy of its peacetime professional base, the complications of equipment, the practice of war as demonstrated by the Germans, the incorrectness of lessons drawn from analyses of German performance and perhaps an unfounded sense of North American superiority. In accordance with previous imperial agreements, the Canadian army adhered to British organizational patterns, staff methods, and operational doctrine. As a result the Canadian army was almost perfectly integrated with the British army, to the extent that units, formations, and even individuals were completely interchangeable. While this proved of inestimable benefit to both armies, both suffered the same tactical and doctrinal dilemmas. Such problems, in turn, were doubtless exacerbated by a general tendency to neglect combined-arms and live-fire training. The Canadians nonetheless enjoyed the advantage of having been trained by General Bernard L. Montgomery, who as commander of Southeastern Army entertained a higher opinion of them than is commonly realized.

Leadership of the Canadian Army Overseas

Probably the greatest weakness of the Canadian army overseas lay in its top leadership, most especially that of General A. G. L. McNaughton, whose focus appeared to be on everything but warfighting. A former chief of the General Staff, McNaughton had retired from that post in 1935 to head the National Research Council. With the onset of hostilities, a public relations campaign mounted on his behalf by the King government had resulted in his being called back to service to lead Canada's volunteer army overseas.

McNaughton had performed brilliantly in the Great War as a counterbattery officer. He was blessed with a compelling personality, and the men continued to love him even after he left the service, much as Union troops in the American Civil War continued to love General George B. McClellan after he was dismissed from command of the Army of the Potomac in November 1862. McNaughton also preferred to focus on national command—that is, on technical and administrative matters—rather than field operations. As mentioned above, Canadian army training consequently suffered, less from equipment shortages, which obviously existed, than from a general lack of professional military application. Collective- and combined-arms training, especially movement and fire coordination, therefore received inadequate attention.

Largely because of his deficiencies as an operational commander, but also because of personality conflicts and policy differences with British military leaders, McNaughton was forced to resign his command of First Canadian Army in December 1943. A successor was not immediately named, and the army was allowed to drift leaderless until Lieutenant General H. D. G. Crerar assumed command in March 1944. As an interim measure, Lieutenant General Ken Stuart, the previous chief of the General Staff named to command Canadian Military Headquarters, was double-hatted as First Canadian Army commander. Stuart reputedly told his own chief of staff, "Don't bother me with details."

McNaughton's removal was for many years portrayed by more nationalistic Canadian historians as a British affront to Canadian sovereignty rather than a militarily justifiable act. Several other Canadian commanders, including Major General R. F. L. Keller, GOC 3rd Canadian Division, also exhibited serious shortcomings as formation commanders. Yet there were still others, Lieutenant General Guy Simonds among them, who were probably the equal of their counterparts in any army. Again, Montgomery's assessments of individual junior and senior Canadian commanders were not all that pejorative and were certainly no more critical than many of the opinions he voiced about their British brethren.

Civilian Leadership and its Impact on the Army

To some degree the situation in the top ranks of the army reflected the state of Canadian political leadership. King insisted on exercising Canadian autonomy independent of the Commonwealth, to the point where he refused to go along with Australian Prime Minister Robert Menzies' proposal for an imperial war cabinet, a fixture of the Great War. Moreover, King had an obsessive fear of the potential threat that conscription for overseas duty posed to national unity and also to his political power base in Quebec. These factors ensured that Canada, from the beginning, would back into the war rather haphazardly.

Initial reluctance to put forth more than a moderate war effort, mainly because of financial considerations and a policy of limited liability, not only condemned Canada's air force to colonial status, but also created two classes of soldiers, one a conscript for home defense and the other a general service volunteer for overseas duty. Furthermore, the Royal Canadian Navy was left to come under command of a neutral power--the United States--a situation that was largely ignored by the Canadian War Cabinet.

At a higher level, Canada's war machinery failed to evolve beyond the level of Cabinet War Committee. King's senior military advisors did not begin to attend committee meetings on a regular basis until three years into the war. Even then they were allowed to attend only the first and third meetings of each month. To the end of war King, the complete civilian, never appreciated the presence of military men in his meetings. As a result the Canadian War Committee collectively tended to either neglect entirely or over-manage military affairs. However, the committee usually subjected military affairs to the most excruciating examinations, often from a mainly domestic perspective.

Because the King government refused to take a more active part in the higher direction of the war, even when the British empire stood alone against the Axis and Canada was Britain's strongest belligerent ally, it was perhaps only natural that the Dominion was excluded entirely from the ABC conversations and membership in the most important Allied combined boards. At a Cabinet War Committee meeting on August 11, held during the Quadrant conference in Quebec and attended by Churchill, King stated that his government had accepted the position that the higher direction of the war was to be exercised by the British prime minister and the president of the United States. He also recorded in his diary that "Churchill and Roosevelt being at Quebec and myself acting as host will be quite sufficient to make clear that all three are in conference together and will not only satisfy but will please . . . Canadian feeling, and really be helpful to me personally." On the basis of this comment alone, one almost has to agree with Canada's greatest military historian, the late Colonel C. P. Stacy, that whereas Churchill gave Britain the flash of steel and the roll of drums, Mackenzie King gave Canada cold porridge.

In addition, Stacy ventured that the lack of political leadership probably caused Canadian soldiers abroad to feel as though they were second-class citizens of the alliance. Indeed, one suspects that the Canadian Army overseas came to think of itself as a neglected army. I am convinced that King would have preferred that the army die quietly in some corner of Europe where it would be unable to disrupt the domestic situation at home.

By the same token, of course, the Canadian soldier serving overseas detested the prime minister of Canada. Ironically, the "Canadianization" of Canada's air force was matched by the less well-known "de-Canadianization" of the army. Many Canadian soldiers, in short, came to look on the White Cliffs of Dover as they might have once looked on the Rocky Mountains—as part of their homeland. There was no rotational system of home leave until 1944, and then only after one had accumulated five years of continuous service overseas. (I remember at the time many soldiers returning to my neighborhood to families that had changed considerably in their absence; children born just before the soldiers left were now six years old.) In many respects the Canadian field force sent overseas was remarkable. Though many of its soldiers did not see their homeland for five years, it never eroded or went to pieces in the field. The honor its soldiers brought to their country, to be sure, was certainly more than their prime minister deserved.

In Canada, at any rate, the public was clamoring for their country to play a more vigorous role in the war. Consequently the King government, anxious to project a favorable image to its citizens—but finding it difficult to do so as long as the army remained inactive--increasingly based its decisions on considerations of status and recognition. Partly in response to calls to get Canadian soldiers into action for reasons of honor, partly to enhance the nation's prestige in the postwar era, and partly to reduce the adverse effect of continued inaction upon troop morale, the Canadian government in 1943 arranged to have the 1st Canadian Infantry Division and the 1st Canadian Army Tank Brigade replace British formations slated for the assault on Sicily. The original intent was to have them return from the Mediterranean to disseminate battle experience throughout First Canadian Army for the invasion of France. But the post-Dieppe perception that casualties were likely to be lighter in Italy prompted the King government to pressure British military authorities into accepting an unwanted Canadian corps, replete with an unnecessary armored division, for service in the Italian theater.

Splitting First Canadian Army hastened the resignation of McNaughton, who had wanted to keep the army united under Canadian command. It also had the effect, already noted, of relegating Canadian forces to a follow-up rather than an assault role in any invasion of Europe. King, of course, never warmed up to that operation. He dreaded the possibility that an invasion would lead to a replay of the Great War, when Canada, which then had population of only 7.5 million, saw sixty thousand of its troops killed in the fighting. As it turned out, the Canadian corps in Italy would not even fight in battle as a corps before the Dominion government commenced agitating in May 1944 for its repatriation to First Canadian Army.

Employment and Performance of the Canadian Army in Normandy

Some fifteen thousand Canadians landed in Normandy on D-Day, over 20 percent of the assault force. Most belonged to the 3rd Division Group, which had been temporarily detached from its parent formation, First Canadian Army, and assigned to I British Corps to take part in the assault on Juno Beach. Also participating in Operation Neptune were thirty-five Royal Canadian Air Force squadrons, and fifty-seven warships and about sixty-nine other vessels of the Royal Canadian Navy.

The 3rd Canadian Division advanced farther inland on D-Day than any other Allied formation. Even so it failed, like all other Allied units, to achieve its June 6 objectives. On June 7 the 25th Panzer Grenadier Regiment of the 12th SS Panzer Division (*Hitler Jugend*) launched three infantry battalions supported by artillery and a tank battalion against the left flank of the 9th Canadian Brigade. This action, which saw the Canadians thrown out of Authie and Buron, might have been avoided had the 3rd Canadian Division's artillery been within range—as it probably should have been, despite congestion on the beach. As it was, the ground lost by 9th Brigade within sight of its final objective, the Carpiquet airfield, was not to be recovered for a full month, and then only after bitter resistance by the 12th SS Panzer Division, which also had to fight the British during Operation Epsom.

On July 11 the 3rd Canadian Division reverted to the command of General Simonds's II Canadian Corps, which had gone into action on Second British Army's front; also in II Canadian Corps was the 2nd Canadian Infantry Division and the Second Canadian AGRA. Subsequently, the effort by II Canadian Corps to exploit the hard-won success of Operation Atlantic, an attack launched in support of Operation Goodwood on July 18, ended in a disaster. Here, failure was due largely to poor tank-infantry cooperation and the arrival of German reserves, most notably the 1st SS Panzer Division, which mustered upwards of fifty tanks. Similarly, on July 25 the Canadian attack on Verrières Ridge during Operation Spring (launched in support of Cobra) foundered on the shoals of inadequate tank-infantry and artillery coordination, a problem exacerbated by extremely poor battle planning by the staff of at least one division.

On July 23—significantly, seven weeks after D-Day—First Canadian Army, which initially consisted of I British Corps, became operational under the command of General Crerar. On July 31 Simonds's II Canadian Corps reverted to First Canadian Army. After the two bloody noses administered to Canadian forces in July, it is not surprising that Simonds chose to mount a major corps attack, if only (in my opinion) to show his subordinates how to implement a proper fire plan. In Operation Totalize (started August 7), described as a mini-Cobra, he actually cracked the German line in a daring night attack that made innovative use of improvised armored personnel carriers. Regrettably, failure to realize that 1st SS Panzer Division had slipped away to Mortain caused him to wait for a strategic bomber strike on positions where he wrongly presumed the Germans to be.

Operation Totalize was finally halted by the 12th SS Panzer Division in one of the few actions in Normandy where German tanks actually played a greater role than antitank guns. Afterward, Canadians were left to ponder what might have happened at this juncture had II Canadian Corps in the early morning of August 8—the anniversary of the great 1918 battle of Amiens—raced immediately toward Falaise. The thought boggles the mind, as such an action would unquestionably have bagged the entire Seventh German Army.

The end of the Normandy campaign came on August 25, following the battle of the Falaise pocket and the arrival of Allied armies on the Seine River. Almost one hundred thousand Canadians participated in the campaign. They left behind five hundred dead and took home eighteen thousand wounded. Any consideration of the Canadian army's operational history in Normandy must take into account the fact that the Caen-Falaise plain was not bocage but perhaps the best antitank country in the world for the fields of fire it offered. Indeed, without the technological advantage conferred by the Sherman Firefly, which was the only Allied tank capable of taking on a Tiger or Panther, it is unlikely that the Canadians would have done as well as they did in this sector.

It is interesting to speculate on what the Canadians might have accomplished had they had more than one Firefly per troop. No doubt tank-infantry cooperation would have remained a major problem, but the highly difficult task of coordinating artillery fire with maneuver arms movement during fluid phases had always presented the greater challenge. At the divisional level the failure by commanders to employ the artillery resources at their disposal in a more effective manner served to impede formation maneuver. At the lower levels of brigade and battle group, lack of knowledge about how gunners operated and a misunderstanding of the benefits of artillery fire ensured the less-than-adequate integration of artillery with infantry and, most especially, with tanks. Notwithstanding these and other shortcomings, however, Canadian armies achieved several spectacular successes in Normandy, enough to at least refute the charge that Canadian failures must primarily be attributed to the inadequacies of regimental officers.

Failure at Falaise
Martin Blumenson

In total war the first rule for the warring parties is to destroy the enemy forces. The history of warfare shows us that the best way to achieve this goal is by surrounding those forces, thereby giving them the option of dying or surrendering. Less than three months after D-Day, in the climactic maneuver of the Normandy campaign, the Allies encircled a large concentration of German troops in the Falaise pocket. Although they won a great victory and inflicted a grievous defeat on the Germans by sweeping the latter from the battlefield, they failed to trap and completely eliminate the enemy combat units. As a consequence, the prospect of winning the war in Western Europe during the autumn of 1944 vanished. The fighting continued for eight more months.

At Falaise the Germans pushed their heads into a noose, but the Allies were unable to pull the string shut quickly enough. Despite considerable success in forming, compressing, and finally closing a ring around the Germans, the Allies acted too slowly and without single-minded concentration. Pursuing less important goals at the same time, they lost the opportunity to liquidate German forces, then muffed another chance to snare them at the Seine River. What should have been an efficient Allied operation was instead inept and bungled, displaying contradictory impulses. Hesitation, wrangling, and uncertainty on the Allied side marred the venture. The Allies let the prospect of complete triumph slip through their fingers.

Most of the Germans escaped the Falaise pocket, then withdrew across the Seine River. During the last ten days of August 1944, about 240,000 German soldiers traversed the Seine and headed for the Low Countries and Germany. How successful the Germans were in this endeavor was soon evident. As early as the first days of September, the Germans established a continuous front more than one hundred miles long between the English Channel and the Ardennes, which permitted formation of a defense line that protected the approaches to Germany. Of the twenty divisions incorporated into these positions, more than half, twelve to be exact, had escaped from Normandy. Though understrength and short of matériel, they were veteran organizations and essentially intact.

Later in September German units that had fled Normandy stopped Allied troops executing Operation Market-Garden, a combined airborne drop and armored drive in the Netherlands, preventing them from gaining the far bank of the lower Rhine River at the Dutch town of Arnhem. In December, in the Ardennes counteroffensive known as the Battle of the Bulge, survivors of the Falaise pocket in large part manned fifteen of the twenty-five German divisions committed to the attack.

A high rate of production—for example, sixteen hundred tanks turned out per month—enabled the Germans to re-equip the formations depleted by the fighting in Normandy. The Germans rebuilt their divisions during the Allies' supply crisis in September, when advancing Allied columns ran out of gasoline.

The fact was, the Allies had the Germans on the ropes in Normandy and had been unable to administer the knockout blow. Allied exhilaration in the form of optimistic intelligence reports foretelling the imminent collapse of Germany quickly changed in tone and substance. Despite disappointment over the outcome of the Falaise battle, there was little bitterness or recrimination on the Allied side, for an immediate succession of heady thrills ensued: the liberation of Paris, the pursuit across northern France, the lightning thrusts toward Germany.

Yet a nagging question remains: why had the Allies been unable to generate a truly cohesive effort and knock Germany out of the war? The answer lies in the realm of three considerations: first, the dubious abilities of the top Allied leaders; second, the nature of the Allied coalition; and, third, the weight given to the Allied invasion plan.

With regard to the first of these considerations, the Allied leaders were mature professionals, but their dissimilar personal traits and habits made it difficult for them to interact harmoniously. For example, Eisenhower chose to be aloof from everyday concerns. Although he was in Normandy much of the time, he took no active role in the affairs leading to and culminating in the Falaise battle; having delegated responsibility for the ground effort to Montgomery, he refrained from meddling. Furthermore, with his headquarters in the process of moving from England to France (where it was located far to the rear of the front), he lacked the machinery of command. He visited his subordinates, listened to them, encouraged them, but never interfered. And though he accurately perceived and assessed the battle situation, he refused to indicate how he thought the Allies ought to exploit their advantages.

Eisenhower can therefore be faulted for his failure to exercise his personal will and mandated authority in order to provide single-minded direction to the Falaise pocket developments.

As for Montgomery, by the time of the Normandy invasion he was an international star, widely regarded as the savior of Allied hopes. A superb commander of British and Commonwealth troops in North Africa, Sicily, and southern Italy, he was at less than his best as head of the Allied coalition forces in Normandy. Concentrating on the battlefield, he ignored the broader problems accruing to his position and thereby made himself vulnerable to criticism. In France his egoism, inflexibility, insensitivity, and lust for power and glory grew into megalomania and delusions of grandeur.

Montgomery can be faulted for his inability to understand how quickly the Americans could move and for his habit of underrating their combat expertise. Moreover, he can be faulted for his failure to set a decisive course for all ground forces in Normandy.

Bradley affected humility and played by the book, preferring to take no chances. In Tunisia Bradley had served as Patton's deputy commander of the II Corps, and when Patton departed to assume command of the Seventh Army, Bradley acceded to the corps command. He served under Patton in Sicily; but as a result of Patton's slapping incidents Eisenhower named Bradley commander of the American ground forces for the invasion and the campaign in Normandy, which made him Patton's immediate superior.

The slapping incidents which occurred toward the end of the Sicilian campaign, when in two hospitals Patton slapped and cursed two soldiers who he mistakenly thought were malingering, were among the most important events in the war against Germany. Patton abused the soldiers because he was at the end of his tether, frustrated by his inability to cut off the Germans in Sicily and because he was forced to fight the battle of Sicily their way. Eisenhower was shocked and angered. Consequently when Eisenhower had to send someone to England in September 1943 to prepare American forces for the invasion of Normandy, he eliminated Patton from consideration even though Patton was the most capable, experienced, and successful American combat general. Eisenhower would certainly have chosen Patton had the slapping incidents not occurred.

Eisenhower considered sending Mark Clark to England. But the Fifth Army, which Clark commanded, was about to invade Italy—otherwise he might have wound up in Omar Bradley's position. Eisenhower thought of replacing Clark with Bradley and sending Clark to England anyway, but decided there wasn't enough time to make the switch. So he was forced, in a manner of speaking, to select Omar Bradley, who was an obscure corps commander and known to hardly anyone outside the army, despite the attempt by Ernie Pyle to make him into a well-known American hero.

The selection of Bradley to be not only the commander of the First U.S. Army in Normandy but also, a little later, the commander of Twelfth Army Group reversed the positions of authority that had existed vis-à-vis him and Patton. Patton had been Bradley's immediate superior in Sicily, but in Normandy he was to be Bradley's subordinate. Historians writing about this phase of the war have devoted insufficient attention to the discomfort felt by both men in this reversal of authority. It was a very difficult situation for both. Bradley had graduated from West Point six years after Patton. Unlike Patton, Bradley had not fought in France in World War I. Having great respect for Patton, Bradley was intimidated by Patton's personal lifestyle and professional assurance. In Normandy he occasionally called Patton "sir" as though Patton were still his superior. Bradley was quite upset when this happened and so was Patton.

In any case, although Bradley had no prior experience as an army commander he did very well in the job. By the end of his stint as an army commander in Normandy, in late July, he had formulated and executed Operation Cobra. And when Cobra, a local operation originally designed to take Coutances on the road to Avranches, broke through the German defenses, Bradley parlayed that success into a full-scale breakout—a move that turned the battle of Normandy into the battle of France as well.

Bradley also had no experience as an army group commander. Therefore, when appointed to head 12th U.S. Army Group (which became operational on August 1), it took him some time to get acclimated to his job and become accustomed to the prerogatives of command at that level. He could hardly believe that he had risen to such an exalted position, and his disbelief proved detrimental to the conduct of Allied operations in the final stages of the Normandy campaign. Even though he was responsible for Cobra and everybody was complimenting him, he manifested an ambivalence during the August campaign that prevented him from deciding and declaring a certain specific course of action.

More to the point, he slowed the tempo of events. Bradley was responsible for initiating the encirclement of the Germans by turning Patton's Third Army north from Le Mans toward Alençon and Argentan, but he was not fundamentally interested in bagging and destroying the German forces. The encirclement occurred because the Germans had attacked at Mortain, and Bradley was anxious to mount a counter-threat to their movement. In other words, he started the encirclement to gain security for First Army and specifically for VII Corps, which was fighting at Mortain. As the situation developed, Patton tried to talk Bradley out of a shallow envelopment, which entailed a hook north from Le Mans to Alençon, Argentan, and Falaise; instead, Patton wanted to go all the way to the Seine River and then drive down the river to its mouth, thereby cutting off all the Germans in Normandy. This would have been a risky maneuver, and Bradley forbade it. Montgomery thought about doing it and then he forbade it as well. Then, just when the shallow envelopment was about to succeed, Bradley stopped it.

Aspiring to public acclaim and glory, Bradley can be faulted for the uncertain course he set, for his contradictory decisions, and for slowing the tempo of events. In Normandy, his actions were disappointing.

Patton, who believed in audacity, thought

Bradley to be tentative in his decisions. The most experienced American battlefield general on the European side of the war and a proven winner, Patton was indispensable in Normandy. No one else could exert such pressure on the enemy or drive his troops with such inspiration and relentlessness; no one had his intuitive grasp of what was possible on the battlefield. Unfortunately for the Allies, he was too far down the ladder of command for his thinking to be followed. Furthermore, well aware of the need to rehabilitate himself after the slapping incidents, he held his tongue. He was the only Allied leader of consequence who was more than willing to take advantage of the opportunity to destroy the Germans in Normandy, in the Falaise pocket and west of the Seine River.

The second consideration explaining the failure at Falaise had to do with the nature of the Allied coalition. Underneath an apparently harmonious surface, the Anglo-American partnership was beset with friction and jealousy. Although Eisenhower made the alliance work, the relationship was marred by mutual misunderstanding and misgiving, plus the difficulties that were bound to arise between two peoples with divergent national histories, traditions, habits, and interests who had to cooperate closely with each other. A contest for domination of the coalition further aggravated the situation. British leadership in the alliance gave way as increasing numbers of American men and quantities of matériel were committed to the European theater of operations. Yet the British always regarded the Americans as inexperienced and incapable. After the Cobra breakout the Americans liberated a large area of Normandy, and in doing so provoked British envy. Some of Montgomery's and Bradley's decisions were made on the basis of, respectively, anti-American and anti-British sentiment.

The third consideration was the invasion plan of Operation Overlord. Covering the first three months of Continental operations, Overlord was aimed at gaining a logistical base for subsequent action. The Allies first had to obtain a lodgement area—the part of France roughly between the Seine and Loire Rivers—for ports, airfields, and maneuver room. These were needed by the Allies to mount the critical offensive that would drive the Germans back to their homeland. Because Eisenhower, Montgomery, and Bradley had their eyes fixed on securing this preliminary objective, they failed to act decisively on the possibility of surrounding the Germans in Normandy and thus bringing the war to a swift end.

*

I want to touch briefly on the use of air power in Normandy. The Normandy campaign consists of the landings, the battle in the hedgerows, the battle for Caen, the Goodwood and Cobra operations, the encirclement at Falaise, closure to the Seine River, and finally the pursuit. Nobody has really researched the effectiveness of using strategic bombers in a tactical role at Caen and in Operations Goodwood and Cobra. The bombardment at Caen accomplished little more than the destruction of the city and damaged the Germans but little. Yet it gave a psychological boost to the British and Canadian soldiers. Whether this result was sufficient to justify the destruction of Caen remains open to question.

As for the Goodwood attack, the tactical use of strategic bombers failed to produce a breakout on the Falaise plain. The precise objective of the bombardment is still unclear. Montgomery deliberately kept the operation orders ambiguous.

On the first day of Cobra American troops following on the heels of the bombardment could not even get across the line of departure, and subsequently the bombardment was judged to have achieved negligible results. But on the next day things started to move, and they moved rapidly.

In conclusion, the Americans are not very good at

encirclement. They let the Germans and Italians escape from Sicily when they failed to cut off enemy forces at Messina. Again, in southern France at Montélimar, they destroyed a lot of German equipment but failed to bag all of the enemy troops. The same thing happened in Normandy.

But the fact that Americans were not very good at envelopment is hardly an excuse for their failure at Falaise. The envelopment or encirclement could have been completed in record time if it had been executed with single-minded resolution. Had this been accomplished, the war would have been over much earlier than it was. Instead the Allies fought in Normandy to gain the logistical base required by Overlord and in doing so overlooked an opportunity to destroy the enemy. The efforts to gain the ground of the lodgement area, provide security to the lodgement area that turned out to be unnecessary, and prematurely plan post-Overlord operations (i.e., the thrust toward Germany) before firmly closing the Falaise pocket, all complicated by national jealousies and frictions on the personal level, led the Allies to forget rule number one, eliminating the enemy and thereby closing out the fighting in the fall of 1944.

The Greatest Thing We Have Ever Attempted

Discussion

John Mountcastle: I would like to ask a question of Joe Balkoski. As you look at the 29th Division on the eve of the assault on Omaha Beach, can you tell whether this is a division that had for some time been set in its D-Day assignment, or was there in the six months leading up to D-Day some question as to whether to assign the 1st Infantry Division to assault regimental objectives and then follow up with the 29th? The reason I'm asking is, I've walked the beach there myself and I've wondered why you didn't see two regiments of the 1st Infantry Division, with a unity of command and so forth, going in abreast on Omaha; and why, in fact, you would have a regiment—the 116th of the 29th Division—assigned a sector. Had that been an issue for discussion with the 29th Division command staff?

Joseph Balkoski: Yes, it was. As far as I know, the 1st Division was specifically pulled out of the Mediterranean for this operation. But as late as the end of January '44 the decision had not been made as to whether there would be a second division on Omaha. Around that time it was decided there would be a second division. There was some debate as to whether it would be the 28th Division of the Pennsylvania National Guard or the 29th Division.

The 29th was eventually chosen because it had been in England since '42 and was the first division to go through the U.S. Army Amphibious Assault Center on the north coast of Devon. (It went through the Slapton Sands center as well.) But the reason why they put two divisions on the front at Omaha was because they essentially had two separate and distinct goals in the post–D-Day stage. The 1st Division was expected to penetrate as far south as quickly as possible and the 29th was expected to link up with the 4th Division. It was fully understood these tasks would have been too difficult for one division to accomplish.

As far as I know, the D-Day objectives were pretty unrealistic. St.-Lô was a D-plus-nine objective for the 29th Division and it ended up being taken on D-plus-forty-two. But the decision was made pretty early on that two divisions would land simply because the penetration inland in the days following D-Day had such distinctiveness.

Orwin Talbott: There was unity of command in the sense that the Omaha assault force was under General Huebner's direction. Then, when more units of the 29th came in, that division broke out under its own separate command.

Joseph Balkoski: Nominally that was the case, although in all my research I never once heard of any meeting between General Gerhardt of the 29th Division and General Huebner of the 1st. Basically what happened on D-Day was that General Cota, the assistant division commander of the 29th, formed what he called a "bastard brigade" of the 115th Infantry and the 116th Infantry Regiments, and he pretty much ran the show on the 29th Division sector. It was good that he did this because the confusion was so great that it would have been unrealistic to expect one man to control the entire assault.

Geoffrey Perret: General McNair and other people complained about the poor standard of training in the guard divisions, and the guardsmen resented that. Do you think the guard could have trained itself up to regular army standards?

Joseph Balkoski: No, they probably could not have achieved the standards of the regular army. First of all, within two months of mobilization, 60 percent of the 29th Division was composed of draftees. These people went into the division without any basic training, so essentially the guardsmen were training the conscripts. And the guardsmen were not training themselves to achieve the standards the regular army had.

I must say, however, that the 29th Division did participate in both Carolina maneuvers, one prior to Pearl Harbor and one after Pearl Harbor, and its performance supposedly was very good. I don't know how it performed in comparison to other divisions. But to expect—well, first you have to judge how prepared the regular army was at that time. I suppose the National Guard in some ways wasn't that far behind the regular army.

But there were extreme deficiencies at some of the high command levels. There were people who were simply too old to have command in the field. And after the Carolina maneuvers there was a massive amount of weeding out of the regiment and battalion COs. McNair certainly believed that the guard was abysmal but Marshall, having a much clearer head vis-à-vis the guard, never really subscribed to that view. However, he did accept a lot of McNair's suggestions about weeding out the older officers and taking units intact out of guard formations and shipping them wherever they were needed, knowing that they would become less of a guard unit as the war went on.

Richard Behrenhausen: I have a question for Professor Blumenson. It was suggested during this morning's discussion that General Eisenhower was perhaps put off of General Patton because he suspected from Patton's efforts in Sicily that Patton was more interested, or most interested, in headlines. Would you comment on that?

Martin Blumenson: Well, Patton wasn't the only one who was interested in headlines. Everybody was interested in headlines. I don't know how else to answer your question. Patton and Eisenhower had been old friends since 1919. They were close friends. They liked each other. They thought alike as far as warfare is concerned.

Richard Behrenhausen: I guess my questions is, do you agree with the premise that a major reason for Patton not assuming Bradley's position was the fact that Eisenhower was fearful of Patton's ultimate motives?

Martin Blumenson: Oh, I don't think so. I think Eisenhower, simply as a result of the slapping incidents, felt that Patton sometimes could not control his temper. And he had the feeling that Patton was hardly going to be diplomatic enough with the British if he went to England; there was the problem of self-control and all that sort of thing.

And yet I must remind people that in French Morocco Patton did very well in a diplomatic mission; he did beautifully with the French officials in North Africa to the point where Harry Hopkins, on his visit to Casablanca, told Patton that they were thinking of transferring him to the State Department. And Patton said, "I'll resign if you do."

The point is that people think of Patton as a hothead, as someone who went flying off the handle. I don't think he was that way at all. I think the slapping incidents were the result of frustration in the Sicilian campaign because of the terrible mission the American troops had at the beginning, and because he had to rush to take Palermo and then advance along the northern shore to get to Messina. This was just tearing away at him and I think he lost control.

Steve Dietrich: This morning Dr. Ambrose gave us reasons why he thought Eisenhower selected

Bradley. He did not mention the slapping incidents. I don't think Eisenhower could have justified selecting Bradley over Patton had it not been for the slapping incidents.

Stephen Ambrose: On that subject, though, let's remember, Ike wanted to cover it up. When it was first reported to him by the surgeon general for the theater, he made Patton go and make the apology, but he asked for and did receive a cover-up. Some reporters got hold of the story and they came to Ike in Algiers and said, "We have this story." Which by itself is a tremendous comment on the difference between the press in World War II and today. Can you imagine in Desert Shield if somebody had gotten hold of a story like that? What do you think the chances are of going to Schwartzkopf and saying, "We have this story and we want to run it, but we wanted to check with you first"? Ike all but got on his knees and he said, "Don't run that story." He said, "If you do, you're going to ruin Georgie's chances in this war, and I've got to have George Patton. When we get into Europe, he is the guarantor of our victory."

So I don't think it would be right to say that Ike reacted to the slapping incident by forming a negative judgment of Patton's abilities. I would contend that he did not think Patton was the right man for what was basically a set-piece battle on June 6, but that Patton was the right man to unleash when there was an opportunity to exploit.

Martin Blumenson: My feeling is that this was a terribly anguished time for Eisenhower, and he did cover the slapping incidents until Drew Pearson let it out in November. But to call Patton indispensable to the war effort is the highest compliment you can give anyone, isn't it?

Now, in the letters that passed between Eisenhower and Marshall, they talked about this, and Marshall said, "Fine, you do what you want." And I think Eisenhower, sort of compromising with himself, said to Marshall, "I will keep Patton because he is indispensable for victory, but I will not elevate him any higher—I will keep him at army command." I think that limiting him to army command comes directly from the slapping incidents. And since the person who went to England would have to command an army group, Patton was kaput.

James Collins: My comment is directed to Mr. Blumenson. You talked about the problems of heavy air bombardment and the consensus that it was no good, and cited Cobra as an example of this. Actually the reason the attack on the first day of Cobra didn't go very well was because the bombs fell short and there was a great deal of disorganization. This was certainly the case with the 30th Infantry Division and to some extent with the 9th.

I was attached to the 9th at that point and I observed two things. One was the disorganization of the troops. Second, the damage was so great that the roads were blocked, making it very difficult to get the tanks or armored personnel carriers through. On the second day they did get through because they'd gotten reorganized, they'd gotten bulldozers to plow out the roads. So I don't think there was really the feeling on the part of the local military that using heavy bombers wasn't a good idea.

Martin Blumenson: Well, the notation in the First Army action report on the night after the bombardment said that its effects were negligible, that it failed to produce the breakthrough. Everyone was discouraged on the evening of the first day of Cobra. I think everyone felt discouraged except Joe Collins, who sized the situation up better than anybody and who committed his armor even though the infantry—I'm talking about the 4th Division, which really didn't take any casualties in the bombardment, as well as the 30th and the 9th Divisions—couldn't get across the line of departure either. Collins doped it out and did the right thing by committing his armor. I think he's responsible, really, for the success of Cobra.

Orwin Talbott: I have a question for Martin Blumenson. In your judgment, if the Americans and the British had been able to close the Falaise Gap, could they have kept it closed or would the Germans have busted through anyway?

Martin Blumenson: Well, I don't know. I think fewer Germans would have escaped; in other words, the probability of capturing more Germans would have been higher. To destroy the enemy means to make him ineffective: you don't have to kill them all.

Clay Blair: I have two comments. First, I look forward to tomorrow to have the opportunity of showing that Bradley might have had some positive qualities that recommended him for the job and that his appointment was not entirely by default. Second, with regard to Cobra: Pete Quesada, who was involved in a lot of the planning for Cobra, told me in an interview I did with him for the Bradley book that the air force totally screwed up the mission that day. He said the air force was supposed to bomb from north to south and it actually bombed from east to west. In other words, the whole bomb run was pivoted 90 degrees. That was his story, anyway.

Martin Blumenson: That story is incorrect, Clay, and Geoffrey Perret will back me up on that.

Geoffrey Perret: Let me say to begin with that I admire Bradley more than Dr. Blumenson does but maybe a little less than Clay Blair. Bradley agreed to the way the bombing was done because he was given a choice. The air force told him, "If it's done quickly, we can do it our way, but if we do it the way you want, it will take hours to funnel all of those planes through that narrow space in the sky. Which way do you want it done?" Bradley said, "I want it done quickly." So the air force said, "Okay. But you understand we are not going to fly parallel to the road." And Bradley agreed. There are at least three reliable accounts of the meeting in which he agreed to that plan.

However, Bradley then tried to cover himself and produced the memo which many people believe is a fake document. He dated it to make it seem that he had objected. But there are three accounts from that meeting which show that he did not object, that he did accept it. Then he said, "They lied to me." But the truth is, I'm afraid, that it was Bradley who lied to try to cover it up.

Steve Dietrich: This is an event that's of great interest to me today because we had this problem in Desert Storm. In Rick Atkinson's controversial book *Crusade* the author faults General Schwarzkopf for bullying his subordinate commanders; he practically ripped the face off some air force commanders because he had ordered them, I believe, to strike enemy frontline units on day one of the bombing campaign. They brought him in to brief him on their plan before the campaign commenced and General Schwarzkopf said, "Excuse me, but I don't see where you're taking out the frontline units like I ordered you to." They proceeded to explain what they were going to do far to the rear, and he exploded. So this problem that we see in Cobra persists today. We've got to get it right. It's inexcusable.

Douglas Porch: I'd like to ask the panel to comment on a remark by Stephen Ambrose in his opening lecture, and that's his explanation for the ultimate failure of the Germans in the Normandy campaign as sort of a failure of military culture, manifested in the lack of initiative and the fact that they always had to refer to higher command before they would do anything.

This struck me as a very interesting explanation because it seems to go against, certainly, what Max Hastings writes in *Overlord*. It certainly goes against what Martin van Creveld writes about the actual efficiency of German military culture. It seems to me that if one gets beyond the Normandy campaign, it goes against what many historians are concluding about the German army in the First World War. For instance, Bruce Gudmundsson's book on the development of stormtrooper tactics shows how much more flexibility the Germans showed in that war. And then there's Bob Doughty's book on Sedan, basically showing that it was German initiative which allowed the breakthrough there to be exploited. So I've got really two questions I'd like to throw out. Were the Germans in fact less efficient than the Anglo-American forces in Normandy; or was this lack of efficiency simply campaign specific?

John English: I have a different view from Professor Ambrose's on the Germans. I do not think they were lesser troops than ours. As in most armies there were good battalions and bad battalions. That was true of the American and British armies and it was true of the German army too. The 12th SS was an extraordinary division. They trained their people well—they trained them with live fire. They did little drill. We were always pounding around parade squares; we were doing smartening-up training. We had a fetish about battle drill without thinking of the bigger picture—we sort of ran around being greatly enthusiastic about things.

They did some extraordinary things. Kurt Meyer's attack, which may have been an ambush, came off the line of march and demonstrated high individual initiative on his part. It may have been a wrong decision. The chief of staff of that division said Meyer should have waited because the SS divisions were twenty-thousand strong; they were much stronger than the army divisions and they had the best equipment. If Meyer had waited, we would have had a twenty thousand-man division attacking us on June 7, and that probably would have taken the Germans to the sea.

Kurt Meyer was also excellent at seizing the initiative at the beginning of Totalize. He wondered why the Canadians were waiting to launch their attack and he said, "Ah, they must be waiting for heavy bombers and that must be the bomb line right there." And he took his troops and went on the other side of it and attacked. This was yet another act of initiative. The Germans did this at all levels.

I've seen lots of reports from the Canadians and reports from the Germans, both indicating that the Germans were very good at showing initiative. The Germans would close up to you at night and they would just raise great pain with you; then they would withdraw come the morning and switch themselves around and you wouldn't know where they were. I think their higher command level, their operational level, was completely fouled up. But I have great regard for the Germans. The German soldier was not an automaton. The German Staff College students of today still have a duty to argue with their senior officers. It is in Anglo-American armies that junior officers sort of say, "Yes, sir, yes sir," dumbly. This is my impression after my service.

Stephen Ambrose: The skills of the individual German soldier are not what I'm talking about; and I'm not saying that the quality of their training was deficient or that at the very lowest levels, from squad up to company, they could not take the initiative. But I just got fed up with Max Hastings presenting these guys as supermen. And do remember that the German army that we ran into was an army on the defensive. The one time they took the offensive against the American army—in the Battle of the Bulge—they got their clocks cleaned even though they sometimes had as much as a ten-to-one superiority.

That this question should come up about the Falaise Gap is interesting to me. What started the Falaise Gap was the Mortain counterattack, and the Mortain counterattack was absolute madness. That any high command anywhere in the world would submit to some psychotic committing them to that kind of attack—well, I don't think we should let the German high command off as easily as we have. They can try to get away with saying it was all Hitler's fault. But they had the guns.

John English: I don't disagree with that. But I think sometimes we overstate our cases, even on Cobra.

Geoffrey Perret: I was shocked by what I considered to be German screw-ups in the Omaha sector. The 352nd Division was a fresh, first-class division. It had seven infantry battalions, ten if you count the three that had been attached from the 716th Coastal Defense Division; and yet only one was really put permanently on Omaha Beach, and only one other came to the defense of Omaha Beach on D-Day. Realistically, the Omaha Beach assault should have been repulsed. The failure to do so was a major screw-up on the part of the senior commanders of the 352nd Division.

If you look at some of the telephone journals of the 352nd on the morning of D-Day you see that the parachute drop—and this is something that's not normally discussed—of the American 82nd and 101st Airborne Divisions completely fooled the commander of the 352nd Division. He pulled out three battalions of infantry to counterattack this drop, which was way out of his sector. This group was known as Task Force Meyer. And this significant group of German infantry was heading off to attack paratroopers east of the Vire River when there were only a handful that had errantly landed there. When it was realized that this was a mistake, the commander of the 352nd turned Task Force Meyer around and sent it off to the British sector, where it was crushed by the 50th British Division. Had they counterattacked on Omaha Beach at anywhere between 1100 and 1400, it would have been bad news for the Americans. And more than those three battalions could have been thrown against the Omaha sector.

Maris McCrabb: I'm going to re-attack the Cobra issue. First, General Quesada did say that Cobra wasn't done correctly because the air force didn't overfly the area before the event. As a result they didn't realize that although it was easy for the ground commanders to see that road and think it was a very prominent landmark, the world does look different at fifteen thousand feet, and it wasn't prominent to the bombardiers. Also, the problems with Cobra showed the lack of knowledge by the ground commanders on what this instrument called strategic bombers could do. I don't think they recognized the difficulties involved.

Dr. Blumenson asked about Caen. Well, because the Allied aircraft had to go to a parallel attack, the psychological effect at Caen was almost dissipated because it took forever for these streams of bombers to get through. There was a lack of appreciation for what the strategic bomber could and could not do.

Clay Blair: One final comment about Cobra. I would like to say that to suggest that Omar Bradley would forge a document is totally preposterous.

Alan Gropman: Let me say something about bombs. There is nothing more capricious than something thrown out of an airplane at altitude. After ten thousand drops with the 101st and the 82nd

Airborne and a bunch of other units in Vietnam, I can tell you that an object in the air for sixty seconds, which is a bomb dropped from twenty-five thousand feet, will drift away from where his bombardier thinks it will fall—350 yards for every ten knots of wind. Now, if you're an aviator, any kind of an aviator, you know what you're dealing with here. You're dealing with the distance between the airfield and the cathedral in Evreaux. Bombing the airfield, they flattened the cathedral eight miles away. You're talking about circular errors in miles not feet. Even when you can see the target, with the techniques they were using in World War II, you're talking about lots of problems. So not only did the army not quite understand what was going on here, neither did the air force. The whole notion of precision bombing is a farce if you know what's involved with dropping things out of airplanes from that particular altitude. So let's keep this in mind when we discuss Cobra.

The air force was very reluctant to use strategic bombers tactically for a number of reasons. But using strategic bombers to help out the army has been very popular from World War II on. Part of the reason for this is the propaganda the air force itself has put out about how accurate it can be; part of the reason is just a failure in judgment. That's how we got McNair—we killed McNair in Cobra, blew him to pieces.

Stephen Ambrose: The Marauders [Martin B-26 medium bombers] did a terrific job at Utah coming in at five hundred to one thousand feet. The B-17s over Omaha dropped inland because they were fifteen thousand feet above the clouds and tried to drop their bombs by radar. It was silly. Why didn't they use Marauders for Goodwood and Cobra?

Maris McCrabb: Spaatz wanted to use the tactical air forces, but they had this notion about command and control of the heavy bombers. They wanted those heavy bombers, and I think it's because they did not understand what the heavy bombers could and could not do. They saw them as flying artillery platforms that could get a lot of tonnage out.

But not only were the weapons, the B-17s and B-24s, inappropriate, the crews weren't trained to do that. This was the same issue that came up in Desert Storm. I was in Desert Storm, and Alan Gropman must have seen my bomb plots. We were trying to tell General Schwarzkopf the same thing, that unless the crews are trained to do it and you have the right instruments, you can't take these weapon systems that string bombs for thousands of feet and expect them to put bombs inside a telephone booth.

Alan Gropman: The B-24s and the B-17s bombed at high altitude for a number of reasons. One was to protect the planes because they were strategic bombardment assets. Eaker and Spaatz and a whole lot of air force commanders didn't think it was necessary to use heavy bombers to support the invasion. Their attitude was that as soon as this silly invasion was over with they were going to go on to take out the oil and the transportation and all those other things. They needed those bombers and therefore they had to bomb at high altitude to protect them. Also, the tonnage, the difference between what a Marauder and a heavy bomber could carry—it was thought that if you wanted to blow a hole in the German lines, you needed a B-17 or B-24 because of the tonnage they could carry. That's the reason they used the heavy bombers.

Geoffrey Perret: The reason the 9th Bomb Division was able to do such terrifically accurate bombing was that it had an absolutely brilliant commander named Sam Anderson. Sam Anderson said, "Look, this is a cloudy continent. We're more likely to have bad weather than good on D-Day." So he took the Norden bombsights out of his B-26s and he put the old bombsights in. These were old-fashioned devices, but they were very accurate at about one thousand feet; more accurate than the Norden. And sure enough, the B-26 crews were able to bomb accurately because they had trained for this type of mission; they had practiced for it, they were prepared for it. They could have brought the B-17s lower, but they couldn't bring them down below three thousand feet, which is where they would have to be in order to see their targets. They probably could have done a better job of linking the radar to the target, but the Eighth Air Force at that point in the war had not really adopted these British bombing techniques—blind bombing, or bombing-through-the-cloud techniques—so they were not that good at radar-assisted bombing. You could bomb with heavy bombers, though, in essentially the tactical role. It was done in the Pacific. Kenney had no qualms about having his B-24s bomb from four thousand feet. LeMay pushed his B-29s down to five thousand feet to bomb Tokyo. It could be done, but there was a kind of a mental block in Europe in 1944 that it couldn't.

John Huston: I thought I could stay out of this. I was there at Cobra at fourteen thousand feet in a B-17. I was a nineteen-year-old officer. Alan Gropman has a point. Our normal procedure was to fly and bomb at twenty-seven to thirty thousand feet. Suddenly, for the first time, on D-Day, we go into the briefing and were told, "You're going to bomb at twelve thousand feet." And we're thinking of those mobile 88s and how accurate they are at twenty-seven, twenty-eight thousand feet, and we're saying, "Hey, I'm ready to go home. This is not for me."

Note with Cobra, then, the one enemy which has not been mentioned here: weather. We are flying in and out of clouds in seventy-two-ship formations. Try flying in formation when you can't see the plane on either side of yours and there's no really effective way to bomb with radar at this stage. You're using a thing called "Gee," and the navigator has to follow the Gee-line down and then he's got to tell the bombardier, "Okay, I think we've come to the crosshair." This procedure was complicated by bad weather, and at in least two units the people turned around, did a one-hundred-and-eighty-degree turn because they thought they'd been recalled. Try that, flying in formation in bad weather with guys coming back through you. Keystone Cops would've had to devise this operation.

Note that Pete Quesada was not a strategic guy. Pete was a tactical guy and he was not there at the time. After the mission they got us out of bed at about 2:30 in the morning saying, "Get dressed, bring your maps." They put us in trucks and took us to division headquarters where we then had to attest, had to sign statements, as to where we had bombed. Of course, we didn't know at the time about the death of General McNair or anything else. These are not meant as excuses, but really—it's a tough thing to use heavy bombers in the tactical role, and maybe it was oversold in terms of what we could do, and maybe there was a lack of appreciation between the ground and the air forces about what was possible.

Conference Participant: Could you know where you bombed?

John Huston: Well, it depends. It depends on the Gee, the navigator, DUC—and that signal was not always a constant one either. H2S was not used at all and would not have been in any way possible to use. Praise H2S because of the land/water return factor; but the bombing for Cobra was all land. We only used Gee at the time.

Paul Stillwell: This is for Dr. English. You mentioned the effect on Canadian morale of the "cold porridge leadership" of Prime Minister King.

What was the effect on both morale and on future assignments of the Dieppe raid in 1942?

John English: The Dieppe raid influenced some of our decisions because it was such a disaster. It certainly destroyed the 2nd Canadian Division. The division had about twenty-two months in England before the Dieppe raid, and after that it had twenty-two months of training to get back into action in Normandy. So the raid definitely affected that division. A lot of people say it never recovered from Dieppe, where nine hundred of its men went down in a few minutes. That explains some of its subsequent actions. It had the second worst day in Canadian military history on Verrières Ridge, where the Black Watch Regiment was wiped out almost to a man in a very painful attack.

Paul Stillwell: Did it take some attempt at rebuilding the morale of Canadian troops after Dieppe?

John English: Yes, I think so. With the other divisions I think there was an attitude, "We're going to get our revenge. We're going to go back at those guys again." And when we finally did seize Dieppe, that caused a little Anglo-Canadian consternation because we insisted on—well, Monty sent the 2nd Canadian Division to Dieppe to march through it. Then Crerar went there to attend that ceremony which for Canadians was quite important. Dieppe continues to haunt us.

The Greatest Thing We Have Ever Attempted

The Greatest Thing We Have Ever Attempted
A Pictorial History

1
In January 1943 Roosevelt, Churchill, and the Combined Chiefs of Staff convened the Casablanca Conference to decide Allied strategy. A group photo of the conferees suggests Anglo-American unity of purpose, but the reality was severe disagreement on several issues, particularly in regard to the invasion of France. Especially at odds were Fleet Admiral King (standing, second from left) and Field Marshal Alan Brooke (third from right), whose verbal sparring at the Cairo Conference in November nearly brought them to physical blows. (U.S. Army)

2

Nor was Anglo-American discord confined to civilian leaders and staff chiefs: Overlord supreme commander Dwight D. Eisenhower and his ground commander, Bernard L. Montgomery, had a strained relationship at best. Here the two generals watch a tank exercise in England, March 1944. (U.S. Army Signal Corps)

3

Lieutenant General Omar N. Bradley and U.S. 1st Division officers observe pre-invasion maneuvers in England. Popularly known as the "GI's General," Bradley possessed the requisite toughness to command the U.S. assault force on D-Day and U.S. 1st Army Group (later 12th Army Group) in Normandy and beyond. (Cantigny Archives)

4

King of the seas: U.S. Fleet Admiral Ernest J. King was Chief of Naval Operations at the time of Operation Overlord. As commander of the largest, most powerful navy in history, he was in large measure responsible for the success of every Allied amphibious operation, including the Normandy landings. (U.S. Navy)

5

Weak leaders for a stout-hearted people: Canadian Prime Minister W.L. Mackenzie King and army commander General A.G.L. McNaughton at Aldershot, England, 1941. King was uninterested in the higher direction of the war, a stance that marginalized Canada in Allied decision-making bodies; McNaughton was an indifferent operational commander who couldn't get along with his British counterparts. (National Archives of Canada)

6

Matériel in vast quantity and, often enough, of superior quality: this was the Allies's trump card in June 1944. In the photo, both quantity and quality are represented by American fighters and bombers lined up for final assembly in England before the invasion. (U.S. Army Signal Corps)

7

Rehearsing for Overlord, troops of the U.S. 1st Infantry Division debark from an LST during exercise "Fabius" at Slapton Sands, England, 28 April 1944. The Allies' ability to land troops and equipment on Normandy's defended shore was the product of months of intensive training. (U.S. Army Signal Corps)

8

A sergeant in the 29th "Blue and Gray" Division sharpens his combat knife just before D-Day. A National Guard unit from Maryland and Virginia, the 29th reinforced the 1st Infantry Division for the assault on Omaha Beach on D-Day and went on to become one of the army's finest combat divisions. As such, it represented America's citizen-soldier tradition at its best. (U.S. Army)

9

Ninth Air Force B-26 medium bombers strike German positions at Pointe du Hoe before the landings at Omaha Beach (located to the left). Allied tactical air forces devastated enemy ground targets and transportation infrastructure, thus providing an effective, sometimes decisive, battlefield counter to German operational and tactical proficiency. (USAF)

10

Rear Adm. Alan Kirk (left), commander of Overlord's Western Task Forces, and Gen. Bradley (on Kirk's left) watch the landings at Omaha Beach from the bridge of Kirk's flagship, heavy cruiser USS *Augusta*. A naval attaché in Britain before the war, Kirk had gained valuable experience in amphibious warfare–and in working with the British–in the Mediterranean theater. (U.S. Navy)

Plate 6

11

A U.S. destroyer braves shallow water and German artillery to provide close-in gunfire support at Omaha Beach, in a painting by Dwight D. Sheplar. Bombardment of enemy positions, one of many tasks Allied warships performed on D-Day, proved vital to the survival and eventual success of the beleaguered Omaha assault force. (U.S. Navy)

12

Troops of the Canadian 9th Infantry Brigade (3rd Division) wade ashore at Bernieres-sur-Mer in the Juno Beach area on the afternoon of D-Day. The 3rd Division advanced farther inland than any other Allied division on June 6, nearly reaching its objective of Carpiquet Airfield west of Caen. (National Archives of Canada)

13

Allied air and naval forces, notwithstanding their tremendous power, could not by themselves accomplish the defeat of Germany; in the end, the Second World War would be won as all wars had been won, "by putting young men into the mud." On 8 June American infantrymen landing at Omaha Beach marched inland to their inevitable rendevous with the ground, and ground forces, of the enemy. (U.S. Army)

14

In the bocage country near St.-Lô, weary American infantrymen rest against a hedgerow while a tank destroyer fires its machine gun at German snipers. The region's dense earth-and-foliage barriers, sunken roads, and small fields favored German defenders, resulting in a tactical nightmare for the attacking Americans. (U.S. Army)

15

British forces on the Americans' left were also experiencing difficulties. Montgomery's troops did not break into Caen, a D-Day objective, until 8 July; the next day, British soldiers clearing away street rubble could look forward to eleven more days of fighting before city was fully secured. (Department of Defense)

16

Canadian 5.5-inch guns fire at German positions near Caen while a troop convoy heads to the battlefront. Some fifteen thousand Canadians constituting over 20 percent of the Allied assault force landed in Normandy on D-Day; eventually, nearly one hundred thousand participated in the Normandy Campaign. (National Archives of Canada)

17

Bocage buster: M4 Sherman equipped with "tusks" to slice through Normandy hedgerows. Made of metal scrap salvaged from German beach obstacles, the device played an important role in the success of Operation Cobra, when it was fitted to three of every five M4s in the U.S. First Army. (U.S. Army)

18

Lieutenant General Guy Simonds (right), commander of II Canadian Corps, was among the Allies' ablest commanders. On the night of August 7-8 his corps spearheaded Operation Totalize, breaking through the German line and driving south toward Falaise. Stiff resistance by 12th SS Panzer Division halted II Corps short of its goal. (John English)

19

Tanks of the Polish 24th Uhlan Regiment, then part of Canadian First Army, advance south from Caen on August 8 during Operation Totalize. In battles rivaling the great clash of armor at Kursk, 21st Army Group (which included Canadian First Army), kept German panzers occupied while Patton's Third Army, exploiting the Americans' breakthrough at St.-Lô, drove fast and far into Normandy and Brittany. (Polish Museum of America)

20

Wreckage of a German column destroyed in the Battle of the Falaise Gap, violent dénoument to the struggle for Normandy. The Wehrmacht's defeat at Falaise was important but not decisive: too many German combat units survived the debacle to fight another day. (Polish Museum of America)

21

While the Western Allies were struggling in France, the Soviet main summer offensive, Operation Bagration, was steamrolling German forces in Belorussia. On 17 July 1944 the Soviets celebrated their triumph by parading some 57,000 prisoners through Moscow.

22

Eastern Front aflame: Soviet infantrymen sprint past a burning German tank, killed in one of the Red Army's 1943 operations. Almost destroyed in 1941, the Red Army's passage to victory in 1945 was a remarkable achievement; how much of it was attributable to the contributions of the Western Allies remains at issue. (U.S. Army)

23

Casemated gun on the Normandy coast. Construction of such emplacements revealed much about the Second Front's impact on German strategic thinking, as formulated by Hitler. Convinced that the Reich's primary threat came from the West, the führer ordered the buildup of defenses and forces in France–to the detriment of his armies in the East. (U.S. Army)

24

Swedish frontier patrol captures a refugee from Norway, October 1944. Realizing that Nazi Germany was doomed, officially neutral Sweden, alarmed by the Red Army's advances and fearful of Soviet domination in the postwar era, silently rooted for a swift and far-reaching victory by the Western Allies, arranged for Finland to quit the Axis–and kept a watchful eye on her borders. (Krigsarkivet, Sweden)

Plate 13

25

"WACs" (members of U.S. Women's Army Corps) change a tire on an army truck. For Allies, total war meant participation of the entire population in the war effort: while women in Axis countries fulfilled traditional roles as wives and homemakers, women in Allied nations served in the armed forces and went to work in defense plants. (U.S. Army Signal Corps)

Panel 3

FACES OF COMMAND:
Evaluating the Generals
and Admirals

Contributors:

Clay D. Blair, John B. Hattendorf,
John W. Huston
Moderated by Paul Stillwell

The Greatest Thing We Have Ever Attempted

Introduction

In June and July of 1944, Lieutenant General George S. Patton achieved one of the most important victories of his career commanding an army that didn't exist, in an invasion that didn't occur, at a place never assaulted, in battles never fought.

His force, dubbed First U.S. Army Group (FUSAG), had a notional strength of thirty divisions. In the weeks before D-Day the Allies made a lot of noise to the effect that FUSAG, ostensibly (and ostentatiously) based in Sussex and Kent, would conduct the long-expected invasion of France across the Dover Strait at the Pas de Calais. The German High Command responded by positioning its Fifteenth Army in Calais. In doing so the Germans fell for one of the boldest sucker plays of all time, a masterly con carried out on an unprecedentedly vast scale.

Codenamed "Fortitude," the scheme was designed to draw the Germans' attention from the actual invasion site in Normandy. FUSAG, its centerpiece, was a total fiction, an army group in name only, as insubstantial as the night fog on the South Downs. The Allies created it literally out of thin air, in the form of radio traffic that filled the ether with a blizzard of counterfeit messages reporting on the simulated activities of an illusory force. The Germans, who were listening in—as the Allies had intended—became convinced that they on to something really big. The Allies led them on this direction—which is to say, in the direction of Calais—by constructing dummy installations and equipment in southeast England, using double agents to spread disinformation, and targeting the Calais area for frequent and intensive bombing. But the key to Fortitude, and its eventual success, was Patton himself.

With Overlord pending, Patton's greatest days were yet to come, but the Germans already regarded him as one their ablest adversaries, the Allied general most capable of fighting as they once did, in the 1939-43 glory days of blitzkrieg and *Vernichtungsschlachten*. Therefore, the Germans concluded, Patton would play a leading role in the Allied invasion of Northwest Europe. And so he did; but, initially, his role was not what they anticipated: they never guessed that he was to be used as the shill in Eisenhower's game of strategic monte. The Germans could not take their eyes off Patton, even after the Normandy landings; assuming the latter to be a feint, they kept the bulk of Fifteenth Army (nineteen divisions, five of them panzer) in Calais, waiting for the main blow to fall. Meanwhile, the battle that would decide the fate of Western Europe—and, arguably, the outcome of the war—was being fought below the Seine. It was not until late July that the Germans finally realized they had been humbugged, whereupon they began dispatching Fifteenth Army's formations to Normandy. Too late. By the end of the third week in July St.-Lô and Caen were in Allied hands; by the end of the month the Allies had broken through the German defenses, with American forces thrusting south past Avranches.

Fifteenth Army's absence from Normandy on D-Day and in the weeks immediately following Overlord cannot be attributed to Patton alone. Operation Fortitude was, after all, a huge production with a cast of thousands. But Patton was the star attraction: and it was his performance that riveted the Germans' attention. In effect Patton tied down an entire German field army, preventing it from becoming a factor during the most critical stage of the war in the West, when Axis and Allied fortunes both hung in the balance, and Fifteenth Army's added weight on the battlefield might have tipped the scales in the Wehrmacht's favor. Patton was a radiant presence who dazzled the audience with his brilliance: blinded by his light, the Germans scarcely saw the man who actually carried the American part of the fight to them and managed it for the duration of the war.

That man was Omar N. Bradley. He had none of Patton's charisma, nor anyone else's for that matter. He didn't need it. He had other virtues that more than compensated for his lack of personal magnetism. These virtues are often overlooked, or misperceived, as is Bradley himself.

He was his own man, but his public persona was media property, created by a sympathetic journalist and perpetrated by other newsmen eager to find a general who possessed, or seemed to possess, the down-home qualities that Americans love to see in people of high standing. In this respect he made "good copy" for war correspondents. But it was not necessarily accurate copy, as Clay Blair points out in his contribution. Its title, "Let Us Not Forget Omar Bradley," should not be taken as a plea for remembrance but rather a statement of intent, fulfilled in Blair's subsequent commentary, to present Bradley as he really was instead of what Ernie Pyle and his fellow journalists made him out to be.

*

Much more than Bradley, it is Overlord's naval commanders for whom a plea of remembrance should be composed. They are truly the forgotten men of D-Day. Not that history has treated their achievements unkindly: the success of Allied naval operations leading up to and through D-Day is a well-established fact. But success did not bring glory to those responsible for it. They did their jobs so well that the many tasks the Allied navy performed were made to look easy, and the many difficulties it encountered were overcome with seemingly equal ease.

Much credit in this regard belongs to Allied ship captains and crews, who carried out their Overlord duties with a deceptively mundane competence. But some credit, if only of a backhanded sort, should also go to the Kriegsmarine for being a virtual no-show on D-Day. With its surface fleet near extinction and its submarine arm reduced to skulking sorties and the occasional mugging of stray Allied ships, the German navy was incapable of disrupting the Normandy landings. Of course, its virtual impotence was also attributable to the Allied navy, which had previously and decisively won the Battle of the Atlantic and had, in doing so, removed the Kriegsmarine as a significant threat. The German navy was still capable of deadly mischief, as it demonstrated in the Slapton Sands incident. But this was the exception that proved the rule. Against the Allies' Overlord armada it was literally powerless. Hence, the Allied navy would fight no headline-grabbing sea battles on 6 June.

Instead, it would fight the German army, if only from a distance. In many instances that distance could be quite short. While the big ships, the battlewagons and cruisers, stood well offshore lobbing massive shells at German emplacements, smaller craft were running right up to the beaches. The result, for the crews of those vessels, was exposure to dangers as harrowing as those encountered in any ship-to-ship duel. At Omaha Beach, for example, landing craft crews were subjected to the same withering fire as the troops they were bringing to shore, while destroyers USS *Satterlee* and HMS *Talybont* were giving new meaning to the term "close-in support" by dashing into perilously shallow waters to fire on German positions. But, for all of its hazards, it was not the sort of activity that puts navy men in the news. It was not even the navy's primary mission, but rather one of many items on a lengthy task-list. In his contribution, John Hattendorf describes the navy's duties on D-Day and explains how and why it performed so brilliantly—thus, ironically, relegating the Allied admirals to obscurity for helping to win one of history's most famous victories.

*

John Huston, the panel's final contributor, discusses the men who commanded the Allied air forces, which dominated the air as thoroughly as the navy ruled the sea. Indeed, it was Allied air power, which had been bashing at the Reich long before D-Day, that set the stage for naval supremacy, and for much else as well, not least the Normandy invasion.

It has often been asserted that opposed amphibious landings are among the most difficult of military undertakings. If this is true, then Overlord, the greatest of all amphibious operations, must be judged an extraordinary achievement. But it was not unique. On the contrary, the success of Overlord was, in a sense, rather commonplace. In the whole of the Second World War, only four amphibious operations—two at Crete, one at Wake Island and Hong Kong, respectively—were turned back before or at the water's edge. All other seaborne assaults and landings, by Allies and Axis alike, were successful.

They were successful because the victors had gained air superiority over the landing zones. The importance of air superiority to the success of amphibious operations is underscored by the fate of two landings that were contemplated, planned, but never launched—the German invasions of Britain and Malta. Both efforts were never attempted because the Germans had failed to wrest air control from the British above and in the approaches to the proposed invasion sites. It could be argued that even if the Germans had won the Battle of Britain in the late summer of 1940, the Royal Navy was sufficiently powerful to stop a cross-Channel attack. But that argument loses credibility when one considers a scenario that would have British warships steaming into the English Channel without air cover, utterly exposed to the swarms of Luftwaffe bombers that would certainly descend on them. An indicator of the disaster that might have been can be found in the battle for Crete, where German aircraft sank nine British warships and damaged several others; and the doomed sortie into the Gulf of Thailand by British battleship *Prince of Wales* and battlecruiser *Repulse*, both sent to the bottom on 9 December 1941 by Japanese dive bombers and torpedo planes.

The Allied fleet assembled for Overlord faced no such threat—not even the hint of a threat. The Luftwaffe put in only a token appearance on D-Day because by then, in Western Europe, it was little more than a token force. It had been literally shot from the skies in the preceding months. Its appearance over the Normandy beaches was limited to *two* fighter aircraft, whose efforts were analagous to mosquitos attacking an elephant: hardly felt and easily brushed aside. Allied air power, by contrast, was devastating to the Germans. It had been so for quite some time. Just before Overlord the Allied air forces, having already neutralized the German fighter arm, had been attacking ground targets—specifically, rail and communications infrastructure—with a fury and frequency that made the Luftwaffe's aerial blitzes of 1939 and 1940 look like child's play.

The battles that produced Allied air superiority were not limited to Continental skies; clashes of a different sort also occurred in meetings between the Allied leaders responsible for formulating air strategy. So far as we know these confrontations were bloodless, although not, one suspects, for lack of enmity or rancor. Predictably, dispute centered on the question of how best to use the Allies' considerable, and considerably varied, air assets. The Allies possessed a fearsomely destructive strategic bombing force that could be (and was) employed for tactical strikes; a medium bomber force that performed in both the strategic bombing and tactical interdiction roles; and a fighter arm equally capable of brawling with German Focke-Wulfes and Messerschmitts and beating up on ground targets. Moreover, Allied aircraft were in just about every category equal to or better than comparable Luftwaffe machines; similarly, Allied pilots and aircrew were, for the most part, more experienced than their German counterparts. The power and versatility of the Allied air forces presented different options for their use, each of which, if implemented, would profoundly affect the way the war in Northwest Europe could and would be fought. Huston discusses these options and their advocates, explaining the terms and course of a debate whose fundamental points of disagreement—the purpose and function of air power—remain at issue to this very day.

Let Us Not Forget Omar Bradley
Clay D. Blair

In the 1970 film *Patton*, the actor Karl Malden portrayed Omar Bradley in a performance that owed less to the historical record than it did to army public relations work in World War II. During the war and afterward, publicists seeking to distinguish this shy, uncharismatic general from his peers fostered misleading images of him. Bradley was often and alternately characterized as a kindly Missouri school teacher, as the "GI's General," and as the "Nicest Guy in Washington." In fact, he was all the things the publicists said but, at the core, he was much more: a tough-minded, brilliant general of enormous stamina and self-confidence, blessed with the capacity to think and act big, an uncanny talent for anticipating the enemy, and a large ration of common sense.

It would be more accurate to describe Omar Bradley as the strictest and most demanding of Missouri school teachers had he actually been one, or as the "General's General" and the "Shrewdest Guy in Washington." Intolerant of flamboyance, immodesty, and incompetence in others, he had a hand in firing more army generals during his professional career than anyone before or since. And yet, the nice-guy image stuck, and that is how he continues to be remembered in many quarters—notably, but not limited to, Hollywood—more than fifty years after the end of the war.

*

I first made Bradley's acquaintance in 1950 during the Korean War, when I was a young reporter on the Pentagon beat. From time to time we met for lunch and he would fill me in on how the war was going. Over the course of several such meetings I got to know and admire the man—and he got to know me. In 1979 he was trying to write the follow-up to his autobiography *A Soldier's Story* (New York, 1951) and invited me to work with him. That book had been about his experiences in World War II, but he felt he still had a lot of things worth saying about the rest of his life, including his childhood, his experiences during the Korean War, and the postwar years. He was having trouble getting it all down on paper, as he was then quite old and in ill health; but he was mentally very sharp and wonderfully good humored. My wife Joan and I spent several weeks with him at Fort Bliss, and they are certainly among the most memorable weeks of our life. The result of our collaboration was *A General's Life*, published in 1983.

What struck us most forcibly about Bradley was how he overcame the impoverished circumstances of his first seventeen years. In a life that spanned eighty-eight years he had many remarkable achievements to his name, but none more so than his rise from a rural, poverty-stricken—and, from age fourteen, fatherless—home to West Point luminary and graduate at age twenty-two.

He was born on February 12, 1893, outside the backwoods town of Clark, Missouri. His father, John Smith Bradley, was the son of a Missouri sodbuster. A self-taught, itinerant backwoods schoolteacher, John Bradley was locally famous for his ability to discipline big, rowdy farm boys, for his marksmanship (which put wild game on the family table), and for his prowess in baseball. He married one of his students, sixteen-year-old Sarah Elizabeth ("Bessie") Hubbard, and fathered two boys, Omar and Raymond. The latter died before his second birthday.

Young Bradley idolized his father, and when John Bradley died of pneumonia at age forty, Omar, then fourteen, was devastated. Unable to meet the mortgage payments on their little house, his mother defaulted on the loan and the house was sold at a sheriff's auction for $441. In 1908 mother and son moved to Moberly, Missouri, where Bessie became a seamstress and took in boarders. Omar, a devout Christian and an A-student in high school, excelled in science and math, starred in baseball, fell in love with Mary Quayle (the daughter of his Sunday school teacher), and helped support his mother with a paper route and other part-time jobs. Soon after his graduation from high school in June 1910, his mother remarried (to John R. Maddox, a farmer and a widower with two young boys of his own), and Bradley made plans to work his way through the University of Missouri and become a lawyer. But when he learned that West Point was free, he instead sought and won an appointment to that institution. He entered the Academy on August 1, 1911, joining a student body of six hundred cadets as a member of the class of 1915.

Bradley found West Point very much to his liking. The school's structured military routine and its abundance of father figures proved well suited to his temperament, and his aptitude for math and science, his superior athletic ability, and his energy and ambition to succeed combined to make him a standout student. He lettered in baseball and football and was inducted into a secret, illegal Greek fraternity, Omicron Pi Phi, whose members—including classmate Dwight D. Eisenhower—were star athletes. Bradley's 1915 West Point baseball team, officially described as the "best team that has ever represented the Academy," finished the season with an 18-3 record that featured an all-important win over Navy. Yearbook editor Eisenhower wrote of First Classman Bradley: "His most prominent characteristic is 'getting there,' and if he keeps up the clip he's started, some of us will someday be bragging to our grandchildren that 'sure, General Bradley was a classmate of mine.'"

After graduation Bradley served in the Mexican border war (1916-17); he also got married, in December 1916, to Mary Quayle. The Bradleys subsequently had two children, a boy who was stillborn and a girl, Elizabeth, who thrived. Bradley did not fight in the Great War; despite requests for overseas duty, he remained in the United States, guarding copper mines in Butte, Montana as an officer in the 14th Infantry Regiment. As a result, he became convinced that his army career was ruined.

Though he believed that he would be lucky to make the rank of lieutenant colonel before being forced to retire, Bradley nonetheless remained in the army, slowly but steadily climbing the career ladder during the interwar years. He served two long tours at West Point (1920-24 as a math instructor, 1934-38 as a tactical officer) and was himself a front-rank student at the Infantry School, Command and General Staff School, and Army War College. From 1925 through 1926 he served with the 27th Infantry in Hawaii, which was then considered a foreign assignment. Also serving in Hawaii at the time was George S. Patton. George and his wife, Beatrice, lived across the street from the Bradleys, and the two couples were a study in contrasts. The Bradleys were very plain, straitlaced people. Bradley did not drink until he was thirty-three. He did not smoke. He was a Christian, baptized by immersion. His wife, a Sunday school teacher's daughter, was similarly inclined. The Pattons, on the other hand, were wealthy and lived on a scale the Bradleys almost could not imagine—George had even brought a string of polo ponies to Hawaii. To have the Pattons for neighbors was quite an experience for Bradley, and one, I believe, that was influential in shaping Bradley's view of Patton later in their careers.

In the early 1930s Bradley had the good fortune to serve for three years as an instructor at the Infantry School under George C. Marshall and Joseph Stilwell, who were promoting what were then considered "revolutionary" curricula and teaching methods. Bradley impressed Marshall and became a member of the latter's elite inner circle, which included other future army luminaries such as Walter Bedell Smith and J. Lawton Collins. He was promoted to lieutenant colonel in July 1936. In 1938 he was sent to Washington, D.C., where he served in the G-1 section of the General Staff and then as assistant secretary of the General Staff in the office of the army chief of staff. He was again working for Marshall, who was appointed chief of staff in September of 1939.

In February 1941, Marshall jump-promoted Bradley to brigadier general and appointed him commandant of the Infantry School. Bradley thus became the first man in the famous class of 1915 to make general. In his new and powerful post, Bradley pushed a number of Marshall's cherished ideas: airborne forces, tank-infantry-air cooperation, the Officer Training School (OCS), and fast, mobile warfare.

In February 1942, just two months after the Japanese attack on Pearl Harbor brought the United States into the war, Marshall promoted Bradley to two stars and appointed him to form, command, and train the 82nd Infantry Division. In June of that year, Marshall determined that this now superbly trained division was to be an airborne unit commanded by Bradley's number two, Matthew B. Ridgway. Bradley was appointed to command and fix a fouled-up National Guard infantry division in training, the Pennsylvania 28th. In February 1943 he was given command of X Corps, which was forming at Temple, Texas.

In the meantime, Marshall had sent Eisenhower to London to command American forces massing for a projected 1942 invasion of France. When the assault on continental Europe was delayed in favor of Torch—the invasion of French North Africa—Marshall arranged for Eisenhower to command that operation, which got underway with landings in Morocco and Algeria on November 8, 1942. Three months later, in February 1943, Marshall countermanded Bradley's orders to assume corps command in Texas and instead ordered him to North Africa, initially to serve as Eisenhower's aide and personal representative in the field.

Eisenhower and Bradley were united in service after twenty-eight years, having last served together as cadets at West Point. They worked in exceptional harmony. Bradley became Eisenhower's so-called eyes and ears in North Africa—Bradley felt that he was being used as a spy—and something of a troubleshooter as well. Subsequently he became the deputy commanding general of II Corps under Patton, who had replaced Major General Lloyd Fredendall as corps commander. On April 15 he succeeded Patton when the latter assumed command of Seventh Army to prepare that force for the invasion of Sicily.

Bradley brilliantly commanded II Corps to the end of the Tunisian campaign and then through the Sicily campaign. In the course of these campaigns he sacked the commander of the 1st Armored Division, Orlando Ward; the commander of 1st Infantry Division, Terry de la Mesa Allen; and Allen's number two, Theodore Roosevelt Jr. In Sicily he watched as Patton went racing off to Palermo and left II Corps high and dry in terms of providing support for its operations. Bradley talked with me at great length about this. He told me he became very angry with Patton. But I don't think he really liked Patton in the first place. He didn't like flamboyant people, which is why he liked the reserved Field Marshal Harold Alexander on the British side but not Montgomery.

At Eisenhower's suggestion, war correspondent Ernie Pyle "discovered" Bradley and introduced him to the American people in a six-part series, which led to the misleading sobriquet the "GI's General." Shortly after the end of the Sicily campaign, Marshall appointed Bradley commander of both the First U.S.

Army and the provisional First U.S. Army Group for the invasion of France. In effect, Bradley would be wearing two hats for Operation Overlord.

First Army Group consisted of Courtney Hodges's First Army, George Patton's Third Army, and William Simpson's Ninth Army. During the writing of Bradley's book, I interviewed William Simpson, who told me a wonderful story that may shed some light on the relationship between the senior army commanders—Patton in particular—and Bradley and Eisenhower. One night Patton came to Simpson's quarters with a bottle of brandy, and the two men had themselves a talkfest. At some point in the conversation, Patton said, "Well, Bill, here we are under Eisenhower and Bradley, both six years our junior. Hodges flunked out of West Point class of 1908 and had to work his way up from enlisted status. I was turned back from 1908 and it took me five years to graduate. You graduated second from the bottom in our class of 1909. Isn't it peculiar that three old farts like us should be carrying the ball for those two sons-of-bitches?"

*

In August 1945 Bradley began a two-year stint as director of the Veterans Administration, leaving that post in June 1948 to replace Eisenhower as army chief of staff. Following the creation of the Department of Defense in 1949, Bradley became the first chairman of the Joint Chiefs of Staff, a job he took at the behest of President Truman.

Bradley had intended to serve as JCS chairman for one two-year term, but agreed to serve a second term when the outbreak of the Korean War in June 1950 resulted in the commitment of American forces to that conflict. Bradley became Truman's chief military advisor for the conduct of the war, a job that soon put him at odds with the commander of American (and UN) forces in the Far East, General Douglas MacArthur. Bradley, like Truman, saw MacArthur as the sum of all that displeased him in a general officer. There can be little doubt that he wanted MacArthur's dismissal or that his thinking in this regard influenced Truman's decision to sack the general in April 1951.

In January 1953 Dwight Eisenhower was sworn in as the thirty-fourth president of the United States. Shortly thereafter Bradley asked his former West Point classmate to be relieved as JCS chairman at the conclusion of Bradley's second two-year term in August of that year. Upon winding up forty-year years of active duty, the sixty-year-old Bradley "retired" into civilian life and became chairman of the board of the Bulova Watch Company, a post he held until July 1973. He died on April 8, 1981, at age eighty-eight, and was buried with full military honors at Arlington National Cemetery.

I'd like to conclude with two statements made by Eisenhower about Bradley that go beyond the usual appraisals and fitness reports. Eisenhower said, "In my opinion you are prominent among commanders of major battle units in this war. Your leadership, forcefulness, professional capacity, selflessness, high sense of duty and sympathetic understanding of human beings combine to stamp you as one of America's great leaders and soldiers."* And in another context he wrote that "Bradley was the master tactician of our forces and in my opinion will eventually come to be recognized as America's foremost battle leader."†

---

*Eisenhower to Bradley, letter, Eisenhower Papers, vol. 6, p. 207.
†Eisenhower to P. A. Hodgson, letter, 6 February 1948, Eisenhower Papers, vol. 9, p. 2,234.

The Greatest Thing We Have Ever Attempted

The Greatest Thing We Have Ever Attempted

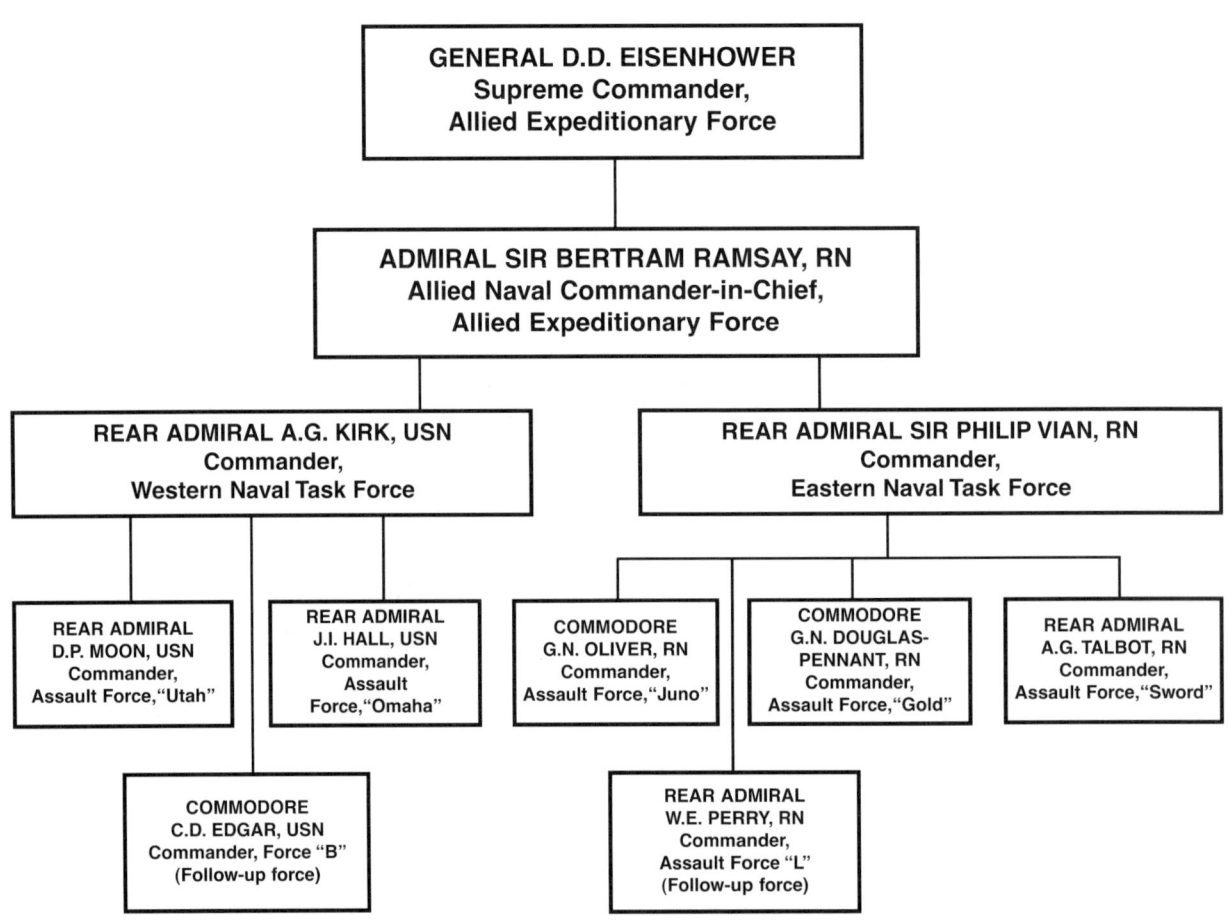

CHART 1   NAVAL COMMAND FOR OPERATION NEPTUNE 6 JUNE 1944

The Admirals
John B. Hattendorf

Professor Ambrose has reminded us of one of General Eisenhower's favorite aphorisms: "Before the battle is joined, plans are everything; the instant the battle is joined, plans are worthless." While Eisenhower and his generals found that true on D-Day, the admirals did not. For them, plans were everything; and, generally speaking, everything worked according to plan. The contrast here between army and navy operations is important and may well explain why today, some fifty years later, few remember the D-Day admirals or anything about them. Who were they?

*

One thing that we on this side of the Atlantic have trouble understanding is that naval command for Operation Neptune was predominantly exercised by the British, as was only proper for an expedition based in Britain and operating in British home waters. Admiral Sir Bertram H. Ramsay, RN, was Allied naval commander in chief; immediately under him were Rear Admiral Philip Vian, RN, and Rear Admiral Alan Kirk, USN, commanding the Eastern and Western Task Forces, respectively. Kirk commanded about 39 percent of the naval assault forces; British commanders, the remaining 61 percent. Some 1,213 combatant ships were employed; 79 percent were British or Canadian, 16 percent were American, and 4 percent belonged to various other Allied nations, i.e., the Netherlands, France, Greece, Poland, and Norway. Of the 4,126 landing craft employed, 21 percent were American; the remainder were British.

Ramsay, who had overseen the evacuation of British forces from Dunkirk in May 1940, had been involved in planning the Normandy invasion since June 18, 1942, when the Admiralty appointed him naval commander of the Allied Expeditionary Force. Shortly thereafter he was assigned to direct the planning for the North Africa landings in November 1942 and then to command the Eastern Task Force in the invasion of Sicily in July 1943. He rejoined the Normandy planning group in October 1943, with Admiral Sir Charles Little and Commodore J. Hughes-Hallet filling in for him during his absence.

Ramsay was not the only Allied admiral to have an important role in Mediterranean amphibious operations. On the British side, Admiral Sir Philip Vian had commanded an amphibious assault force in the invasion of Sicily, and subsequently a force providing fighter cover and tactical support to the landings at Salerno. On the American side, Rear Admirals Alan Kirk and John Hall had commanded task forces in the same landings under the command of the most experienced American expert in amphibious warfare, Admiral H. Kent Hewitt. Kirk's and Hall's Mediterranean experience was significant not only from an operational standpoint but also because it had entailed working with the British, hence acquiring some familiarity with British command and planning procedures. Such familiarity as well as their experience were important factors in their being chosen to command naval forces on D-Day. In addition, Kirk had been the American naval attaché in London before the war, which further weighed in his favor.

The application and refinement of naval thinking, in light of the Allied experience in North Africa and the Mediterranean, as well as the American experience in the Pacific, is important to understanding and evaluating the naval aspect of the Normandy operation. And it is an area that, to my knowledge, naval historians have not yet carefully studied.

In order to evaluate the admirals, one first needs to grasp the vast scope and complexity of the operation and the role that naval forces would play in bringing it to a successful conclusion. In February 1944 Ramsay issued the preliminary plan, which contained some seven hundred pages of detailed instructions encompassing the directions to captains of the 5,339 warships and landing craft involved. The plan clearly outlined the basic naval functions: ensuring the safe and timely arrival of the assault forces at their beaches; covering these landings; and subsequently providing for the support, rapid buildup, and maintenance of forces ashore.

As outlined, the naval functions have a deceptive simplicity. But there was nothing simple about them, in that they required a range of undertakings and tasks to be performed. Ramsay was responsible for exercising general command and control over all naval forces other than those requiring distant cover and also for exercising direct command within the assault area off the French coast. This meant that he was in charge of the following:

* Movements of naval forces designed to deceive the enemy as to the actual place and timing of the landing.

* Defense of the invasion force from enemy attack. This entailed:

1. Harbor defense, both in the ports of embarkation and in the landing areas.
2. Defending against light craft on the flanks of the immediate assault area.
3. Maintaining sufficient surface forces to meet the German fleet if the latter should make a determined counterattack at the eastern approaches to the Channel.
4. Escorting the convoys to guard against air and U-boat attacks in the Channel.
5. Preventing U-boats based in ports on the Bay of Biscay from reaching the Channel by patrolling the southwestern approaches to the Channel.
6. Sweeping mines from the German defensive minefields in the cross-Channel passage and in the landing anchorage areas.

* Organizing and assembling the ships from numerous landing points into the appropriate five assault groups so that the proper forces sailed and arrived in correct sequence, at the right beaches at the right time, for unloading.

* Providing gunfire support for the pre-landing attack and the landing itself, until field artillery could be brought ashore and placed in operation.

* Moving and constructing (by the sinking of ships) five landing craft shelters (Gooseberries), two of which would later be enlarged and incorporated into artificial harbors (Mulberries).

* Providing bulk fuel oil supplies by tanker and by laying and maintaining cross- Channel pipelines.

* Conducting offensive sweeps with aircraft carriers off the Norwegian coast to interdict German inshore traffic, while also contributing to the deception plan.

* Establishing efficient naval organization on the beachhead as quickly as possible after the landings in order to organize boat traffic, instituting ship-shore communications, operating shore fire-control parties, and otherwise meeting the army's requirements as soon as possible.

* Preparing for subsequent operations, including the formulation of immediate plans for:

Faces of Command: Evaluating the General and Admirals

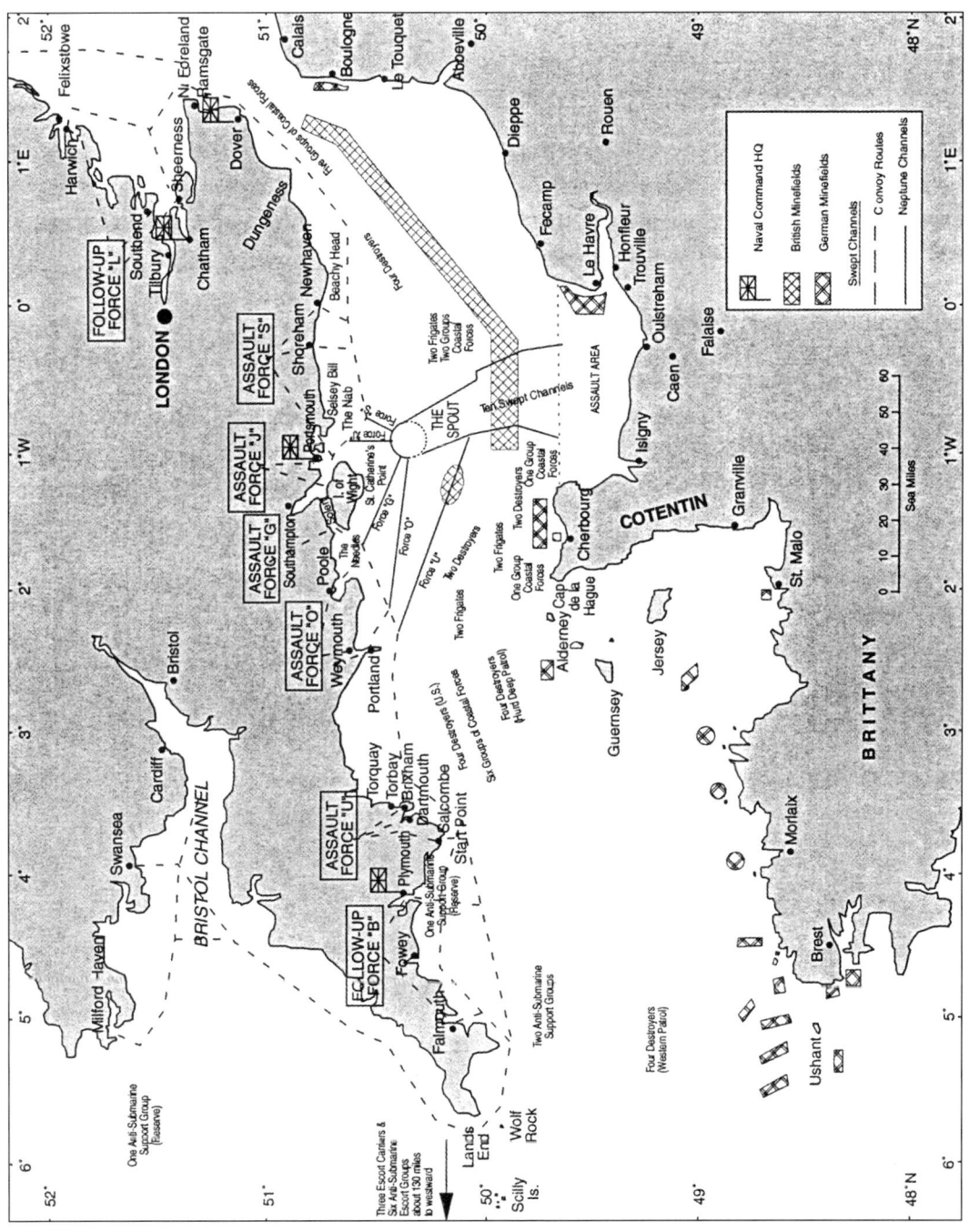

CHART 2   OPERATION NEPTUNE CONVOY ROUTES AND NAVAL FORCES

1. Restarting the Arctic convoys as soon as the success of the invasion operation seemed assured.
2. Detaching ships for duty with the British Far East and Pacific Fleets as soon as possible.

The admirals achieved all of the naval objectives, largely according to plan. Nevertheless, it was not an entirely flawless operation. Problems arose in the following areas:

Planning. British and American naval commanders discovered, if they had not already done so, that there were some essential differences in their respective planning procedures. The British in higher echelons prescribed details which in normal U.S. practice were left to responsible commanders at lower echelons. In addition, the U.S. Navy used a standard order form and issued specific types of orders at specific points, while the British did not. This proved to be a practical factor in the execution of the operation, as each of the five assault areas presented differing conditions on landing. In trying to adapt to the British approach, the U.S. Navy found that the higher echelon's dependance on details and information which only the lower echelons could provide resulted in delay and lack of firmness in planning–which in turn complicated issues at the lower echelons where the U.S. system was still in use. At the same time, responsible lower commanders found their freedom of action curtailed as the plans formulated at the higher levels became directives.

Intelligence. German naval forces never launched the major counterattacks the Allies had prepared for. To an extent, the admirals clearly overestimated the risks they faced and allowed unduly large margins of safety.

Naval gunfire. Naval gunfire successfully reduced German counterbattery fire but nevertheless failed to destroy well-protected casemated guns with anything other than direct hits. The immediate postwar studies of the naval gunfire suggested that there were many improvements to be made in this area, particularly with regard to timing, intensity, organization, coordination, and target selection.

The Great Storm. The unexpected storm that swept up the Channel from June 18-21 was the most effective enemy the invasion force faced. The admirals lacked plans and preparations to deal with extremes in weather even though fierce storms were known to occur in the Channel at this time of year.

Despite these problems, the admirals commanding the naval phases of Operation Neptune achieved greater success than even they had anticipated. Success turned not only on good fortune but on good planning. As Admiral Sir Charles Little, the commander in chief at Portsmouth, wrote to Admiral Ramsay, "Your orders for the operation have of necessity been voluminous but . . . so explicit that their successful implementation was assured."

Further Reading

Elsey, George M. "Naval Aspects of Normandy in Retrospect." In *D-Day: The Normandy Invasion in Retrospect,* the Eisenhower Foundation, 170-197. Lawrence: University Press of Kansas, 1971.

Hartcup, Guy. *Code Name Mulberry: The Planning, Building, and Operation of the Normandy Harbours.* Newton Abbott: David & Charles, 1977.

Morison, Samuel E. *History of U.S. Naval Operations in World War II,* vol. 11, *The Invasion of France and Germany.* Boston: Little Brown, 1947-1962.

Roskill, Stephen W. *The War at Sea, 1939-1945,* vol. 3, part 2. London: HMSO, 1954-1961.

Schofield, Brian B. *Operation Neptune.* Sea Battles in Close-Up Series. Annapolis: Naval Institute, 1974.

Faces of Command: Evaluating the General and Admirals

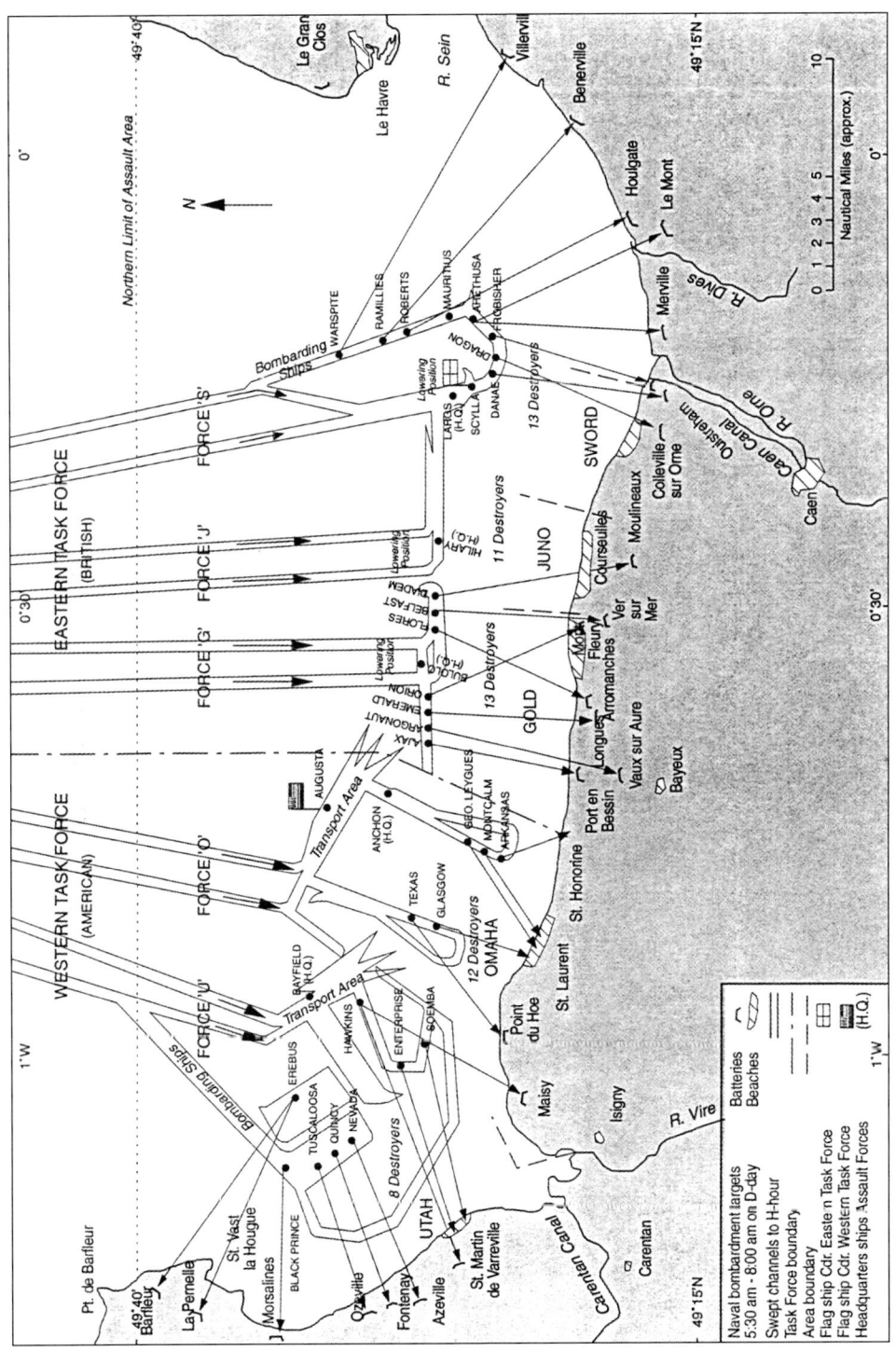

CHART 3 OPERATION NEPTUNE: THE NAVAL BOMBARDMENT

The Greatest Thing We Have Ever Attempted

Air Leadership and Overlord
John W. Huston

Written in 1951, the USAAF's official World War II history summarized the role of air power and, by implication, its leadership in Overlord. The authors concluded:

> So much of air's contribution to the success of the Normandy landings depended upon the cumulative effects of operations extending back through the days, months, and even years which preceded D-day, that D-Day itself, though providing an obvious climax to this preparatory work, seems almost like an anticlimax.

The result of Allied air operations conducted in the months leading up to D-Day was total air superiority over the landing sites and sea lanes. The Allies' control of the air exceeded the most optimistic projections of those involved. Even the supreme commander, Dwight D. Eisenhower, had to have been surprised at such a complete redemption of his promise to the invasion troops: "if you see fighting aircraft over you, they will be ours." For example, the Eighth Air Force, in which I was privileged to fly on that day, launched 2,362 heavy bombers in support of the invasion and lost only one aircraft to enemy action. This same air force put up 2,185 fighters with losses of only 25. These figures do not include the operations of the U.S. Ninth Air Force, the British Second Tactical Air Force, and Bomber and Coastal commands. The aggregate was the appearance in the air that morning of at least eleven thousand planes that flew more than 14,600 sorties, probably the largest concentration of aircraft ever.

This air armada, in spite of a ceiling that rarely rose above two thousand feet, lost a total of only 113 aircraft, mostly due to antiaircraft fire. It was opposed by a German Luftwaffe, once the master of the skies over Europe, that flew only 319 sorties that day. On D-Day the commander of German fighter defenses in the area possessed but 160 planes, of which only 80 were operational. The absence of air opposition and the overall initial success of the landings convinced the U.S. Chiefs of Staff, on the day following the invasion, to go ahead with their plans to visit the Normandy beaches only five days later.

Note that one aspect of this air war that was different from the ground and naval operations was that the action in the skies on June 6 did not constitute a baptism of fire for the vast majority of airmen, either the "crew dogs" or the leadership. On D-Day the airmen ended up doing what they had been doing all along. There were some minor changes, such as the drastic reduction in operating altitude from over twenty-five thousand to twelve thousand feet. But for most airmen, D-Day was pretty much just another day at the throttle.

*

This unexpected air superiority masked many of the problems and much of the acrimony, not always in microcosm, that had beset the Allied alliance (and, for that matter, the German leadership as well) for some months before the invasion. These difficulties involved, *inter alia,* commanders and command relationships, force composition and deployment, and the identification and nature of the targets to be attacked. To some the issue represented a reappearance of ghosts and ideas of the 1920s and bore importantly on the future of land-based air power. Even before Eisenhower arrived in England to assume his responsibilities as supreme commander, he presciently anticipated problems from the airmen. On January 5, 1944, he told his chief of staff: "I anticipate that there will be some trouble in securing necessary approval for integration of all air forces that will be essential to success for Overlord." Ike's deputy, Air Chief Marshal Sir Arthur Tedder, has recorded that the American supreme commander, in assessing his air problems, "saw rocks ahead."

Who were the leaders of the Allied air forces? In 1944 the bulk of the leadership represented a reunion of the "classes" of 1942 and 1943 from the Mediterranean. Air Chief Marshal Sir Arthur Tedder, Air Vice Marshal Sir Arthur Coningham, Lieutenant Generals James Doolittle, Carl "Tooey" Spaatz, and Lewis Brereton, and Major General Hoyt Vandenberg had all worked with, beside, and for Eisenhower in the Mediterranean; hence they brought with them to England a knowledge of each other and a rapport which did not exist among the army and navy commanders.

The two exceptions in this regard are, of course, Air Chief Marshal Sir Arthur "Bomber" Harris and Air Vice Marshal Trafford Leigh-Mallory. The latter, a former head of RAF Fighter Command, was the commander of the Allied Expeditionary Air Force (AEAF) on D-Day. He was probably the first airman named to a command position for the invasion, receiving his appointment when it was thought the only role for Allied air forces would be to provide fighter air cover for the invasion. He had been a controversial figure during the Battle of Britain, and his quarrels with Air Vice Marshal Keith Parke are well known and need not be elaborated on here. A fighter pilot, he embodied many of the characteristics that Americans viewed as haughty among Britishers. He seems to have caused the only real friction between American and British air leaders. John Tremaine, the historian of the RAF, says the choice of Leigh-Mallory for an Overlord command was a mistake. Winston Churchill has used the term "weak" to describe him. But Leigh-Mallory was in a difficult position. He was an outsider, not one of the Mediterranean alumni. In any case, it is possible that he has been ill treated by history because of his untimely death in November 1944. After D-Day he was kicked upstairs and sent to an important assignment in the Far East but was killed in a plane crash en route. As a result he did not live long enough to answer his critics, who have not been kind to him in their writings.

Tedder was the actual leader of the AEAF and he enjoyed Ike's full confidence. He quickly became a convert to and proselytizer for the Transportation Plan, which was inspired by Professor "Solly" Zuckerman, a British zoologist who served as the AEAF's scientific advisor. Tedder pushed the Transportation Plan through despite formidable opposition from Air Chief Marshal Sir Charles Portal, Spaatz, Harris, and Winston Churchill. Among his other virtues, Tedder was able to work around and ignore the roadblock that was Leigh-Mallory.

Harris and Spaatz were the strategic air commanders. On D-Day Harris was, theoretically, in control of the U.S. Ninth Air Force and the British Second Tactical Air Force; Spaatz was the commander of U.S. Strategic Forces in Europe. As proponents of strategic bombardment, both opposed the Transportation Plan. They knew each other quite well and were close friends, despite their vastly different personalities. Spaatz was the complete opposite of Harris: he was inscrutable. Eisenhower wrote that he really didn't understand Spaatz but felt that he was the "best damn airman" in the world. It seemed to Eisenhower that Spaatz was mostly interested in playing poker and in drinking with his colleagues. But Eisenhower had great faith and confidence in this man.

Spaatz, it is interesting to note, had served in England as an observer during the Battle of Britain. "The damn Germans," he wrote at the time, "are setting strategic bombardment back a hundred years. They're dropping bombs everywhere, without consideration for strategic targets." When he returned to Britain in 1942 as commander of the Eighth Air Force, he lived with Harris and his wife and established his headquarters near that of Bomber Command. Asked what his relations with Spaatz and the U.S. strategic forces were, Harris replied that "we had no relations. The word is inapplicable to what actually happened. We and they were one force."

*

More than a year before the invasion, differences with regard to what strategic bombing should entail had surfaced with the issuance of the Pointblank directive implementing the Combined Bomber Offensive agreed upon at Casablanca. The American draft called for the "offensive against German fighter strength" to be an "intermediate objective second to none." When finally accepted, after modification by Harris, it called for a "progressive destruction of the German military, industrial, and economic systems, and the undermining of the morale of the German people to the point where their capacity for armed resistance is fatally weakened."

Harris insisted that bombing of the German homeland, in terms of both matériel loss as well as morale collapse, would invalidate the need for a land invasion. This became an article of faith not only with Harris, who sought to achieve his goals through night operations by RAF Bomber Command, but to a slightly lesser degree with Spaatz and Lieutenant General Ira C. Eaker (who commanded the Eighth Air Force in 1942-43 before succeeding Tedder as commander in chief of Allied air forces in the Mediterranean). Harris, having drunk deeply of Sir Hugh Trenchard's doctrine, constantly reminded Churchill that the success of Bomber Command would prevent the recurrence of the terrible British World War I losses on the Western Front. (Trenchard, Britain's air chief of staff in World War I, had theorized that strategic air forces, by striking at industrial and civilian population centers, would prove the decisive factor in winning future wars.)

Only nine months before D-Day, Harris wrote to the prime minister: "We can wreck Berlin from end to end if the USAAF come[s] in on it. It will cost between 400-500 aircraft. It will cost Germany the war."

Through RAF night attacks, adopting what one author has called "if not the role of rapier . . . that of bludgeon," Bomber Command set out to destroy German morale. In the process Bomber Command became Harris's virtual fiefdom, responding only in a desultory fashion to signals from the RAF staff, but enjoying direct communication with Churchill.

The U.S. bomber commanders agreed with the long-term aims of Harris, insisting, however, that they could be achieved by complementing the RAF night attacks with U.S. daylight raids by B-17 and B-24 heavy bombers. Echoing Harris's assertion about wrecking Berlin, Spaatz claimed as late as March 1944 that if he had thirty clear days in which to bomb Germany, the invasion would be unnecessary. As junior officers, both Eaker and Spaatz had assisted and testified on behalf of Billy Mitchell during his 1925 ordeal; consequently, they were keenly aware of the role of strategic bombardment in establishing a *raison d'etre* for a postwar United States Air Force. In many ways this rationale, rarely articulated outside AAF circles, was a major component of their thinking, which benefitted from the encouragement of their chief in Washington, General Henry H. "Hap" Arnold. But Eaker, Spaatz, and Doolittle, as well as Arnold, failed to appreciate that German morale might prove as resilient as that of the British, which had not cracked under the Blitz, although the duration, scope, and intensity of the Luftwaffe's attacks were not precisely comparable to the Allied air offensive.

The other Achilles heel in the arguments of the strategic bombing enthusiasts was time. Once a relatively firm date was established for implementation of Overlord, the calendar became an important part of the strategic bombing equation. As late as March 1944 Spaatz conceded that it would require an additional six months of bombing to deny the Germans enough synthetic oil to significantly affect the immediate outcome of the war. In the meantime Overlord would have been launched.

A major question was resolved in March 1944 over how best to gain and ensure air supremacy before, on, and after D-Day. Spaatz even more than Harris argued for a continuation of the strategic bombing offensive, insisting that only attacks on targets such as oil production facilities would be sufficiently valuable to the Germans to risk defense by their fighter forces. He had been encouraged by the results of the intensive bombing offensive that had taken place during "Big Week" in February 1944, when German manufacturing plants had been the targets of major AAF and RAF bombing. However, Spaatz and Harris were unaware of the extent to which the Germans had moved their industry underground, particularly after the two Schweinfurt raids in 1943. The success of this effort resulted in a monthly increase in German fighter production throughout 1944.

*

The counter-argument to advocates of strategic bombardment was put forth by Tedder and Leigh-Mallory. They were joined by Solly Zuckerman in calling for all available aircraft, including the heavy bombers, to concentrate on railroad and communications targets. Their aim was to isolate the beaches and battlefields from adequate German reinforcement. The argument was resolved in favor of the latter option by Ike himself. But sufficient latitude was given to Harris and Spaatz to utilize their bomber forces in both strategic and tactical roles.

Problems of organization and the interplay of personalities vexed the planners and the planning, but for the most part did not present a major impediment to operations in the pre-invasion period. Except for Leigh-Mallory, who quickly proved ill-suited for his position as AEAF commander, Eisenhower's operational air leaders had worked closely with or for him in the Mediterranean. As mentioned, Arthur Tedder, whose experience lay mainly in the realm of tactical aviation, became for the most part the air commander, particularly when friction developed in the relations between Leigh-Mallory and most of the other air leaders, both American and British. Spaatz, for example, announced at one point that he would not take orders from Leigh-Mallory. The fact is, the lines of authority on the AEAF's "wiring-diagram" were not clearly drawn. This could have resulted in considerable confusion, but many observers, among them British Lieutenant General Frederick Morgan, have commented that it did not adversely affect the use of air power. One reason for that was, of course, the bypassing of Leigh-Mallory, which Americans achieved by doing business with his American deputy, Major General Hoyt Vandenburgh.

Personality differences reached the highest levels. Eisenhower threatened to go home if he was not given command (although the word agreed on later was "direction") of the strategic air forces, which were, in theory, under Leigh-Mallory's control. It was probably not an idle threat. Churchill, always the self-styled strategist (termed an "amateur coach" by at least one American general), was not always a positive factor. The student of D-Day finds it difficult to comprehend Churchill's motivation in appealing to Roosevelt concerning the possible killing of French civilians living and working in and around targeted French railroad and communications sites. It is particularly incomprehensible when his request for support from the White House was only made nine days before the invasion was scheduled to be launched.

*

No assessment of Allied air power for Overlord would be complete without calling attention to the role of the German leadership in the D-Day period, but this is unfortunately beyond the purview of this paper. It is difficult to account for the myriad mistakes the German leaders made. These include their continued belief long after reality had set in that the main Allied attack would be in the Calais area and their failure to perform effective reconnaissance over English coastal areas in the final pre-invasion days. In addition, the failure to push development of the Me 262 jet-powered aircraft bears close scrutiny, as does Hitler's decision to pull back the bulk of the remaining German fighters to defend the Reich after "Big Week." Allied Strategic force leaders felt that air superiority on D-Day had been gained by the success of Big Week, and they were correct, the 1944 increases in German fighter production notwithstanding. Adolf Galland, then commander of German fighters, reported that between January and April 1944 the Luftwaffe fighter force lost over a thousand pilots. In April he was quoted as saying, "Each incursion of the enemy is costing us some fifty air crews. The time has come when our weapon is in sight of collapse."

The Allies' air leadership in Overlord was extremely successful in spite of national, doctrinal, and personality differences, but the achievement of air superiority was a function of many months of air battle in European skies. Among the major results, at least insofar as American land-based air was concerned, was the forging, as soon as the battle was joined, of a close, successful relationship between the ground commander and the tactical air commander. This resulted in most of the World War II army ground leadership, including Eisenhower, vigorously supporting the demand of the army air force for sovereignty in the immediate postwar period. At the same time the Overlord experience temporarily, but only temporarily, weakened the claims of the strategic enthusiasts that the war could be won in the air; with the advent of the atomic bomb the strategic advocates rose to a position of dominance in the postwar United States Air Force.

The Greatest Thing We Have Ever Attempted

Discussion

Thomas Buell: This is for Jack Huston. That statement by the leaders of the strategic air, that they can win the war without having to land troops ashore—it sounds like such absolute arrogance. Did they have data to support that, was it wishful thinking, was it bluster? Did they really think if they kept bombing German industry that the umpteen German divisions were one day just going to wave the white flag and say, "It's all over"? It's just such a blunt statement. How did they envision the war was going to end if they were given thirty days of good weather?

John Huston: You'll find Churchill saying somewhat the same thing as late as 1941. How much of this was whistling in the dark or arrogance? As far as Spaatz was concerned, strategic air was going to be the postwar *raison d'etre* for an air force. There's no doubt that Arnold firmly believed in the war-winning capabilities of strategic air; it's hard to say whether Spaatz believed it, but I think both he and Bomber Harris did. It certainly was an article of faith with them. I think they ignored the resolve of the German people and their ability, as we found out after the second Schweinfurt raid, to move their industry underground. But the American and British air commanders really believed in the possibility of ending the war with strategic air alone, although they may have been whistling in the dark to some degree.

Alan Gropman: There are people out there that still believe it. Possum Hansell went to his grave saying that. There were people called "air power airheads" who expected Desert Storm to end in six days; John Warden and others said they could use 150 planes to hit 84 targets and end the war in six days. That particular concept is still alive.

John Huston: Not to belabor this, but in World War II they felt they were working with empirical data identified after the promulgation of the CBO in 1943. They said, "Here are the sensitive targets—if we hit them, we can shut these guys down." Particularly with oil. This is why Ploesti in August of '43 becomes so important to them. They said, "If you'll only turn us loose, we'll bring this thing to a screeching halt." And they did achieve a degree of success. In Italy you do find German trucks running on fuel other than gasoline. Strategic air's war-winning capabilities were an article of faith for them, for reasons we've indicated. But they felt they had empirical data to support it.

Paul Stillwell: It is truly surprising how far that doctrine spread, in part urged on by Seversky's book, *Victory through Air Power*. To cite an example of how widely believed it was, I remember seeing a retrospective on TV a few years ago, called *Hollywood Goes to War,* which showed an animated feature trumpeting this same doctrine from that great military strategist, Walt Disney.

Kenneth Hagan: My question is for John Hattendorf. The other two panelists sketched in the common background of leaders in either the Mediterranean or in the army. I wonder if you could do the same for those American rear admirals that were in command at Normandy. Were they typical in their career patterns? Had they had previous command of major combatants or had they made their career in the amphibious forces all along? And secondly, just a brief word if you would about their postwar careers. Did they go on to three and four stars?

John Hattendorf: No. In that regard, they didn't go on at all.

Kenneth Hagan: But Kirk probably did the best.

John Hattendorf: Kirk went farthest. The others—they're just not distinguished. They had fairly typical careers.

Paul Stillwell: Just to give a human face to one of those rear admirals, Don Moon, who was the task force commander at Utah Beach. A few years ago, somebody brought his cruise box to the Naval Institute. Moon's house in Annapolis was on fire and the firemen had discovered this box and wanted somebody to have it before the house burned down. Among the treasures it contained was Admiral Moon's checkbook from about 1930, one of those huge ledger-type things. He had very neatly pasted each canceled check back onto his check stub. This fits in with everything I've heard about his personality: he was an extremely controlled type, wanting to master every detail himself. That's reinforced by the story I heard from General Talbott of landing at Utah Beach to find Admiral Moon in a chateau propped up against the wall sound asleep, and General Talbott wondering who was in charge if the admiral was asleep. Probably he was totally exhausted after several sleepless nights worrying about the invasion.

General Collins in his memoir talks about the cautious Moon wanting to cancel the landing on the afternoon of the 6th, and Collins being resolute on his behalf and telling him to pour some cement in his shoes and keep it going. Admiral Moon was plagued by the memory of Exercise Tiger, which he had commanded. He had been called on the carpet for it and seemed to take the whole burden of Tiger on his shoulders.

I talked to his senior surviving staff officer and he told me that with Moon you had on the one hand an extremely conscientious man, while on the other hand you had a type who wants to control every detail and felt that he had perhaps lost control. After D-Day he went into a clinical depression and had a staff physician but not a psychiatrist looking after him. The doctor tried his best, but what Moon really needed was to be taken out of the theater, to get a rest, to get some competent psychiatric care. But it just wasn't available. And so on the 5th of August in Naples, with yet another invasion coming up, southern France, and with Admiral Moon, again, feeling extremely conscientious, feeling a big burden—he shot himself. He thus became the only U.S. Navy flag officer in World War II who was known to have killed himself. So there's what became of one of the rear admirals of Normandy. He was a very real casualty even though his death occurred two months after the battle.

Maris McCrabb: I have to make a couple of points about strategic bombing not only in World War II but today as well. Essentially from the fall of France up until the invasion of Northwest Europe, the strategic bombers were taking the war to the Germans; they were dropping bombs on Germans' heads. Yes, the Luftwaffe produced more airplanes in 1944 than in any other year, but at a tremendous cost. It's not a very efficient thing to disperse your plants, so the slack capacity that the strategic bombing theorist thought wasn't there in the 1940-42 time frame was there in 1944. In late 1944, when the German economy collapsed, it collapsed in a heap. That's what the strategic bomber guys accomplished by the fall of 1944: the absolute collapse of the German war economy.

Stephen Ambrose: I have a problem with that assessment. In December of 1944 the Wehrmacht launched the biggest offensive on the Western Front of the entire war, with brand new tanks. And I think it needs to be said that with regard to these admirals who were in the Normandy operation, there wasn't an aircraft carrier there and that's why there wasn't any glamour to it, and that's why they didn't get promoted after the war. The Pacific guys just hogged everything the same way the big bomber boys hogged everything in the air force after the war. What saved the day, by the way, at Omaha Beach—Tom Buell knows because he commanded one himself—were the destroyers.

It's interesting. There's quite a lot of evidence to suggest that putting those old battleships in the invasion fleet was done just to provide targets for those huge German coastal guns. The Allied planners figured that if there were battleships out there, German artillerists wouldn't fire on the beaches, they wouldn't concentrate on the transports—they would got after those battleships. So they were there as targets, and their fire really wasn't very effective. But those destroyers were going in right where they were scraping bottom off of Omaha and firing pointblank at German tanks. The *Harding* actually fired a five-inch gun at an individual: they saw a German with binoculars up on the bluff and they turned the five-inch gun on him, and then he wasn't observing anymore.

On strategic bombing, it seems to me that its advocates didn't know economics. They had that idea that there was a key somewhere and all they had to do was find it. They thought the key was ball bearings, so they bombed the hell out of those ball bearing plants. But it wasn't that hard to make ball bearings, and there were ball bearings in the pipeline, and the factories all had ball bearings in storage. It just wasn't that hard for the Germans to make good their losses.

Orwin Talbott: On D-Day I was on the *Susan B. Anthony* headed toward the beaches with a low ceiling. There were aircraft going to Normandy and aircraft coming back. They were so thick, I made the comment to the man behind me that you could walk from England to France on the back of the planes. It was an incredible sight. Now, a question. With regard to the strategic bombing goals of General Spaatz and the others, was any thought given to the idea that, if they had been successful, the Iron Curtain might have wound up on the English Channel because the Russian troops were on the Cotentin and there would have been no Allied troops there?

John Huston: Not on Spaatz's level. Spaatz was not a geopolitician. Spaatz was, in effect, an operator of aircraft.

Paul Stillwell: Just to follow up on Steve Ambrose's comment about the battleships. I talked to a marine who was on board the battleship *Arkansas,* and he very much had the feeling that they were expendable. He felt a sense of relief that there were in fact no guns on Pointe du Hoe to threaten the battleships. In effect, he had a panoramic view of the invasion without the threat that was expected.

Alan Gropman: On the stage of the Air War College—Possum Hansell, Curtis LeMay, and Ira Eaker were on the panel, and I interviewed them for the student body back in '77—Possum said, "We never needed to invade. Three thousand bombers would have done it." As soon as he stopped talking, I turned to General Eaker and I said, "Comment on that." He said, "The goddamn Russians would have been on the North Sea if that's what happened." I don't know if that's post-World War II thinking, but certainly the general air power enthusiast as opposed to the strategic bombing enthusiast thought of it.

There's no question that air power made a signal contribution. That's why Eisenhower supported its independence—but only, by the way, if the air force would create a tactical air command. Air power certainly damaged German production. It certainly shut down a good part of their oil production. The question we're discussing here is not what air did. It made the dominant contribution. It was supposed to. This was part of Roosevelt's strategy. The question is the difference between the promise of the strategic bombing doctrine of the 1920s and '30s, the claims of Spaatz and the others in 1943 and '44, and the reality. That's all we're talking about. And there is a big gap between what the air force promised and what the air force actually accomplished.

John Huston: Strategic bombing enthusiasts had to continue to make their promises in order to politically justify and defend the vast amount of resources that would be committed to the strategic effort. The navy was always saying, "you're wasting that money by pouring it into strategic bombardment." But there was a certain amount of self-defense here, maybe looking to the future for a *raison d'etre*.

Geoffrey Perret: I have a question for Dr. Hattendorf. I read a transcript a few years ago in which the person being interviewed said that the reason why the German E-boats were able to penetrate the protective screen of Allied warships and sink those LSTs at Slapton Sands was that the Americans were forced to follow British doctrine, and the Royal Navy was trying to run the screen from Portsmouth. He also that the U.S. Navy had a commander on the spot who controlled the screens and that we knew that there was an E-boat threat, but by the time Portsmouth had decided what to do about it, it was too late. Is there any truth to that?

John Hattendorf: I've heard the same story.

Paul Stillwell: Part of the problem also was that one of the British destroyers was damaged and a replacement that might have helped ward off the E-boats did not get there in a timely fashion. I talked to a physician who was on one of those LSTs, and he gave me one of the most horrifying stories I've heard. He went down below decks on the LST and when he got to the tank deck it was totally engulfed in flames. He heard ammunition going off, saw fuel burning, and heard screams of agony from the soldiers trapped in that inferno. He said he knew the sooner they were asphyxiated, the sooner they'd be out of their misery, so he deliberately closed the water-tight door to hasten their end.

Clay Blair: Yesterday when we were discussing the shore bombardment by the navy—the softening up process for Omaha Beach—we should have remembered that in the British sector, owing to the reefs offshore, the British had to land on a flood tide, the highest possible tide. This gave Montgomery an hour and a half extra time for shore bombardment by the navy over what was done at Omaha.

The other point I wanted to make yesterday and didn't have an opportunity to do so was that in the choice of landing sites, although it's not an overwhelming consideration, we must remember that the Germans still had formidable naval bases in Brest, Lorient, La Rochelle, and La Pallice in Bordeaux. We inflated the threat of U-boats, but those places had to be captured, it was then thought, in advance of the landings. Bradley also had the idea that those places would be converted into major logistical support bases for all operations of Twelfth Army Group.

John Hattendorf: Tidal conditions at all the beaches were different and a major consideration. One of the aspects which the navy had not planned for and did not realize—all the previous landings that had been done in the Pacific and in the Mediterranean had been done in areas where there was relatively low tidal range. They had not thought about the effect of the high tidal range in the Normandy area and the idea that you could even dry out a ship, an LST and off-load in that way. So that was a great surprise and one of the great lessons learned.

To go back to gunfire support. In October 1944 the navy sat in review of the initial reports from Normandy and made an interesting comparison between the landing at Kwajalein and the Normandy landing. And they point out, and I read from this October 1944 document in which they say, "The ratio between Omaha and Kwajalein of troops landed was approximately 4:1; of defensive strength of positions assaulted, roughly 3:1; and of naval gunfire support, 1:3. Using Kwajalein as a basis for a rough comparison, and disregarding other considerations, the landing of four times the number of troops against approximately three times the defensive strength would call for an amount of naval gunfire support at Omaha many times greater than that employed at Kwajalein. Yet the weight of metal delivered at the Omaha defenses was one-third that used at Kwajalein." And they conclude from that, again, that more gunfire should have been used.

Clay Blair: One final comment on that, if I may. We should remember that General Gerow, who commanded V Corps, said in his first message from the beach to Bradley: "Thank God for the U.S. Navy."

Paul Stillwell: Amen to that. Mr. Rooney?

Andy Rooney: Who was responsible for the diffused targeting of our strategic bombers? It seemed to me that the problem here was that they didn't ever decide on what they wanted to hit, and even after the invasion they were whip-sawed by the infantry commanders demanding their support on the ground. We would go after ball bearings one day and oil the next. We didn't even take out the bridges over the Rhine. It seemed to me there was an awfully bad targeting job done.

John Huston: There was a combined targeting committee, British and American, that worked this out.

Andy Rooney: They didn't work it out.

John Huston: Okay. That was their job, in any event, and they worked on it. Note, Mr. Rooney, that the bridges over the Rhine were not their responsibility. That was a job for tac air as opposed to strategic air. Maybe in the final analysis, in terms of ball bearings and other things such as that, Steve, there's no doubt that such industries were an Achilles heel and the problem was the Allies didn't go back and actually destroy them. But your point is right, there were other sources for ball bearings—Switzerland and Sweden—and there were some in the pipeline. But in answer to your question, Mr. Rooney, there was then a combined British-American targeting. They would choose a target, work about two weeks ahead, in effect send out planes to see who was most effective, the RAF at night (which normally wouldn't go after a strategic target), or the U.S. Air Force by day.

The Greatest Thing We Have Ever Attempted

Panel 4

INTERNATIONAL PERSPECTIVES:
Did Normandy Matter?

Contributors:

Bruce Menning, Werner Rahn,
Klaus-Richard Böhme, Vitalii N. Bogadanov
Moderated by Kenneth Hagan

The Greatest Thing We Have Ever Attempted

Introduction

On 17 July 1944, fifty-seven thousand German prisoners of war were paraded through the streets of Moscow. A contemporary photograph, shot from above, shows a horde of prisoners moving toward the camera in a dense but loosely organized column extending endlessly back down the middle of a wide boulevard. Russian soldiers walk on either side of the column, token guards for men who pose no further threat to the Soviet state; the sidewalks are crowded with civilian onlookers. Bedraggled and unshaven, obviously docile and doubtlessly demoralized, the Germans remind one of cattle in a herd on the final leg of its journey to the slaughterhouse. But though many would die during the years of captivity that awaited them, they were, in fact, survivors of a slaughter rather than imminent victims of one. Captured in Belorussia during the Soviet offensive codenamed Operation Bagration, they were the human wreckage of Army Group Center, a once-mighty force that had, in the preceding weeks, suffered a defeat of almost unimaginable magnitude. German manpower losses in the Soviet main summer offensive (which included, in addition to Bagration, the Lwów-Sandomierz and Brest-Lublin operations) have been estimated at 445,000; and though far greater numbers of Soviet soldiers were killed or captured in the encirclement battles of the 1941 campaign, the Red Army's triumph in the summer of 1944 was, unlike the German victories in the Barbarossa offensive, strategically decisive—and, more significant, irreversible.

The Germans called what happened to them in Belorussia the "Destruction of Army Group Center," but however much historians are obliged to respect the definition that victims of a catastrophe assign to their experience, it should be remembered that Army Group Center was not destroyed but rather slightly more than halved in strength; and that the German army in the east (Ostheer), grievously wounded but by no means broken, would fight on for another nine months, inflicting tens of thousands of casualties to the Red Army right up until the final hours of the war, in the battle for Berlin. Nevertheless, it also bears mentioning that while the Soviets were smashing Axis armies left, right, and center on the Eastern Front, and, in doing so, liberating immense swathes of their own territory and conquering vast tracts of foreign lands in an arc extending from Finland through the Baltic states, Poland, Rumania, and Bulgaria, the Allied armies in Normandy were having a hard and slow go of it against forces that H. P. Willmott, in a later panel, would deem unfit for the Wehrmacht's "starting lineup." And when the Western Allies finally broke out of Normandy and were presented with their one and only opportunity in 1944 to encircle and annihilate the bulk of the opposing enemy forces, they botched the effort, failing in the performance of an operation that was fundamental to warfare and at which the Red Army excelled.

*

In his contribution, Bruce Menning provides insight into the Red Army's demonstrated excellence in Bagration by examining that operation in terms of its scale and resources; its context in the efforts of the Allied coalition as a whole and its strategic implications; its position as an example of the maturation of the Soviet operational art; and the results it achieved and the lessons to be derived from it, particularly for today's armies. Operation Bagration was not one but a series of offensives in the center of the Eastern Front, and, as Bruce Menning pointed out in the panel discussion, this series was itself a subset of multiple offensives "rippling" across the vast expanse of the front, from Finland to the Black Sea, through the summer of 1944. But Bagration was intended to be the centerpiece of the summer campaign, and its awesome achievements mark it as one of the mightiest and most successful military operations in history, while providing a fitting counterpoint to the debacle suffered by the Red Army on the same ground in the summer of 1941.

But even Bagration's success had limits. The Soviet offensive ran out steam in the late summer of 1944 with the Red Army halted on the Vistula, Western Poland and much of the rest of Central Europe still in German hands, and Germany continuing to resist major penetration from Allied armies both east and west. In his presentation Captain Dr. Werner Rahn alludes to this situation when he quotes a 1943 speech by Hitler in which the Führer states that the greater danger to the Reich lay not in the East but in the as-yet uninvaded West. Hitler's logic was formed by a simple calculus based on territory: the Wehrmacht could give up more land in the East than it could in the West without fatally endangering the continued existence of Nazi Germany. In 1943 the disaster at Stalingrad, followed by withdrawal from the Caucasus and defeat at Kursk, must have demonstrated, at least to Hitler's satisfaction, that he was correct on this point; the Red Army's halt on the Vistula in 1944 might have been taken as further confirmation that the Wehrmacht could be decimated on the Eastern Front and pushed back hundreds of miles while leaving Germany with the means and the will to fight on.

But any optimistic thoughts Hitler entertained about the future of his regime after Bagration were grotesquely out of synch with reality. The reasons for this, Rahn observes, were to be found in the West. It was as Hitler feared: for once, he was right. By 1942 the mere threat of a Second Front in Northwest Europe forced the Germans to begin fortifying a three thousand mile-plus coastline against invasion—an undertaking that seems, in retrospect, to reflect an almost fantastical belief by German military and civilian leaders in the ability of the Wehrmacht to forestall an action that everyone on both sides knew to be inevitable. Fantastical or no, this was Germany's only means of dealing with its ultimately insoluble strategic dilemma of fighting a war on two fronts. But fortifying the coastline did not accomplish this aim, and not only because the Allies were able to pierce the shore defenses in one day on 6 June 1944. Rahn makes the significant and oft-overlooked point that as early as summer 1942 the Germans were fighting a war on no fewer than three fronts, the other two, in addition to the war in the East, being the naval war in the Atlantic Ocean and the North Sea, and the Allies' strategic bombing campaign in the skies over Germany. In this scheme the Normandy invasion amounted to the opening of a fourth front.

*

While Army Group Center was undergoing its approximation of Armageddon, the question of what to do about Finland was becoming increasingly more insistent in Allied circles. In Sweden, officially neutral in the conflict, the issue weighed heavily on the minds of military and government leaders and was recognized by one and all to be fast approaching the crisis stage. In advance of Operation Bagration the Soviets had launched a major offensive against Finland with the twofold aim of recovering territory lost to the Finns since June 1941 and driving that country from the war. Starting on 9 June, the two armies of the Soviet Leningrad Front went on the attack in Karelia, breaking through the defenses of the Finn's Mannerheim Line on the 18th and capturing Vyborg two days later. The Finnish army, as always, resisted stoutly, but to little avail: though it could slow the Soviets, it could not stop them. The Finns have a saying: "One Finnish soldier is as good as ten Russians, but what do you do when the eleventh comes along?" The proverbial eleventh Russian joined the fray on 21 June in the form the Soviet Karelian Front, which struck north of Lake Ladoga on both sides of Lake Onega. The Finns had their answer, and it was the same one forced upon them in the Winter War of 1939-40: make peace.

As Klaus-Richard Böhme explains, the course of events in Finland was of vital concern to Sweden, which viewed with alarm the possibility that the Soviet Union might grab all of Finland rather than settle for a return to the 1940 status quo or some approximation thereof. Such a move, the Swedes realized, might drag their own country into the war, with unfortunate consequences not only for Sweden but for all of Europe as well. How the Swedes dealt with this problem is the subject of Böhme's paper, and in addressing it he provides another perspective on the importance of the Normandy landings to Europe. His is the perspective of a neutral that saw danger coming from all sides, but most especially from the East, in the form of the Red Army and the regime that directed its actions. By the summer of 1944 Swedish leaders were convinced that the defeat of Germany was only a matter of time—they were already looking ahead to the postwar era and how the world might then be structured. The Red Army's recent victories pointed toward an irresistible Soviet surge into the heart of Europe, eventually resulting in the establishment of Soviet hegemony over the entire continent. The Swedes, under no illusion as to what this would entail for their own sovereignty and way of life, dreaded the prospect. But what action could they take to prevent it? Very little, as it turned out: they could broker a peace between Finland and the Soviet Union; after that, they could only hope that the Western Allies would advance fast enough and far enough from their Normandy lodgment to check the Soviet advance in Central Europe. This hope was fulfilled, but at great cost to the nations that fell under Soviet domination: these would have to wait another forty-six years before their redemption was accomplished.

*

The title of this panel implies that the Normandy invasion and the campaign in Western Europe was not a critical factor in Germany's defeat. Vitalii N. Bogdanov propounds this view in his paper (contributed to these proceedings despite a scheduling conflict that prevented him from attending the conference in person). In this regard he is entirely representative of Russian historians and, it is worth noting, of Stalin himself. After repeatedly and vehemently demanding a Second Front in the early stages of the Russo-German war, when things were going very badly indeed for the Soviet Union, Stalin, says Bogdanov, underwent a change of heart—if that is the appropriate term to use for this most ruthless of dictators. Around midpoint in the war, before Overlord, Stalin ceased to regard an invasion of Northwest Europe as vital to the outcome of the war in the East, although he recognized that such an operation was desirable because it would necessarily reduce Wehrmacht capabilities in his sphere. Bogdanov dates Stalin's conversion to about the time of Bagration—that is, summer-autumn 1944; interestingly, Marshal Georgii Zhukov puts it earlier, after the July 1943 Battle of Kursk, when Stalin told his top commander that, regardless of what the Western Allies did in the coming year, "our own forces are sufficient to complete the rout of Germany."

This is, to say the least, an arguable assumption. What is not arguable is that the Soviet Union, which lost 27 million lives in the war, would have lost millions more without the Western Allies fighting on its side. The very prospect should be reason enough to assign a high value to the Western Allies' contributions in general and to the Normandy invasion in particular. Another reason is that it prevented the establishment of Soviet hegemony over Western Europe—the sure outcome of a solo Soviet victory. In other words, Normandy saved the West, including a majority of Germans, from Soviet tyranny. Eastern Europe was not as fortunate: there, the Soviets would dominate until the collapse of the communist regime in 1989, leaving behind a legacy of despotism and misrule that should forever dispel any doubt about Normandy's importance or the wartime contributions of the Western Allies.

Swedish Prognoses Concerning the Outcome of the Second World War
Klaus-Richard Böhme

During the Second World War the Swedish Department of State and the Defense Staff made no official prognoses concerning the outcome of that conflict. Before 1942 the Defense Staff did not even summarize its collected intelligence; instead, it merely circulated whatever information was readily available, for example, reports by Sweden's military attachés. The Department of State continuously informed the Committee on Foreign Affairs of the *Riksdag* about the war situation but was extremely reluctant to comment on the possible outcome of the war in these briefings.

However, one of the high-ranking officers in the Department of State, the Deputy Director of the Political Office, Ragnar Kumlin, on three occasions—in August 1941, March 1942, and October 1943—wrote memorandums addressing Sweden's situation vis-à-vis the course of the war. Although Kumlin did so with the approval of Secretary of State Christian Günther, these memorandums were not signed by the latter and therefore did not express his official views. Even so, they were circulated not only within the Department of State but also among the important Swedish embassies in Berlin, London, Moscow, Rome, and Washington, D.C.

The memorandum of August 1941 dealt with two issues: Sweden's situation following the German attack on the Soviet Union in June of that year, and the sort of pressure that might put on Sweden by Germany and the Western Allies. The other two memorandums discussed the likely outcome of the war and the European, especially the northern European, situation after the war. In the context of this conference the second memorandum of March 16, 1942, is of the most interest.

Some days before this date the Department of State had briefed the Committee on Foreign Affairs, but had restricted itself to asserting that 1942 would reveal whether Germany or the Soviet Union would dominate Central Europe. Not long before this briefing, in December 1941, the German offensive to take Moscow had failed; the Japanese had attacked Pearl Harbor, thus dragging the United States into the war in the Pacific, and Germany had declared war on the United States, thereby ensuring the eventual use of American forces in Europe. Mindful of these developments, Kumlin began his memorandum by stating that he would be much more precise than the state department's briefing. He then discussed two possible outcomes of the German-Soviet conflict in 1942: a German or a Soviet victory. He concluded that the Western Allies would be unable to make a landing in Europe if Germany defeated the Soviet Union in 1942, but made it clear that he thought a Soviet victory more likely than a German one.

Kumlin noted that so far the Germans and the Swedes (whom he politely referred to as "neutrals") had underestimated Soviet fighting power and, what is more, had little knowledge of the Soviet Union's military potential. He then pointed out that not only had the Soviets halted the German advance into Russia, they had also counterattacked successfully and, as of March 1942, were still on the offensive. So why then, asked Kumlin, were so many in Sweden convinced that 1942 would see the Germans launch a great and successful offensive against the Soviet Union? Wasn't a continuation of Soviet offensive operations the more likely scenario? But in the event the Germans did mount an offensive in the summer of 1942, it was conceivable that they might achieve initial success; they would, however, certainly fail to win a decisive victory. The Soviets, wrote Kumlin, would then counterattack, and the Germans would eventually run out of resources and be defeated within about three years.

Kumlin explicitly ruled out any possibility of the conclusion of a separate peace between Germany and the Soviet Union or between Germany and the Western powers. Nor did he believe there would be a coup d'etat in Germany to remove Hitler and the Nazis from power. He also was convinced that Germany would be completely occupied by the victors, contrary to the situation in 1918.

Kumlin expressed grave concerns about what an Allied victory might entail, surmising that it would establish the Soviet Union as the dominant power in Central Europe, with the Soviets occupying large parts of Germany—probably as far as the River Elbe—in order to deter another war with that country. It was true that the Western powers, especially Great Britain, would try to check the Soviet advance into Central Europe; Stafford Cripps, the British ambassador to the Soviet Union from 1940 through 1942, had signaled his country's feelings on this matter when he told the Swedish ambassador in Moscow, Wilhelm Assarsson, that Britain would not like to see the Russians in Berlin. But Kumlin doubted whether Britain and the United States would be able to do much to halt a Soviet advance into Germany, and he did not believe they could prevent the Soviets from dominating Germany and large parts of Eastern and Central Europe. Kumlin's thinking in this regard was influenced by his awareness that the defeat of Germany could not be accomplished without the Soviet Union. The Western powers, he knew, understood this only too well, which was why they were trying to convince their own people that the Soviet Union was making a huge contribution to the struggle against Germany. Kumlin realized that such propagandizing efforts might not prove entirely successful, but felt the American and British peoples would nonetheless care little about Germany's fate once the Allied victory had been achieved.

But there were other more important reasons for the inability of the Western powers to prevent the Soviets from dominating Germany and Central Europe in the postwar period. First, the Western powers—in particular, the United States—were also fighting a war in the Pacific, which necessarily diminished the size of the forces they could commit to the war in Europe. Second, any peace treaty with Germany would have to be negotiated not only by Britain, the United States, and the Soviet Union, but by all the nations that had been attacked and occupied by Germany. These nations would hardly dare to oppose Soviet demands concerning Germany. By the same token Britain and the United States could not, for what can best be described as psychological reasons, bring themselves to argue on Germany's behalf. This, despite the very real possibility that the Communists might gain power in Germany, resulting in the sovietization of the country and the likelihood that it would side with the Soviet Union in any future struggle with the Western Allies.

Kumlin did not say what Soviet dominance over Central and Eastern Europe would mean for Sweden, but one can assume that both he and the Department of State felt that such an outcome was only marginally better than a German victory. In the third memorandum, dated October 15, 1943, Kumlin evaluated the possible position of the Scandinavian countries after the defeat of Germany, by that time regarded as a virtual certainty by Swedish observers. According to Kumlin, the Soviet Union would control the entire Baltic shore from Leningrad to the Danish border, making it the dominant power in the Baltic as well as Central and Eastern Europe, with little chance that Britain could counterbalance Soviet hegemony in the region.

The main concern of Kumlin and the Swedish

foreign policy establishment was to save Finland from Russian occupation, and to prevent the Western powers and the Soviet Union from agreeing to establish spheres of interest in the Nordic countries. Swedish foreign policy was therefore directed toward neutralizing the entire region. The problem confronting Sweden, however, was that this objective could not be spelled out just yet because it was not known what the Soviet Union intended to do about Finland or whether the Western powers would maintain their alliance with the Soviet Union. If Sweden acted precipitously and too actively, the Russians might make a claim against Finland, which in turn might cause Britain and the United States to try to get a foothold in Denmark and Norway. This, in turn, might cause Germany to attack Sweden in order to secure its position in northern Europe.

As remarked above, Kumlin's memorandums were circulated to a select group of Swedish embassies, including the one in Berlin. They could hardly have come as a surprise to the Swedish ambassador to Germany, Arvid Richert, or to the military attaché, Colonel Curt Juhlin Dannfelt. To the contrary, Kumlin's prediction that Germany would be defeated by the Soviet Union was probably based in part on Dannfelt's reports.

Dannfelt was appointed the military attaché to Germany in January 1933, shortly after Hitler took office as chancellor. Well mannered and fluent in several languages—he was a graduate of English, German, French, and Russian from the University of Uppsala—Dannfelt soon established excellent contacts in Berlin, which enabled him to gain extraordinarily accurate and detailed information about the German military. So skilled was he in this endeavor and so knowledgeable were his sources that he was able to continue collecting valuable information even after the Germans tightened security in 1937. He quickly became aware of the German rearmament and at least by 1938 was convinced that Germany wanted war. He was also convinced from the beginning of the German rearmament that Germany could not win another world war. But when he first learned that the Germans were preparing a campaign against the Soviet Union, he did not believe it would come to pass because of his intense conviction that such an undertaking would result in Nazi Germany's downfall.

Kumlin had access to even better information than that which appeared in Juhlin Dannfelt's reports. After their occupation of Denmark and Norway in April 1940, and again before they invaded the Soviet Union in June 1941, the Germans had forced Sweden to open her telephone lines so they could communicate with German forces in the Nordic countries. The Swedes almost welcomed this request, as it gave them access to classified German reports. The Swedes rather quickly managed to break the German code used in transmitting such reports and were thus able to acquire excellent information about the difficulties the Germans faced in Russia.

The German reports in 1941-42 were amazingly candid about the situation on the Russian Font, revealing, for example, that Soviet resistance had stiffened with the onset of winter and that the Germans lacked cold-weather equipment, were sometimes short of ammunition and fuel, and had suffered much heavier losses than they cared to admit in their public pronouncements. In order not to arouse German suspicion, however, only a small group of high-ranking Swedes were made privy to this information. Juhlin Dannfelt was not included in that group. But as we have seen, he nonetheless managed to form a good picture of the situation in the East and consequently never believed in a German victory over the Soviet Union.

In this respect Dannfelt was an outsider within the Swedish military. Among the high-ranking officers, colonels and above, only one man held the same view—Colonel Carlos Adlercreutz, the commander of the Defense Staff's Department of Intelligence. How isolated Juhlin Dannfelt and Adlercreutz were from their colleagues is shown by the fact that Adlercreutz did not share his opinion with the Swedish military's commander in chief, General Olof Thörnell. Thörnell, of course, did read Juhlin Dannfelt's reports but distrusted the judgment of Sweden's most competent military attaché, as it contradicted his own belief that Germany would defeat the Soviet Union. Nor did Thörnell believe the German reports. Like most Swedish officers, he was initially convinced that Germany would defeat the Soviet Union in the autumn of 1941. When that did not happen, he and the majority of his officers did not doubt official German assurances that the Soviet Union would be defeated sometime thereafter.

Once it became apparent that Germany would not defeat the Soviet Union, the aim of Sweden's security policy was to get Finland out of the war and thus preclude German efforts to keep her as an ally, and to resist German pressure on Sweden to help defend Norway against an Allied invasion. Sweden was aware that Hitler feared an attack by the Western Allies on Norway. Swedish military leaders believed the Allies would land in France because it made strategic sense to do so, but they could never be sure of Hitler's thinking on such matters.

The Allies took advantage of Swedish and German concerns about the defense of Norway. In the spring of 1944 the British stepped up intelligence and diplomatic activities in Scandinavia, thus conveying the impression that Norway was a primary target for an Allied attack. Obviously, the British hoped the Germans would be deceived into thinking an Allied invasion of Norway was likely. The Swedish military attachés in London and Washington were unable to gain any information whatsoever about the Allies' plans; therefore, the D-Day landings came as a big surprise to Stockholm. And in the days immediately following the Allied landings Sweden still expected the Allies to mount operations against Norway in order to divert German forces from the Normandy beachhead.

The Swedish Department of State at this time did not make any prognoses about the possible advance of American and British forces into Germany. This was partly due to the fact that Ragnar Kumlin had, earlier in the year, been appointed ambassador to Brazil, and after he left Stockholm nobody at the State Department wrote memorandums of the kind he did. However, the main reason why the State Department was not much concerned with this issue was that those responsible for the formulation of Swedish foreign policy were occupied with getting Finland out of the war by mediating an armistice between Helsinki and Moscow.

On June 9, 1944, the Soviets launched a new offensive against Finland. By September the Finns, facing defeat, asked for peace negotiations, using Sweden as an intermediary. In this context, from the Swedish and Finnish point of view, the Allied landings in France and advance in Normandy was of great importance. The assumption was that the Soviet Union wanted to occupy as much German territory as possible and might, therefore, be willing to settle for an armistice with Finland on rather favorable terms for that country in order to concentrate entirely on the fight against Germany. This assumption proved to be correct. On September 19, 1944, the Finnish-Soviet armistice was signed. Finland lost some territory but was not occupied.

In particular, Ragnar Kumlin's prognosis of March 1942 about the situation in Central Europe and Germany proved to be remarkably prescient, even though he had doubts about the military strength the Western Allies would bring to bear in Europe. Notwithstanding the landings in Normandy and the subsequent movement of the Allied armies through France and into Germany, the Soviets advanced to the

Elbe River and beyond. As Kumlin had predicted, the Soviet Union became the dominant power in Central Europe and remained so for most of the second half of the twentieth century. But his worst fear, that all of Germany would be sovietized, was not realized, because contrary to his fears the Western Allies did amass enough strength to check the Soviet Goliath in the middle of Germany.

In spite of the fact that Kumlin's second memorandum was published in 1977 by the director of the archive of the Swedish State Department, Professor Wilhelm Carlgren, it was hardly noticed and used by scholars. Carlgren himself referred to it in a paper given at a conference in Western Germany in 1987. So did I in an essay about Sweden and the battle of Stalingrad, published by the *Militärgeschichtliches Forschungsamt* at Freiburg, Germany in 1992.

References

Riksarkivet, Utrikcsdepartementets arkiv: 1920 års dossiersystem vol. HP 39A, HP 1 Er.

Böhme, Klaus-Richard. Tysklands expansion böjar. In *Stormvarning*, ed. Bo Hugemark. Stockholm: 1989.

Böhme, Klaus-Richard. Fölora Tyskland kriget? I så fall när? In *Vindkantring,* ed. Bo Hugemark. Stockholm: 1992.

Böhme, Klaus-Richard. Stalingrad und Schweden. In *Stalingrad: Ereignis, Wirkung, Symbol,* ed. Jürgen Förster. Munich: 1992.

Carlgren, Wilhelm M. *Svensk utrikespolitik 1939-1945.* Stockholm: 1973.

Carlgren, Wilhelm M. Småstadsdiplomati I stormaktskrig. Promemorior från krigsåren av Ragnar Kumlin, (Svensk) *Historisk Tidskrift* 1974.

Carlgren, Wilhelm M. Svensk underrättelsetjänst 1939-1945. Stockholm: 1985.

Carlgren, Wilhelm M. Die Einschätzung der Lage Deutschlands in der zweiten Kriegshälfte aus schwedischer Sicht. In *Die Zukunft des Reiches: Gegner, Verbündete und Neutrale (1943- 1945)*, eds. Manfred Messerschmidt and Ekkehart Guth. Herford and Bonn: 1990.

The Greatest Thing We Have Ever Attempted

Stalin's Response to Overlord: The Belorussian Operation

Bruce Menning

Between June 22 and August 29, 1944, in answer to Allied requests to divert German resources from Normandy, the Soviets began and completed their Belorussian operation. This operation is known to the Russians as "Bagration," codenamed in memory of the dashing Georgian-born general who fell at Borodino in 1812, and to the Germans as "The Destruction of Army Group Center," in recognition of the results produced.

More than fifty years later, Bagration remains a subject of study for officers at the U.S. Army Command and General Staff College at Fort Leavenworth, Kansas. Soviet operations in Belorussia were notable for the following:

Scale and resources. Bagration was an immense effort that covered an expanse measuring five to six hundred kilometers deep and five hundred kilometers wide. It lasted nine weeks and involved 2.4 million Soviet soldiers in fronts comprising twenty combined-arms armies, two tank armies, five air armies, and one naval flotilla. Arrayed against Soviet forces were 1.2 million Germans in elements of three army groups and supporting air and naval units. Primarily the offensive involved First Baltic and First, Second, and Third Belorussian Fronts executing a series of six break-in operations through defensive belts, then conducting a series of both shallow and deep encirclements. Upon completing the encirclements, which bagged the main strategic/operational reserve of German Army Group Center east of Minsk, Soviet forces then plunged off into the deep exploitation phase.

Strategic/coalition context. Bagration shows what the Soviets were willing to do within the larger strategic and coalition context. Despite all of the carping on Stalin's part about opening the Second Front, Overlord almost caught the Soviets by surprise, to the extent that they had paid little heed to promises by Roosevelt and Churchill that the Western Allies would soon invade Northwest Europe. In early April of 1944 representatives of the Allied military missions in Moscow informed the Soviet high command (*Stavka*) that the Second Front would become a reality in June. At the same time the Allies asked the Soviets what they would do to relieve some of the pressure that was anticipated in the West. Accordingly, Overlord triggered a frantic planning effort by the Soviets. Stalin had to decide how to support the Western Allies while simultaneously gaining political leverage for the termination of the war. This meant resolving the issue of where to strike following the Soviet successes of early 1944. The Soviets had to focus on that strategic direction which promised the greatest results in terms of the follow-on military and political benefits that would accrue as a result of the operation.

From about April 7 to the early part of June 1944 the State Defense Committee, the General Staff, and the various Red Army fronts were busily at work on the strategic, operational, and tactical planning for Bagration. The offensive kicked off on June 22, the anniversary date of the German invasion of Russia (Operation Barbarossa) in 1941. So the Soviet offensive came after Overlord but, significantly, the time-lag was short—a little over two weeks.

Maturation of the Soviet military art. Bagration demonstrated that the Soviets now had adequate resources to conduct multi-front strategic offensive operations, and that they had learned how to conduct multiple encirclement operations followed by deep exploitation. Bagration further demonstrated the refinement, through a combination of hard experience and on-the-job training, of Soviet operational formations and structures, with command and control elements adapted to ends, forces, and methods.

Decisive results attained. Bagration's payoff was enormous in terms of what it did both for the coalition effort and for the position of the Soviet Union vis-à-vis the Western Allies. The Soviets reconquered Belorussia and gained a foothold in East Prussia and Poland, which put them in a position to press forward with follow-on operations into Germany itself. In achieving these results the Soviets had tied down large German formations on the Eastern Front; destroyed seventeen German divisions and three brigades; inflicted 50 percent losses on fifty additional German divisions; and placed the Soviets in a commanding position in Central Europe.

Lessons derived. Bagration demonstrated aspects of concepts of operational design, e.g., center(s) of gravity, decisive points, lines of operation, and culminating points. Moreover, Bagration incorporated elements of operational design, including objectives, sequencing, resource application, and operating systems, especially operational maneuver, fire, and protection (including deception, or *maskirovka*).

Relevance to today's armies. Bagration is taught at Fort Leavenworth because it addresses a series of issues the army believes that mid-level officers should know about and understand. Through the example of Bagration, the U.S. Army hopes to foster an ability to engage in operational planning; the army also hopes to instill in officers an understanding of the operational art as that aspect of military art which lies between strategy at the high end of the military spectrum and tactics at the lower end.

MAP 1
Russian summer offensive, 23 June-7 August 1944
(*The West Point Atlas of American Wars*)
(opposite page)

International Perspectives: Did Normandy Matter?

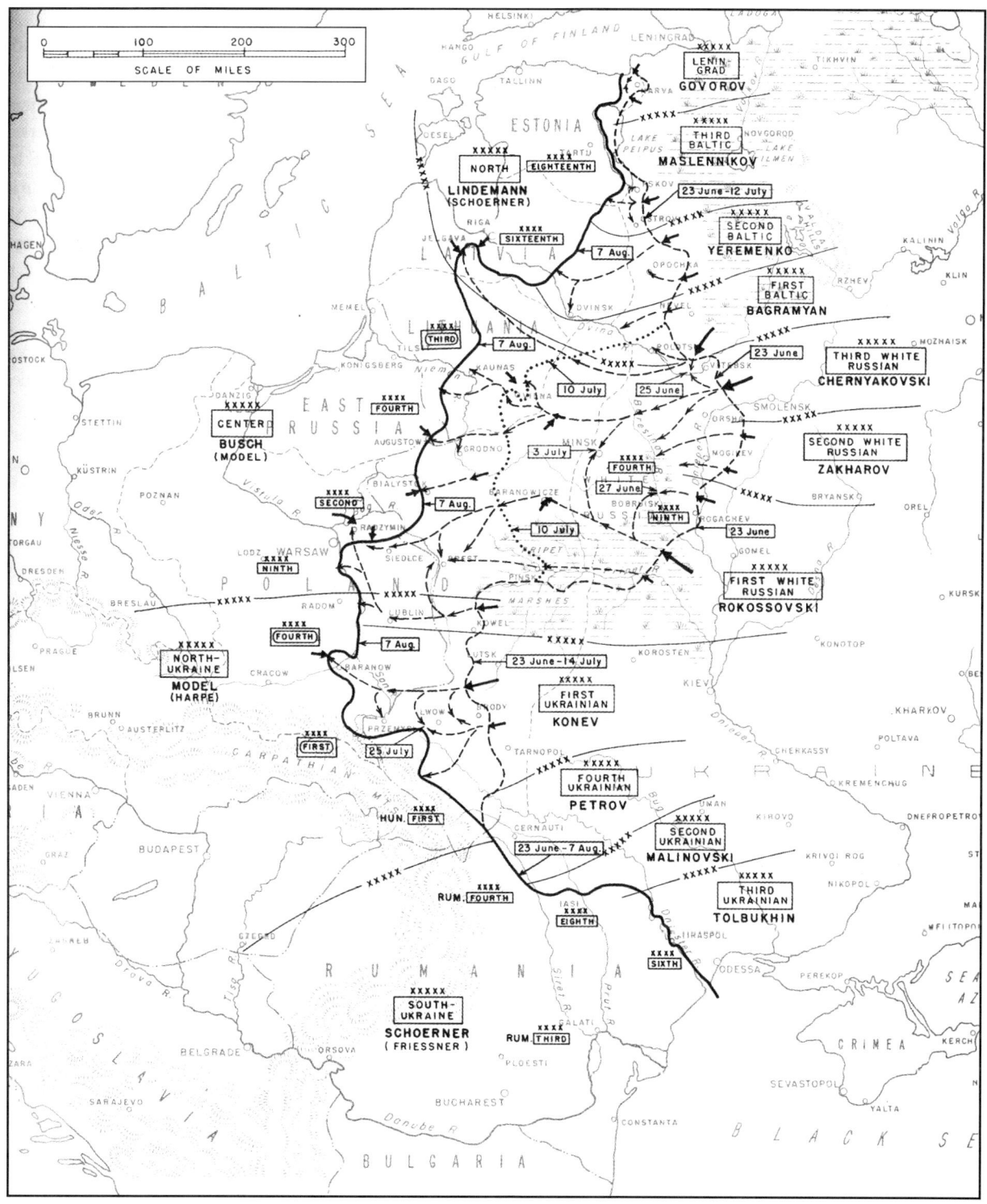

The Greatest Thing We Have Ever Attempted

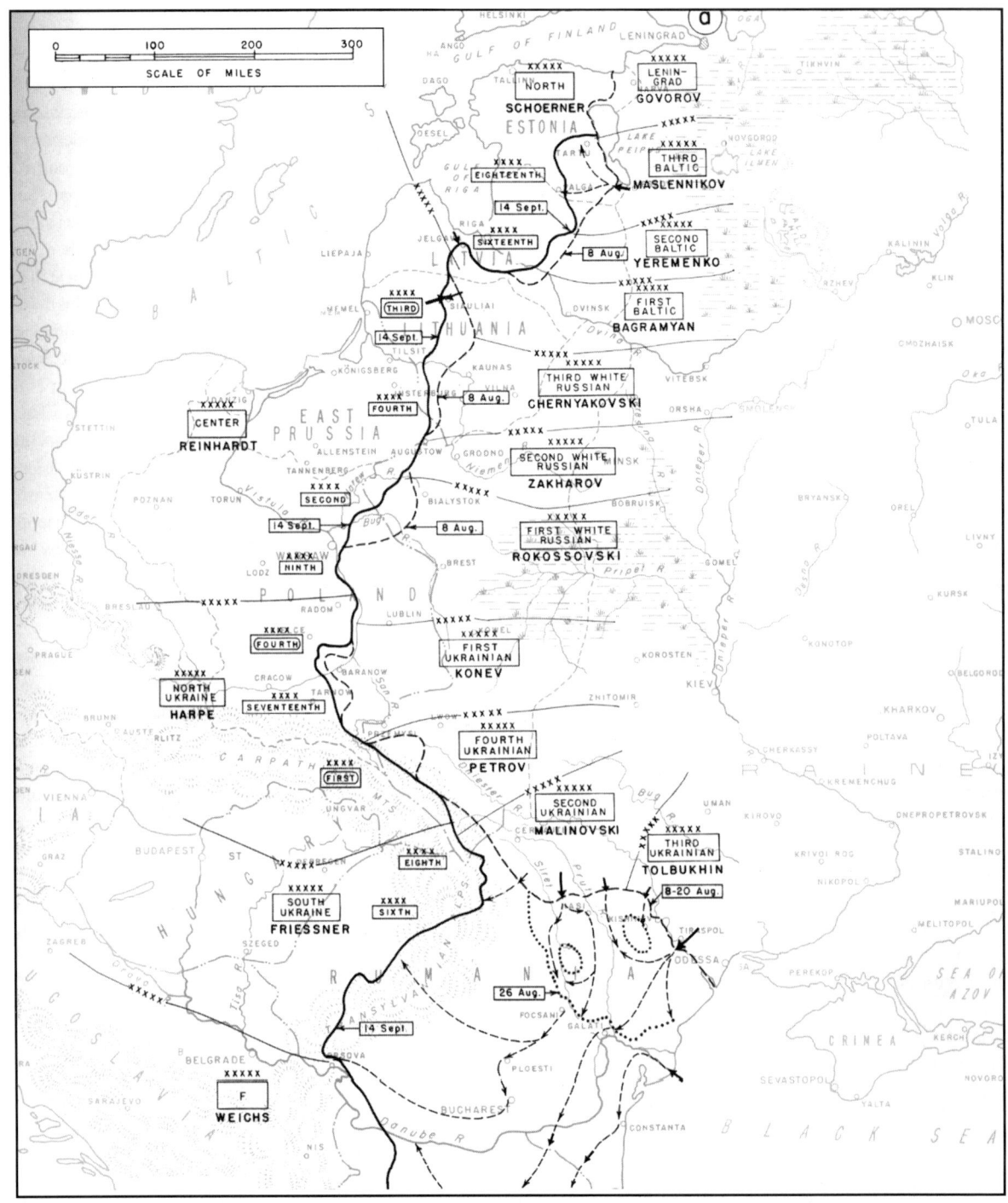

MAP 2
Russian summer offensive, 8 August–14 September 1944 (*The West Point Atlas of American Wars*)

The Impact of the Second Front on German Strategy, 1944

Werner Rahn

Until 1943, Hitler's strategic concern was to vanquish the Soviet Union and subsequently exploit it economically so as to be able to wage a prolonged war against the United States. However, as early as August 1942 Hitler was skeptical about the prospect of decisive victory over the Soviet Union. This, coupled with his belief that the German warmaking potential was sufficient for only one front, led him to the logical conclusion that a second front had to be prevented at all costs. Therefore, he planned to fortify the coastal areas, making them into a new "Siegfried Line" or "West Wall." Also, he deployed a rather small number of fast divisions in the West in the hope that they would be able to ward off possible Allied landings. Yet plans for fortifications did not take into account the third dimension, leaving a weak spot which Hitler himself recognized: because the Luftwaffe could not be withdrawn from the East, Allied air superiority in the West had to expected.

Essentially, naval warfare in the Atlantic Ocean and the North Sea, and in the adjoining coastal waters, had turned into a second front by the spring of 1942. At the time the Allies possessed only limited naval transport capacity, a situation exacerbated by heavy losses, chiefly to U-boat attacks. This posed a serious problem for the Allies, in that sufficient maritime transport was not only vital for Britain's survival, it was also the single most important prerequisite for the buildup of a strong base for supporting any offensive against the Axis in Europe. By the end of 1942, however, the threat to Allied shipping had been virtually eliminated. The immense military and industrial might of the United States had been brought to bear against the U-boats with telling effect, forcing Admiral Karl Dönitz, the head of the U-boat force throughout the war and commander of the German navy from January 1943, to break off the submarine campaign in May 1943. From then on the strategic bridge across the North Atlantic became an increasingly secure route for Allied convoys, permitting growing quantities of matériel to be delivered to the British Isles without major German interference. Thus the Allies were able to turn all of Britain into an arsenal for the planned invasion of Normandy while further enhancing its role as a launching pad for the ongoing bomber offensive against Germany.

The bomber offensive had by the summer of 1942 established a third front in the skies over Germany. The offensive forced steady augmentations to German air defenses, which nevertheless failed to effectively shield the armaments industry. The Germans never made the necessary radical U-turn in armaments production toward air defense weaponry and equipment, thus opening a wide strategic gap into which the Allied bomber offensive could strike. Still, before 1944 the Allies neglected to concentrate their bombing on the weak spots of the German war economy (synthetic oil plants, reservoirs, engine plants, ports), which allowed production to increase considerably until the summer of 1944.

German-held territory possessed a coastline extending 5,100 kilometers (3,200 miles) from the North Cape to the Pyrenees. This formed a front line that had to be controlled and secured continuously to repel attacks in their early stages, to retain freedom of operation for the U-boats, and to allow for the use of coastal waters by military and commercial traffic. But the German military was unable to control the coastal waters to any great degree. The Allies took advantage of this weakness by conducting commando raids which increased German insecurity and tied down additional defense forces. The Germans' swift success in pushing back the Allied landing at Dieppe in August 1942 seemed to prove that their coastal defenses were up to the job. It led the Germans to underestimate the Allies and to become overconfident about their own capabilities.

The so-called Fortress Europe would have provided a substantial means of defense in the medium run had the overextended front lines been made to conform to Germany's warmaking capacities. But a clear decision in favor of strategic defense was never made. In 1943, after the final offensives in the East had failed, the bulk of German manpower and equipment remained concentrated in the East. Meanwhile, the threat in the West was growing quickly, resulting in an ever-deepening dilemma for the German high command. The future of Fortress Europe had by then become a foregone conclusion; it was only a matter of time before it fell to Allied assault. The withdrawal of U-boats from the Atlantic, the seizure of the North African coast in November 1942, and the Allied landing in Sicily sharply illustrated the Allied determination not to lose the strategic initiative again. The Allies intended to wear down the German potential from several points of the compass before eventually delivering the decisive stroke from Britain—the invasion of northwest Europe. The Axis powers could only counter with short-term, mostly ineffectual measures. They had their backs to the wall in virtually all areas of warfare, and no alternative to ultimate defeat was in sight.

In November 1943 Hitler issued a directive concerning the strategic defense of Fortress Europe which led to the redeployment of Germany's scarce resources:

> The hard and costly struggle against Bolshevism has demanded extreme exertion. . . . The danger in the East remains, but a greater danger now appears in the West: an Anglo-Saxon landing. The vast extent of territory in the East makes it possible for us to lose ground, even on a large scale, without a fatal blow being struck to the nervous system of Germany. It is very different in the West. Should the enemy succeed in breaching our defenses on a wide front here the immediateconsequences would be unpredictable. Everything indicates that the enemy will launch an offensive against the western front of Europe, at the latest in the spring, perhaps even earlier. I can therefore no longer take responsibility for further weakening the West in favor of other theaters of war. I have therefore decided to reinforce its defenses, particularly those places from which long-range bombardment of England with pilotless missiles will begin.

Hitler's directive was an attempt to create the conditions in which an invasion could be repelled, thereby securing Germany's rear in the fight against the enemy in the East. In the spring of 1944 Hitler and the Supreme High Command believed that the army formations then at their disposal would be sufficient to fight a second battle for France. In formulating this belief they ignored or forgot their own experience of 1940, which demonstrated that victory had been achieved by the combined efforts of air and ground forces. By the spring of 1944 there was no Luftwaffe left worthy of the name, and any hopes raised by the effects of the long-range bombardment of Allied bases by V-weapons were soon shown to be illusory.

The Germans did manage a considerable reinforcement of their coastal defenses. However, the deployment and contingency planning for their mobile units, in particular the few remaining panzer divisions, had laid bare the weaknesses of the German command structure. German military leaders never came to a unified assessment of the situation, and were therefore never able to develop a coherent defensive concept. The issue was further confused by the success of Allied efforts to deceive the Germans as to the time and place of the pending invasion. The Germans never agreed on where the invasion would likely occur and delayed the concentration of available forces for weeks even after the Allied landings. As H. P. Willmott observed in *The Great Crusade:*

> This German intelligence failure was very much part of that institutionalized weakness which affected the strategic direction of both the war and this campaign by the German High Command and which embraced the doctrine, command and organization of the German forces; in their turn these flaws were to be compounded by a succussion of all but impossible dilemmas that arose during the Normandy campaign with each German failure—how to contain the Allied beachhead without committing the armor needed for the counterattack; whether to concentrate against the British or the Americans; whether to cede or try to hold the Cotentin; whether to continue to fight a holding action or to withdraw to a shorter and more easily defended line. . . . The argument over doctrine was never resolved by a German High Command that could provide no answer to the initiative and superior firepower of the Western Allies, and this lack of policy led to and was reflected by a hopelessly confused command structure of the Wehrmacht in the West. (H. P. Willmott, *The Great Crusade* [London 1989], p.358)

The question remains why the German command, despite the obvious disparity of forces, still believed in the possibility of a successful strategic defense. The answer can be found on several levels of military thinking and reveals four major deficits in the professional judgment of the military elites:

1. *Incorrect assumptions about the probable landing site.* The German staff could not imagine that the Allies would land anywhere but on the most propitious shore, or that the Allies would not want to conquer a major port right from the very start.

2. *Exaggerated trust in the superiority of the few panzer divisions.* The German command underestimated the effects of Allied air superiority on the transportation infrastructure, upon which the mobility—and superiority—of these formations depended. Both before and after the invasion, Allied air forces inflicted such destruction on the road and rail networks that army units could only be moved at night, with frequent and major delays severely hindering their progress.

3. *The inability of the German command to comprehend the vast preparations for Overlord, the energy and determination that went into making the landings a success, and the sheer numbers involved.* Surprisingly, the Germans learned little in this regard from their experience in the Mediterranean, else they would have realized that the Allies meant to conduct their assault on Fortress Europe as a rather low-risk battle of attrition.

4. *Over-confidence in the deterrent effect of the Atlantic Wall.* Many German officers believed the Allies would never dare to invade. But should the Allies run the risk after all, they were to be beaten in another battle of France, in which the vastly superior Allied forces would be countered by the fanaticism of the superior warrior and strategist. This was believing in miracles, but the era of "miracle weapons" had already begun and sheer military reasoning had

already had its day. (M. Salewski, *Die deutsche Seekriegsleitung 1935-1945*, vol. 2 [Munich: 1975], pp. 431-32)

During 1944 Germany's strategic situation was so seriously affected—and not only by Overlord and the battle of Normandy—that defeat was only a matter of time. In the east, Army Group Center collapsed only weeks after D-Day, with the loss of twenty-eight divisions and more than 380,000 men. In the south, the Allies gained ground swiftly, conquering Rome and advancing as far as the line Pisa-Florence-Rimini. The systematic bombardment of synthetic oil plants that began in May 1944 eventually deprived the Reich of resources vital for military mobility, without which it could not sustain a viable war effort.

After the German offensives in Russia had failed, the chance for a final victory had been lost. The military command began to live in a world of shadows in which any reference to the real situation was perceived as a depressing interference, since it implied that the war could no longer be won. The supreme German military leaders gave in to wishful strategic thinking despite the dismal war experience so far and often against their better judgment. This may have been the gravest failure of the German high command.

The weakest spot in the German decision-making process was certainly Hitler himself. After the winter of 1941-42 the influence of the military on the conduct of war was gradually eroded. Responsibilities were split up, each agency jealously guarding its own sphere of influence. The overall strategic responsibility resided in Hitler alone. In view of the complexity of modern warfare, a command structure designed to suit one person was destined to fail.

But Hitler was convinced of his military genius. And he was unwilling and unable to delegate authority and to reduce the workload of decisions at the top level. In particular, during the battle of Normandy he interfered directly with the commanders at the front on numerous occasions. This was bound to have negative effects on the conduct of operations.

Concentrating command decisions from a strategic level down to the operational or even tactical levels in the single person of Adolf Hitler could only have one consequence, that of permanently overburdening the dictator. As a result, there were critical moments when the decision-making process was blocked at its center and start-point, i.e., the Führer himself. In the summer of 1944 the only solution to the problem was to remove Hitler physically. The attempt to do so failed on July 20, 1944.

The Second Front: A Russian Perspective

Vitalii N. Bogdanov

In the spring of 1944 the overall situation in Western Europe was favorable for an Anglo-U.S. invasion of Normandy. For Stalin the issue of an Allied landing in France was an aspect of the war closely associated with great expectations, disappointments, suspicions, distrust—and hopes. Since the beginning of the war he had nurtured especially high hopes for the role Great Britain and the United States might play in defeating Germany. In one of his first messages to Churchill (July 18, 1941) Stalin made his feelings on the matter known in no uncertain terms: "It seems to me . . . that the military position of the Soviet Union, and by the same token that of Great Britain, would improve substantially if a front were established against Hitler in the West (Northern France) and the North (the Arctic)." In all his subsequent negotiations, correspondence, and telegrams Stalin couldn't help reminding his Allies of the need to open a second front.

In the long run Stalin succeeded in obtaining support from the Allies in the form of armaments, materials, and foodstuffs. However, his efforts to sway the Western Allies into opening a second front were less successful. Stalin approached Churchill with the idea of a second front as far back as June 1941, yet the invasion did not take place until June 1944. By then Soviet forces were preparing to liberate Byelorussia, the Western Ukraine, and the eastern regions of Poland and Czechoslovakia, and advance up to the frontiers of Germany. The Western Allies opened the second front at a time when there could be no doubt that the Soviet Union was capable of crushing Germany without their help.

Stalin understood that Great Britain and the United States were acting in accord as representatives of a common Western force, and was concerned and indignant over the Allies' postponements and delays in opening a second front in northwest Europe. It was obvious to him that the principal concern of the United States in 1942 was securing its military and economic positions rather than opening a second front. Theoretically, the United States and Britain began to give thought to planning for a second front in northwest Europe from the end of 1941, but they took no practical measures in this regard until 1944. Stalin saw that the desire of the Allies to undertake combat actions in Europe would only be realized when they were certain that Germany and its armed forces were in critical condition. He didn't conceal his disappointment, irritation, and displeasure about this, as demonstrated by his message to Churchill on July 23, 1942: "As to a second front in Europe, I fear the matter is taking an improper turn. In view of the situation on the Soviet-German front, I state most emphatically that the Soviet government cannot tolerate a second front in Europe being postponed until 1943."

Up to the middle of 1944 the issue of a second front was at the center of Stalin's diplomatic efforts, although in 1944, with victory on the horizon, Stalin didn't bring the issue to a head as he did in 1941. In 1942 Stalin spelled out his attitudes vis-à-vis the relationship between his country and the Western Allies. In his view, the situation of the Soviet Union, which was carrying the main burden of the war, gave him the right to occupy a special place in the anti-Hitler coalition.

In protecting his nation's interests, Stalin showed himself to be a cruel, uncompromising politician, yet one who also enjoyed the universal esteem of his Western partners. During the Big Three summit in Teheran (November 1943) he did everything possible to put the issue of a second front at the center of attention. In response Churchill and President Roosevelt declared that an Anglo-American landing in northern France—Operation Overlord—would be undertaken in May 1944 and supported by a landing in southern France. This satisfied Stalin, who promised to organize a large offensive against the Germans at several points in order to pin down enemy divisions on the Eastern Front and thus deny them the opportunity for creating any complications for Overlord.

During the war the Soviet high command closely followed the actions of American and British forces. They saw how skillfully Eisenhower and Montgomery commanded Allied forces in the Normandy invasion and the advance to the Seine. And they recognized the valor of the officers and men of all the armies of the Allied Expeditionary Forces in Europe.

The landing of American and British forces in Normandy was the largest amphibious operation in the Second World War. It undoubtedly influenced the subsequent course of the armed struggle in Western Europe. However, the Normandy operation had some problematic aspects. The most significant of these was the sluggish movement of Allied forces. The expeditionary forces needed a month and a half to form a strategic bridgehead in northern France one hundred kilometers long and thirty to fifty kilometers in depth. In that time the enemy was able to restore its combat formations and organize its defenses on the German frontier.

According to Marshal Georgii Zhukov, the Allies' actions in Western Europe were generally successful. But because no major enemy forces opposed them, they did not—and could not—conduct offensive operations in the full sense of the word; that is, operations involving penetration of a deeply organized defense or fighting against operational reserves and counterattacks, as was the case on the Eastern Front.

A second front in Western Europe changed the ratio of German divisions fighting on both the Eastern and Western Fronts. But it did not change the significance of the Eastern Front as the main theater of war. In July 1944 the Red Army faced 174.5 German and 60.5 satellite divisions. U.S. and British troops were opposed by 135.5 German divisions. Moreover, German formations in the West were on the whole less battle worthy than those on the Eastern Front. As a result, after crossing the Rhine the Allied Forces did not engage in heavy fighting with the Germans. German troops retreated quickly and surrendered to American and British forces without offering much resistance.

On September 27, 1944, Churchill wrote to Stalin: "I shall take the occasion to repeat tomorrow in the House of Commons what I have said before, that it is the Russian Army that tore the guts out of the German military machine and is at the present holding by far the larger portion of the enemy on its front."

Discussion

Thomas Buell: This question of the effect that Operation Bagration had on Normandy is kind of a cause-and-effect sort of thing. I think it was implicit that because the Russians did launch a major offensive, this somehow helped out the landing in Normandy. But nothing specific was said about how it helped. Again, it's a case of cause and effect, because the landing at Normandy was intended to relieve the pressure on the Russian Front. I heard that there weren't many German aircraft on the Western Front because they were in Russia. I also heard that maybe there weren't as many Germany troops in Russia because they were being sent to the Western Front. I wonder if any of the speakers would go into a few more details on the cause and effect between those two simultaneous operations and how one affected the other or how one helped the other.

Bruce Menning: It's hard for me to address the situation in the West. But from the perspective of the Eastern Front, even if you have some decisive results in the East, you have a situation which is unlikely to bring about an immediate victory. At the same time you have a situation which will hold resources in the East so they cannot be applied to the West. The problem is that you don't have something like you had in World War I, where you could yank a corps out of the offensive in 1914 against France and transit across Germany in ten days or two weeks, because the units you're talking about are much larger and the difficulties of transiting, especially given the problems with control of the air, are much more difficult. So if you look at the way that resources can be parceled out between the fronts, what you have is a situation that contributes to a more rapid attrition rather than a slow attrition. In very immediate terms, look at the number of mechanized and armored division equivalents the Germans have in the West. In the East, about thirty of those units are being tied down. I would say that unless the Soviets had applied pressure, you would probably have seen some of those units beginning to seep over to the West in a period of, let's say, several months at least. So that's at issue.

Another issue is one of outright attrition. With Operation Bagration you have something like thirteen hundred German aircraft and nine hundred tanks destroyed. That's only part of what's being taken out of the German war effort. Plus, even though Hitler can speak glibly about how Germany can't get hurt that badly in the East, if you take two successive operations that go five hundred and six hundred kilometers respectively, you're in Berlin. The Soviets made it halfway with Bagration; the other half was the Vistula/Oder operation, which was launched ahead of schedule to relieve the pressure on the Allies from the Battle of the Bulge. Now, the Battle of the Bulge was over by the time the Soviets could kick off the Vistula/Oder operation, but all the same, it was somewhat the same kind of see-sawing back and forth that's speeding up the attrition we're talking about. There are other things that are imponderable. The psychological impact of Bagration had to be devastating.

Werner Rahn: You are right. Weakening the Eastern Front several months before Overlord was the wrong decision for the Germans to make because the only consequences would have been to shorten the overstretched front line in the East. Even with their poor intelligence the Germans saw the danger and the threat to Army Group Center, and especially in the weeks before the beginning of the Soviet offensive they made a lot of proposals to reduce the lengths of front line, to go back many kilometers. Maybe a timely decision in this regard would not have resulted in such catastrophic consequences later on. But Hitler said, "No. We have to hold, and we have to hold at this line."

Klaus-Richard Böhme: I would like to add another point. The Russians actually started to attack on the 9th of June. On that day they attacked the Finnish lines and by the 19th of September Finland signed an armistice which turned the Finnish forces against the Germans. So they achieved a lot.

Bruce Menning: Yes. What I had neglected to say was that you have a series of offensives. The Soviets liked to ripple their operations across the front, and they had already started the ripple, as Dr. Böhme correctly notes, in early June. Part of that was not only to achieve "real" objectives, but also to obscure what the axis of the main strategic advance would be. It was that old saw, where do you hide an elephant? You hide it in a herd of elephants. So the Soviets rippled a series of smaller offenses to create a herd of elephants to hide this big one.

Thomas Buell: Wouldn't the Russians have launched a major offensive in 1944 in any event, regardless of Normandy?

Bruce Menning: Yes. But what happened was that both the diplomacy and the military planning effort that preceded the Normandy landing caught the Soviets flatfooted because they had just come off a series of successful operations. The close-out of winter operations in the north had opened up the Leningrad Front. They had had some momentous offenses in the Ukraine that actually put the first Soviet troops in Czechoslovakia--some Russian soldier just stepped over the border in a kind of symbolic gesture. Then they were waiting to see what the Allies would do and wrestling with the problem of what does "unconditional surrender" mean. Stalin was never really crazy about unconditional surrender before the Second Front opened. He looked at that and said, "What does that mean to me and the Red Army? If the Allies are talking about unconditional surrender it means we're going to face stiffer and stiffer resistance the closer we get to the German homeland."

But what then makes unconditional surrender somewhat more palatable to him and changes the entire calculus is the Allied landing at Normandy. Suddenly he had to think, "Oh, this is serious. The Allies are serious. Now what do we do?" The Russians have a big salient which they've developed down in the Ukraine. This is where the bulk of their armor is. Their five big tank armies are down here—they kept them there on purpose to deceive the Germans into thinking that this was the main strategic axis—and they could have flooded on into southeastern Europe and the Balkans. That's one of their strategic options. But if they do that, they're looking at an extended flank, and they're thinking that's not a very good idea. The other thing they can do is reposition the forces in the Ukraine and drive north. Then they see that the bulk of the German forces are still up north, and they decide that's not a good idea either. So what they want to do is to make the Germans think that the main effort will be in the south and that the all other objectives are secondary, and then just simply blow away the center. Which is what they did.

They had to figure out where to strike next, and not only were they looking at that decision from a military-strategic perspective, but from the political-military perspective as well. Now, Stalin didn't make any public pronouncements about his intentions, but when examining this issue you have to deduce which operations will, at their conclusion, leave him in a position for the next series of operations. When you're stringing operations together, it's like playing a game of eight ball: while you're taking the shot, you're lining up your next shot. If he's going to line up his next military shot, he's got to figure out what's going to bring him in closer to the ultimate decision. He does a very good job of that. Then, if you look at the political side of the equation, you see Stalin calculating what will give him more leverage in conflict termination. Now the Soviets can actually begin to think in terms of what kind of postwar settlement they want all this to produce. So these are extraordinarily important issues. I must say, from looking in the archives, that we actually know very little about them. If Russia doesn't go down the tubes, and if we can keep prying open the archives and so on, we're going to get better answers to some of these questions.

Werner Rahn: I want to add a small explanation on the correlation between land warfare and naval warfare, especially with regard to naval training in the Baltic. One reason for keeping Army Group North in position and not withdrawing it toward the German frontier was to keep the Baltic free for training exercises of the late-model U-boats. So Grand Admiral Dönitz pushed Hitler and the army command to hold the coastline as a precondition for maintaining a free exercise area in the Baltic. When the Russians reached this coastline it would be nearly impossible to conduct training in the Baltic.

John English: General Montgomery's Epson operation was hit by the 9th and 10th SS Panzer Divisions, which came from the Eastern Front from an operation around Tarnopol. This was quite a significant movement of two major formations. Also the 12th SS claimed on D-Day that they had no trouble moving; they lost only their bridging equipment. Panzer Lehr is the one formation that we always think about as being destroyed by air action.

But the 12th SS moved at night and had a very clever way of doing it, quite different from ours. That's just an observation. My big question to you is, have you ever seen any evidence that in 1943 that the Russians began to believe that they could take Germany out alone, that they didn't need us?

Bruce Menning: No. Remember they're at Kursk in July and August of 1943 and they're still talking about standing on the strategic defensive. What they do is employ the strategy of the defensive counteroffensive: let the enemy hit you, absorb the shock, wait till his operation culminates, then sledgehammer him in return. It's only when you get into 1944 that you can talk about self-standing offensive operations that are not intended merely to absorb the shock of a German attack and then counterattack. They now have much more confidence, and many more assets. Lend-Lease is an issue that will come up here. Lend-lease was not really decisive in itself, but if you look at the way these operations were mounted and you look at their five- and six-hundred-kilometer deep exploitations—the way they could maintain offensive momentum was because their assets now included a lot of Dodge and Studebaker trucks. Those trucks made a big, big difference for the mobility of these huge formations. In a Western sense--you look at Western heavy divisions—the Soviet units are runt formations: a Soviet corps is really more like a division, an army is more like a corps, and a front is like an army group. But all the same, to get all of that jammed on and put a good bit of their support and so forth on wheels is something else that they now do extraordinarily well.

Geoffrey Perret: I wonder if you'd be willing to comment on one of the most controversial aspects of this whole operation, that of the Red Army stopping on the Vistula and watching from across the river while the Warsaw uprising was going on. They just sit there for several weeks while the Germans crush it.

Bruce Menning: I don't have anything more than conventional wisdom. I know that's one of the chief issues they are attempting to attack with the assistance of the archives. We talked with the military archivists about what we could get out of those archives. These are the Ministry of Defense archives at Podolsk, about twenty-five miles southwest of Moscow. Access is only won by small increments and indirect actions. However, I don't feel that the Eastern Front archives as such are any longer sensitive from a military or a political-military point of view. It's more a question of getting into those materials. They have maybe eight thousand boxes of materials they captured from the Germans that they haven't even looked at yet. They haven't even catalogued them. And they're suffering from budgetary reductions, they're barely keeping themselves moving, they're letting people go, they're not paying employees on time. So the ability just to get in there and do fundamental work and to uncover more about the issues that you're talking about is limited. You're very correct in pointing this out: what happens is, the offensive brings them up to Warsaw, where they sit and watch the uprising be destroyed by the SS and other elements. But I haven't uncovered any secrets about that. In fact, the thrust of my research has been basically on preparations for war—war planning, troop mobilization, development of strategy—and not on the strict operational aspects of either this or other conflicts.

Werner Rahn: I can agree with this assessment. Our colleagues have a lot of problems getting access to the archives, but the main problem is the organization of the archives and the bad shape of the documents.

Alan Gropman: This may be the opening shot of the last panel discussion. By this time the war was over; it's just a matter of when it's going to end. If you peel the onion back and you keep peeling it back, it turns out to be a strategic failure on Hitler's part. If you read *Mein Kampf* you know that when Hitler isn't talking anti-Semitic gibberish; what he's railing against is a two-front war, a mistake he said he would never make if he came to power. Starting on the 1st of September 1939, Hitler got all the wars he didn't want. Strategically he had planned for a completely different war, and he got none of the wars that he wanted and all of the wars that he didn't want. One of the problems with the seminar up to this particular point is that we've been relentlessly operational in our outlook. Every now and then we need to take a step back. If the strategy is bad, the war is lost. And Hitler's strategy was bad because he was a very bad strategist. And incidentally, his admirals and generals were not strategic thinkers; they were great operational thinkers, but not strategic thinkers. That's the lesson those of us who teach at the National War College have got to emphasize: that strategic thinking is essential.

Bruce Menning: I would argue that Hitler's generals were in many respects not even good operational thinkers. Their model of the war was the single strategic operation used against Poland and France, where you had an obvious anvil you could hit on the other end and you never had to plan for successive operations, you never had to plan for protractiveness. That was accepted as the norm until they got to Russia.

Werner Rahn: I can't accept this. From a strategic point of view, I think the war was lost in the winter of 1941-42, and I think Hitler knew this very well. And his second offensive against the Soviet Union in Operation Blue in the summer of 1942—the aim of this operation was to get economic assets from certain regions of the Soviet Union. If you compare the efficiency of the German army of the summer of 1941 with the spring of 1942, if you look at the readiness of the divisions, you find that the German army in the spring of 1942 was a shadow of the army of the summer of 1941. And so from the strategic point of view the war was lost in the winter of 1941-42. In the naval staff there was strategic thinking but there was no material basis for it. There was one-sided thinking about "tonnage warfare" in the race between the sinking and building of Allied ships, but this race was lost in autumn 1942, as revealed by a comparison of the ship-building capacity of the United States with the monthly sinking rate of the U-boats.

Stephen Ambrose: I think Alan Gropman is quite right, but let's move even beyond strategy and into politics. You look at the map of the Eastern Front and you think about Belorussia, which the Red Army is overrunning. Hitler had been in control of that country since the summer of 1941, when it was primed for recruits to fight against Communism. So was Poland and France and the Ukraine, and all this territory he had occupied with these fabulous people who just hated Stalin and hated the Soviet Union and hated the Russians. And what did Hitler do with this asset? He turned it into partisans who were a drain on his resources, turned them against him. So it's more than just that the Germans were awfully bad strategists. Hitler was just mad. Think about it: on December 11, 1941, when the counteroffensive is starting outside Moscow, Hitler declares war on the United States. That's when he lost the war. The guy was just a madman.

I wanted to share with you something on these Russian archives. I was with Colonel Vitalii Bogdanov in Moscow three years ago at a conference the Eisenhower Institute sponsored, and we asked him, "What are you coming up with?" One tidbit he gave us was a Zhukov-to-Stalin memo in February of 1940 that said Hitler was going to attack in France as soon as the road was dry. There's our chance, said Zhukov: we ought to strike the Germans and hit hard. Hit them in the back within a few weeks after they invaded France. Talk about what-ifs.

Bruce Menning: There are two issues here. Number one, I must agree with the assessment of 1941-42 being a breaking point. If you're looking operationally, I might even argue that the preview of coming attractions occurs in the crisis of July and August of 1941, when the initial offensive operations of the Wehrmacht run out of steam, they have the big meeting at Orsha, they have an operational pause, they have to draw their log up, they have to regroup their forces. If you read Halder's war diary—Halder, every few days, if not on a daily basis, keeps a running tally of the good guys and the bad guys—you'll find that for the good guys, the Fascist good guys, through the first weeks of Barbarrosa everything is rolling along and the successes are much greater than the Germans ever anticipated. Then you get to mid-August 1941 and Halder had listed the German reserves and the Russian reserves. He looks at the situation for about August 5th and records that the Germans have two divisions in reserve while the Russians have reserves consisting of eight armies. That's when you know that they've reached the stage of looking at what their plans were and what they had to do for the successive operations, and so on.

One more important point on the issue of the axes. Stalin felt (though you can't find it in any one writing) that if the war between the Soviet Union and Germany was going to be a systemic war—and by definition a war between Bolshevism and Nazism would be systemic—it would be protracted. He puts himself in Hitler's shoes and says, "I've got to have the Ukraine and the Caucasus." So in the fall of 1940 and the spring of 1941 Stalin repositions his main defensive belts to put the preponderance of his forces south of the Pripet Marshes. Thus when Hitler attacks with Army Groups North, Center, and South, what you find is you've got a major Axis army group—Army Group Center—that really does not have any of the heavy armor opposition in front of it. As a result, Guderian and the boys are blowing the Russians away left and right until suddenly they reach the operational pause. Then they look at the Ukraine, and the offensive in the Ukraine is having trouble because here are all the heavy units that Stalin put down there, figuring that the Germans are going to have to take the Ukraine because this war is going to be protracted and it's going to take Russia two or three years to win it. So there's one instance where Stalin had the right strategic judgment and then almost lost the war because he actually was right.

Kenneth Hagan: My question is for Klaus-Richard Böhme. Was there ever a concern in Sweden that the Red Army just might continue rolling on through Finland and into Sweden?

Klaus-Richard Böhme: No, not into Sweden, but into Finland. It was a main concern, what would happen to Finland. The Swedes had tried to keep Finland out of war against Russia. They supported Finland when Finland was attacked in 1939 by Russia. Then in 1941 when Finland sided with Germany the Swedes opposed that move and relations came to a crisis between Sweden and Finland. But the main concern of the Swedes, and this is why Sweden couldn't bother much about D-Day, was to get Finland out of the war as soon as possible, out of the pending German catastrophe. They started such efforts after Stalingrad. But they had to be careful because the Germans were strong in the north, and the concern was that the Germans would attack Sweden in order to back up their defense in Norway and to make the Finns stay with Germany. That was a problem. D-Day was good, in that respect, for Sweden's political situation. The Swedish assessment was that if the Western Allies were pushing hard, then Stalin would not be so concerned to get as much of Germany as he might want, and he might agree to more lenient conditions for Finland. And that was exactly what happened. Finland was not occupied. Finland was the only country which Stalin could have occupied but did not. The Finns got hard conditions and they lost some territory and they had to fight Germany. But they got out of war.

Werner Rahn: I want make a point about the targeting of strategic bombing. If you read the memoirs of Albert Speer and his assessment of the German war economy, and if you look at the building of the U-boat pens on the Atlantic Coast, you will find that these pens were weak targets for a long time, during the building phase, when the wooden scaffolding was up for the pouring of concrete. But they were never attacked during the building phase—they were attacked when they were hard targets. And with regard to the water supply for the Ruhr district—which was critical to the German war economy--the Royal Air Force made one attack on a main water reservoir. It was successful, but the RAF did not launch a second attack while the reservoir was being repaired. The same thing happened with the synthetic oil plants. The first concentrated attack against the synthetic oil plants was made in May 1944. The monthly output of such plants versus the consumption of fuel they produced resulted in a shortfall of more than seventy thousand tons. This prompted Speer to tell Hitler that Germany couldn't fight a war when fuel production lagged so far behind demand and consumption.

Clay Blair: I have a question for Professor Rahn. After the war the Allied view of Admiral Dönitz was that he was not really a dedicated Nazi, and this was reflected in his sentence at Nuremberg. More recently, however, we've had British scholars taking the opposite view. What do German scholars have to say on this point?

Werner Rahn: I think there is the opinion that Grand Admiral Dönitz was a Nazi. He had a very positive view of Nazi ideology. If you look at his speech to a navy group after the attempted assassination of Hitler—it was a very frank speech, and if you look at what he said about Jews you must come to the conclusion that Admiral Dönitz was a convinced Nazi. I think there is no question of this. There has been a different opinion of this in the U-boat community up to now, and this must be taken into account. But if you look at his speeches to navy cadets as well as to his commanders, you can see that he was convinced that it was right for Germany to follow the Führer. It was only after the death of Hitler that he changed his mind. For example, five days before the death of Hitler he organized an operation to send more than 180 young naval cadets by airplanes into encircled Berlin. I interviewed the commanding officer of these cadets, and he has published an account of his experience of coming into the center of Berlin by plane with the cadets. Upon arriving he went to Hitler to report that he had brought this group of cadets into Berlin to fight. His description of his last talk with Hitler was very impressive. It was Dönitz's decision to send highly qualified personnel into Berlin even though his staff must have known that this was stupid thing to do from a military standpoint. But it was done, and Dönitz had obeyed the orders of Hitler.

Geoffrey Perret: I would like to make a comment on strategic bombing. From a German point of view it did seem random and haphazard, but there are explanations for most of it. There were not many heavy bomb groups in the ETO until the end of 1943. And at this point everything was really focused on the preparations for D-Day. At the same time the British were obsessed with the German V-weapons. Churchill was leaning on Eisenhower throughout this period to attack the V-weapon launch sites. So a lot of air assets, the heavies and the mediums, were dedicated to hitting Crossbow sites. The strategic bombing of Germany does not really begin until September of 1944. Now they're not attacking Crossbow sites, they're attacking Transportation Plan sites. That one raid in May 1944 against the synthetic oil plants was pushed through by Spaatz because he was determined to attack oil. But there were so many other competing priorities. In September of 1944 Tedder and Zuckerman pushed another Transportation Plan and Spaatz said, "Enough is enough; I'm going to attack oil." And he did. It's not really until September and October that you really get the strategic bombing of Germany. Once it starts, it becomes very effective. And it did bring about the collapse of the German war economy. But the irony is, it did not bring it about until some thirty days before the war ended and the Allied armies were overrunning Germany.

Bruce Menning: Fundamentally, the problem with the Schweinfurt raids and so on, in September 1943, was that we couldn't get mass. If we had kept it up, we wouldn't have had any air force left. And then if you look at the weather patterns you will find that we only had about seven or eight days in the whole fall period when we could put planes over the target with any degree of precision. It was ridiculous in light of the results that were attained.

In contrast to the Western Allies, the Soviets had since the 1930s held a more limited vision for the strategic use of air power. Lapchinskii was their great guru for air power in the 1930s, and one of his fundamental sayings—and I always remind our air officers at Leavenworth of this—was that an air operation starts and ends on the ground. In Bagration the Soviets committed five-plus air armies to the fighting and they flew 153,000 sorties. Most of it was close-air support and what a couple years ago we would have called battlefield air interdiction; there were almost no deep targets. But when you look at what they thought before the war when they had some large multi-engine bombers, you will find that Soviet strategic targeting first of all involved striking at the ability of opposing forces to mobilize and concentrate and undergo strategic deployment. That was their target. They didn't worry about Douhet's notion of breaking the will of the people and all of those other eerie concepts. They had a real firm idea of what they wanted to do with strategic air power.

Luncheon Address

"Never That Young Again"

Andy Rooney

The Greatest Thing We Have Ever Attempted

"Never That Young Again"

I am both pleased and daunted to be here today among this distinguished group of historians. I am in no way a historian—mostly my expertise is having been in Normandy and Europe during World War II. I did see close up and in detail what so many of you write so well about in broader terms.

First, I would like to say I was not on the beaches on D-Day. On D+4, I came into Utah, and I was pretty proud of that. It was still not a safe place to be. I have heard so many people say they were there on D-Day that the beaches would have been crowded with newspaper people alone if all the people who claimed to be there were there. We wouldn't have needed the infantry that day.

On the third day I was there, I was over around Caen, driving between the hedgerows in my jeep, following three tanks along. There was a machine gun position up ahead, and I was trapped in this tank parade. Some wounded, some dead, Americans were lying in the path between these two eight-to-ten-foot high hedgerows, just wide enough between them for the tank to pass. The order came for the tank to go ahead. This was my introduction to war: watching those tanks roll over these bodies in the hedgerow country. I was never that young again.

I was lucky. I never graduated from college but was drafted at the end of my junior year. I looked forward to playing football another year at Colgate, but was drafted. One of two million American soldiers dumped into the British Isles, I was sent to England with an artillery battery.

The decision was made to make *The Stars and Stripes* a daily newspaper, and a sign was posted in every barracks: "All newspapermen report here." So I claimed I was a newspaperman—I had worked two summers for a newspaper in Albany, New York, and edited my college paper—and I got the great break of my life. I was assigned to *The Stars and Stripes*. We had a very good group of experienced newspaper people who had come from the best papers in the country. I was really the only novice there.

I remember walking into *The Stars and Stripes* on my first day—we had offices with *The Times* of London. We had two editors, the city editor and the national editor. The city editor covered the war, the other editor covered the news of America and everything else. Over their heads in huge letters scribbled all over the wall was "It's Adolf, A-D-O-L-F, not A-D-O-L-P-H." Certain things you never get over.

I just barely held my job while I learned how to do it. I was sent to Eisenhower's press conferences—I guess the theory was that nothing much would happen that I could damage. I loved to go in and talk to Kay [Summersby]—she looked better in her uniform than Ike looked in his. I remember one of the first times we sat around this big table, and Eisenhower spoke to us. I was taking notes, everyone was taking notes. I wanted to be one of the fellas.

Before I got back to the office, I saw the story that Associated Press reporter Gladwyn Hill already had out, and I was just shocked to find that when you go to a press conference you do not write a story in the order the man gave it to you: you pick from here and there. I said, "My gosh, that was the last thing Eisenhower said—and Hill's leading with that." I was a slow learner in the newspaper business.

I finally ended up covering the Eighth Air Force and the Ninth Air Force. When the P-47 was operational out of the British Isles, the military knew the press knew it was there, but the information was still restricted because the Germans had not given us confirmation that they had actually captured one and therefore knew for certain we had one. One day the Ninth Air Force took a big press group to the airfield to see the P-47, showing us everything about it—after we promised we would not write about it until we got the official release.

Meanwhile, Bud Hutton, *Stars and Stripes* editor, had been collecting everything ever written about the

P-47 in the United States and England. One of those nuts about airplanes, he had everything that was public about airplanes. We had two censors in our office. One of the rules was that if you could show the censor that the information already had been published, then there was no question, you could use it. So Bud—just like a spy, the stuff he gathered—he collected all this material, and three days after I swore not to reveal anything, he publishes this two-part piece about the P-47. *Everything* about it. Well, there were really no secrets that were damaging to anyone. But I had just promised not to release the information.

As the editor of the paper—he was a sergeant—Bud saw all incoming mail first, and he would go through it every morning. So about four days later comes this official heavy document from General Hunter, the Ninth Air Force Fighter Commander, demanding his court-martial. After Bud leafs through this demand for his court-martial, he just wrote at the top of it—as he did so often—"Disapproved, BH." He put it back in the system. and nothing was every heard about it. That's how we won the war.

I am trying to write a book called *My War,* and I just can't get over how infrequently my memory of the event coincides with the facts of the matter. I have concluded that the facts are wrong, of course, in almost every case.

One good thing for me is I have *The Stars and Stripes*. I have hundreds of stories and each one reminds me of something else I didn't write. It's as if I have taken notes, and I have all the bound copies. I was writing this chapter about bravery, and I thought I must have something to illustrate this bravery theme.

If you are just dumb and foolhardy, that's not very brave, and there s a lot of that that passes for bravery, I think. Brave in my mind is when you knowingly risk your own life to help someone else, and there was so much of that in the air force.

I found a story I had written about a man named Raymond Cheek. He had flown twenty-four missions, and this was his twenty-fifth, and at the end of it he was finished. The squadron group doctor decided to go on this mission, too, as a gunner. The assistant base commander, a lieutenant colonel who had also been a pilot, decided to go as copilot. But the regular copilot also was about to fly his twenty-fifth mission. This one was over Ste.-Nazaire or some easy target, so he wanted to go ahead and get his twenty-fifth mission out of the way. He went as a waist gunner.

The pilot Raymond Cheek's head was shot off with a 20mm shell, and fire erupted in the oxygen system. The copilot, the assistant base commander, his arms were just shredded, and he was trying to fly the plane with his elbows. The navigator jumped, and someone went back to get the regular copilot who was flying as waist gunner. He came up and got the copilot out of there. There he is between his friend with his head shot off and the burned copilot, and he flew the plane back. I read this story, and thought I did a pretty good job—"Gee, it's all there," I thought to myself. I even had the names of the people on board the flight. I set out to find these people—this was just last month. Of course, many of them were dead, but I did find some of them.

I found the regular copilot who had brought the plane in, finally, under terrible conditions. He had landed with the wind—this was in my story—but there was no explanation of such an odd thing. And here I thought I had done this good job.

I asked him, "How come you landed, with the plane in that bad shape, how come you landed with the wind? You didn't know?"

He said, "Raymond Cheek was marrying the nurse on the base the next day. She was waiting for him at the end of the runway, and they were having a party. So I landed the other way."

I had missed the story completely, and this keeps happening to me in the course of doing this book.

As I talk to my kids about war, I tell them if you don't get killed or wounded, there is no experience like it. The whole nation became so motivated, I wish there were some substitute for war for getting us going in this country.

In college I had a professor named Kenneth Boulding, a distinguished economist who died about a year ago out in Colorado. He was a Quaker, and I had decided, though I had to submerge my strong agnostic inclinations to do it, that he was onto something. He believed any peace was better than any war.

Kenneth Boulding didn't believe in war under any circumstances, so I thought for a while in college that I could be a conscientious objector. I finally decided I could not. I didn't want to go to war, but I was not a conscientious objector, and I submitted to the draft.

Shortly after we crossed the Rhine (I don't know where the press camp was), Jack Thompson came in with Hal Boyle. These were two great reporters. I mean there were none better. They came in, and I was the only other reporter in the room. They had just come from Buchenwald, and before they sat down to write, they told me the whole story of the camp. "Go ahead," they said, "write the story."

I don't know as I have ever been so ethical in my life, but I just decided it was not the kind of story I could take secondhand. So I didn't write it, and my paper wanted to know where I had been. I often think now that the day I finally did get to Buchenwald, I realized that I was wrong in college, when I thought that any peace was better than any war. Now I knew that any peace was not better than any war . . .

The Greatest Thing We Have Ever Attempted

Discussion

Thomas Buell: Sir, a little more about Buchenwald. Did you have any idea what was going on there before you saw it?

Andy Rooney: No. We began to get stories about it, but I did not accept as fact what I heard. I did not believe it. There was no way, until we came across the first place, that any of us could have believed that it was as bad as it turned out to be. What I did see is something you never forget.

John Mountcastle: We are at the point where the written word is getting to be less and less the source of information to inform people. They don't read the newspapers anymore. And if they do, they just might glance at the headlines or look at USA Today. How do you see us communicating if we have anything as big as World War II again?

Andy Rooney: I'm not sure you are right. I hate to see newspapers disappearing because I write a column and I have fewer newspapers—I write for 200 newspapers today and I had 327 five years ago. So it does bother me a lot. People, however, are reading a lot, we are publishing more books than ever. My children are all in their late thirties and forties; my father was in World War I and I was born in 1919. By the time I was twenty, I had heard about the kaiser and the gas but I knew very little about World War I. My children today—none of the names mentioned in today's panels would be unfamiliar to them. So you have to say something good about the knowledge expansion in this country. We are doing something right. I have great faith in the written word. I like it a lot and I think we are lucky in this country because English is a better language. English is the second language of every country in the world. Not because we are culturally dominant or socially dominant but because English is a better language than any other. It is five times bigger than any other in the world and, unlike the French, we have been very American about language, very democratic. We all object to the slang words we hear, but if they aren't any good they die, and if they don't die they're useful and we take them into the language and improve and enrich our language with them. I wouldn't write off the written word that soon.

Richard Behrenhausen: You covered your relationship with the military in World War II; will you give us your thoughts on the relationships between the military and the media today?

Andy Rooney: It is a little difficult for me. My son is a correspondent and he covered the Middle East and he came home just so furious with the military. I don't know what's happened; I don't know why the military thought they could control things or not trust us. During World War II we had censors in the press camp—Jack Thompson and I were talking about this at lunch—and we knew what the rules were. We knew what side of the war we were on too. There was no ambivalence about that. I think the Pentagon has made a lot of serious mistakes. Most news people in my business think in broad terms. If everybody in the world knew all the truths about everything it would be a better world. The military doesn't believe that. They are just so secretive. There are certain things they can't reveal, we all know that, but they protect things that are absolutely absurd just for the sake of protecting them. Certainly, news organizations have some bad people, inadequate people who don't know what they are doing. But, still, we need more openness. Openness almost never hurts anything.

The Greatest Thing We Have Ever Attempted

Panel 5

NORMANDY AS HISTORY:
Have We Learned The Right
Lessons?

Contributors:

Stephen E. Ambrose, D'Ann Campbell,
H. P. Willmott
Moderated by John W. Mountcastle

The Greatest Thing We Have Ever Attempted

Introduction

In his opening remarks, panel moderator John Mountcastle observed that, in looking at the lessons to be learned from Normandy, we must ask whether we are involving ourselves at the right level of warfare, and then identify, in the context of Normandy, some of the critical aspects of joint and combined warfare. At the Army War College, when using Overlord and the Normandy campaign as vehicles for discussing these significant issues, Mountcastle said that students often focus on the timing and the linkage between strategic goals and operational goals, and the question of whether an even grander strategic concept for defeating Germany should have been developed earlier in the war before the formation of COSSAC.

Students also study Normandy for the insights it provides into the nature and problems of command unity in coalition warfare, an issue of growing importance not only to the army but to all service branches. The nation's military leadership, said Mountcastle, anticipates that most future action by the armed forces will be undertaken in the context of multinational efforts involving units from several allied countries: "the norm will be combined operations and, increasingly, interagency operations." What is more, those operations will become increasingly diverse in nature, demanding flexibility by those assigned to carry them out.

Mountcastle concluded by saying that students at the Army War College have become increasingly concerned about the relationship of Normandy—the lodgement, the breakout, and the subsequent exploitation of that breakout—with follow-on plans. "Phased strategic operations are of great interest to them," he said; and, inasmuch as land operations are their chief concern, most of the students, even naval, air, and marine officers who participate in the program, are "inclined . . . to subscribe to a statement made by T. R. Fehrenbach in his book *This Kind of War* in which he said, with regard to the impact of the other services: "You may fly over land forever, you may bomb it and strafe it, but if you want to control it, if you want to hold it, you must do it as the ancient Romans did, by putting your young men in the mud."

*

For Stephen Ambrose, the panel's first contributor, the young men who stormed ashore on D-Day were advertisements for their own courage and dedication to democratic principles; and, as the embodiment of such virtues, proof of the moral superiority of the democracies for which they fought. Reading from his book *D-Day June 6, 1944: The Climactic Battle of World War II* (Simon & Schuster, 1994), he described his remarks on Overlord as "a love song to democracy," one that paid tribute to a system of government that was more humane yet nonetheless stronger in every aspect than the German model. Ambrose takes aim at the belief, much in vogue before the Second World War, that fascist states were better able to compete in what was seen as a Darwinian struggle for survival among the nations and peoples of the world. It was a belief based on three suppositions: first, that social Darwinism can and does explain the dynamics of human history; second, that the national struggle for survival, although fought in the economic, political, and cultural spheres, will ultimately be decided on the battlefield; third, that fascist states, because of their very nature, produce superior fighting men hence superior armies. From 1939 through 1945 the first two suppositions, however dubious in the long run, demonstrated a certain short-term validity: the

Second World War was indeed a Darwinian conflict, a matter of life or death for the nations involved that was settled, not by diplomacy or mediation, but by force of arms. But the third supposition was disproved with a completeness and finality that put an end to fascism as an intellectually respectable ideology. According to Ambrose, the German army's failure was inextricably linked to the uniquely and profoundly flawed character of Nazi society: the Western Allies defeated their enemy in every important area of warfare, and, significantly, they did so because and not in spite of the fact that they were democracies.

*

D'Ann Campbell picks up where Ambrose left off, discussing how the Allies' concept and practice of total war proved superior to that of the Germans. This despite the fact that Germans had long been perceived as the experts at total war. Such was their reputation that, in the Great War, German soldiers were branded as "Huns," and never mind that throughout the conflict the Germans behaved, on balance, no better or worse than their enemies, or that they lost the war and were disarmed. The reputation stuck, and the fear of Germans—or, more precisely, of German military prowess and practices—remained. In the 1930s Adolf Hitler played on that fear, using it to help score bloodless victories in the Rhineland, Czechoslovakia, and Austria. It was bolstered in April 1938 when warplanes of the German Condor Legion, fighting on the Nationalist side during the Spanish Civil War, terror-bombed the Basque town of Guernica.

The incident shocked the world; but for many it was a shock of recognition rather than surprise, the dismaying fulfillment of prophesies concerning the nature of the next large-scale war. Since the end of the Great War air power theoreticians such as Guilio Douhet and Hugh Trenchard had produced disturbing visions, widely publicized in the media, of the bomber as a destroyer of cities, a waster of civilizations. Not flights of fancy but terror informed their views: in future conflicts, they declared, civilians would be subjected to apocalyptic doses of death and destruction from above. The impact would be decisive: the victimized populations, their morale shattered by a fatal rain of high explosives, would force their governments to sue for peace at any price. Consequently the clash of armies, if it occurred at all, would become mostly irrelevant, as would the armies themselves. Thus the age of battles would finally pass into history.

The example of Guernica was still vivid when the Second World War began on 3 September 1939. It was expected that the Germans would from the very start wage total war, which meant, among other things, mass air assaults against civilians; and in Poland, they did not disappoint. Elsewhere, however, and with the notable exception of Rotterdam, the Germans behaved with restraint. It was not until 7 September 1940 that they began the terror-bombing of British cities. But the British were not so easily terrorized by what they called the "Blitz," and besides, the Germans lacked aircraft suitable for the job. The Blitz raids caused widespread damage and inflicted tens of thousands of casualties, but did nothing to bring Britain closer to defeat. After a massive raid on London on 10 May 1941, the Blitz was ended. Hitler had determined that he could make better use of his bombers elsewhere, and in the role for which they had been designed: namely, smashing hostile armies, this time in Russia, which the Germans invaded on 22 June 1941.

It was in the conflict with the Soviet Union that the Germans fully prosecuted their version of total war. In essence, what this meant was war without mercy. Prisoners were killed or maltreated, civilians murdered and brutalized, villages razed and earth scorched—all in addition to the "normal" ferocity of the actual fighting. This was the military's interpretation of total war, the *furor teutonticus* in modern dress. It was all of a piece with the harrowing of Poland, the bombing of Rotterdam, the Blitz, and Guernica. The basic premise was that war, if it is to be total, should express its totality in military action beyond the nation's frontiers, on foreign soil, against enemy soldiers and civilians; and that such activity should be carried to extremes of violence and destruction in order to achieve victory quickly and repress conquered people more thoroughly.

The problem with this approach is that it often backfires. The law of unintended consequences is invoked: victimized populations are enraged by terror rather than subdued—they fight back. In the Second World War the Allies fought back, if not with everything at their disposal—poison gas and biological weapons, for instance, were not employed—than with more than the Axis powers might have used. Specifically, observes D'Ann Campbell, the Allies made more and better use of their human resources, including women. In Germany and Japan, by contrast, most women were uninvolved in the war effort. For those two countries, total war was to be anything but total on the home front, where all the talents and energies of what amounted to a little over 50 percent of the adult population were largely allowed to go to waste. Uninvolved in the war effort but not uninvolved in the war: it came to them first in bombers and then in armies, both of which were equipped with weapons and machines built in part by women from nations that knew, really knew, what total war was all about.

*

Of course, the Allies were not blameless when it came to inflicting civilian casualties. Hundreds of thousands of German and Japanese civilians were killed and wounded in Allied air raids on their cities. Attacks on Hamburg (27/27 July 1943), Dresden (14-15 February 1945) and Tokyo (9-10 March 1945) claimed the lives of around forty-four thousand, one hundred thousand, and eighty thousand, respectively. The atomic bombs dropped on Hiroshima and Nagasaki each killed, in a single explosion, an estimated 187,000 outright; tens of thousands more subsequently died of injuries and radiation sickness. Few conventional battles were as lethal: one has to go a long way back in history (in the West, at any rate) to find clashes between armies where so many died so quickly. This was terror bombing at its literal best, outdoing by many orders of magnitude the destruction inflicted on Guernica, Rotterdam, and the cities of Britain. Historians have not ignored this aspect of the Allies' total war concept. Many have grappled with the moral issues it raises. The question of whether the Allies were morally much less militarily justified in targeting the enemy's civilian population centers for air bombardment defies resolution: to this day it remains a topic of controversy and debate. The right lesson to be learned from the Allies' use of air power has, accordingly, proved elusive.

The same can be said for many aspects of the war, a problem that H. P. Willmott tackles in the final presentation of the conference. In Willmott's view, learning the right lessons are of secondary concern to asking the right questions, because the former follow naturally from the latter. Willmott takes his American colleagues to task for their failures in this regard, citing examples from preceding contributors of faulty analysis and offering his own interpretations in their stead. In part Willmott's objective is to set straight an historical record bent, mistakenly or otherwise, by many of its compilers and keepers. But his is also a cautionary tale of the consequences, particularly for a nation's armed forces, of misinterpreting the past. Where hindsight is flawed, foresight is clouded: the result can be bad decisions and ill-considered strategies that, when implemented, lead to military failure as well as the failure to achieve the policy objective for which military action had been undertaken. The danger here, Willmott seems to be saying, is not so much that of repeating the past, as Santayana famously observed of those who forget it, but rather of making a fresh new mess of the present and laying the groundwork for future disasters.

The Meaning of D-Day
Stephen E. Ambrose

The lesson of Normandy is that there is nothing a democracy cannot do once it agrees on what needs to be done. No power in the world can match that of an aroused democracy.

I now want to read from a book I've got coming out next month.[1] The book starts with a prologue that gives brief biographies of the first two Allied officers killed on D-Day—Lieutenant Dan Brotheridge of the Oxfordshire and Buckinghamshire Light Infantry Regiment, killed on the bridge that crosses the Orne Canal at Bénouville, and Bob Mathias of the 82nd Airborne Division, who lost his life in the pre-dawn parachute assault on Normandy:

> It was an open question, toward the end of spring 1944, as to whether a democracy could produce young soldiers capable of fighting effectively against the best that Nazi Germany could produce. Hitler was certain the answer was no. Nothing he had learned of the British army's performance in France in 1940, or again in North Africa and the Mediterranean in 1942-44, or what he had learned of the American army in North Africa and the Mediterranean in 1942-44, caused him to doubt that, on anything approaching equality in numbers, the Wehrmacht would prevail. Totalitarian fanaticism and discipline would always conquer democratic liberalism and softness. Of that Hitler was sure.
>
> If Hitler had seen Dan Brotheridge and Bob Mathias in action at the beginning of D-Day, he might have had second thoughts. It is Brotheridge and Mathias and their buddies, the young men born into the false prosperity of the 1920s and brought up in the bitter realities of the Depression of the 1930s, that this book is about. The literature they read as youngsters was anti-war, cynical, portraying patriots as suckers, slackers as heroes. None of them wanted to be part of another war. They wanted to be throwing baseballs, not hand grenades, shooting .22s at rabbits, not M-1s at other young men. But when the test came, when freedom had to be fought for or abandoned, they fought. They were the soldiers of democracy. They were the men of D-Day, and to them we owe our freedom.

But not just to them. They had to be got over there. They had to be equipped. They obviously had to be led. But first of all there had to be that miracle of the American republic in the twentieth century, the prodigies of production, that made it possible for these men to do what they did. There were more airplanes in the sky on D-Day than on any other day in human history, and more ships on the water. As Admiral Samuel Eliot Morrison put it, "We sent more ships across the English Channel on D-Day than existed in the world fifty years earlier."

On D-Day, a vast majority of the American people was directly involved. Most of them had made a direct contribution, as farmers providing food, as workers in defense plants making planes or tanks or shells or rifles or boots or any of the myriad items the troops needed to win the war, or as volunteers doing the work at hundreds of agencies. The bandages they had rolled, the rifles they had made, were being put to use even as they heard the news. They prayed that they had done it right. . . .

Very few Americans were without personal worries on June 6, 1944:

Nearly everyone in the country knew someone in the Army, the Army Air Force, the Navy, or the Coast Guard stationed in the European Theater. Only a handful knew if the soldier or sailor or airman was in action on D-Day or if he was going in later, but they all knew that before the war was won their loved one would be in a combat zone.

Now it had started. The buildup phase was over. The United States was committed to throwing into the battle all the vast forces she had brought into existence over the past three years. That meant their boy, brother, husband, boyfriend, employee, fellow student, cousin, nephew was either already in combat or soon would be.

In Helena and New York, throughout the nation, they sat and wondered and listened to the radio and dashed out on the streets for the latest edition of the newspaper, with a front-page map of the French coast. . . .

On D-Day, Franklin Roosevelt used the power of radio to link the nation in a prayer. Throughout the day the networks broadcast the text, which was printed in the afternoon editions of the newspapers; at 2200 hours Eastern War Time the president prayed while Americans across the country joined him:

"Almighty God, our sons, pride of our nation, this day have set upon a mighty endeavor. . . .

"Lead them straight and true; give strength to their arms, stoutness to their hearts, steadfastness in their faith. . . .

"These men are lately drawn from the ways of peace. They fight not for the lust of conquest.

They fight to end conquest. They fight to liberate. . . . They yearn but for the end of battle, for their return to the haven of home.

"Some will never return. Embrace these, Father, and receive them, Thy heroic servants, into Thy kingdom. . . ."

The editors of the *New York Times* tried to put some perspective on D-Day in their lead editorial for the June 7 edition. "We have come to the hour for which we were born," they wrote. "We go forth to meet the supreme test of our arms and of our souls, the test of the maturity of our faith in ourselves and in mankind. . . ."

In New York and throughout the land, bells tolled. The greatest of these was the Liberty Bell. It had last been tolled on July 8, 1835, for the funeral of Chief Justice John Marshall. At 0700 on D-Day, Philadelphia Mayor Bernard Samuel tapped the bell with a wooden mallet, sending its voice throughout the country over a radio network. Then he offered a prayer. . . .

In Ottawa, Prime Minister Mackenzie King reported to the House of Commons that the landings were making good progress. He warned that there was still much to do. Opposition leader Gordon Graydon said there were no divisions of opinion on this day. From the ranks of the French-speaking members, Maurice Lalonde rose to acclaim, in French, "the historic fact that from the belfry of time has rung out the hour of the deliverance of France."

On D-Day, Canada, like the United States, was united as never before. French-Canadians and English-speaking Canadians had equal stakes in the invasion and were single-minded about the goal. Monsieur Lalonde asked special permission of the House: Could the "Marseillaise" be sung? For the first time in Canadian parliamentary history, all the members joined in singing the "Marseillaise," followed by "God Save the King. . . ."

"When can their glory fade?" Tennyson asked of the Light Brigade, and so ask I of the men of D-Day. "Oh, the wild charge they made. /

All the world wondered. / Honor the charge they made."

General Eisenhower, who started it all with his "OK, let's go" order, gets the last word. In 1964, on D-Day plus twenty years, he was interviewed on Omaha Beach by Walter Cronkite.

Looking out at the Channel, Eisenhower said, "You see these people out here swimming and sailing their little pleasure boats and taking advantage of the nice weather and the lovely beach, Walter, and it is almost unreal to look at it today and remember what it was.

But it's a wonderful thing to remember what those fellows twenty years ago were fighting for and sacrificing for, what they did to preserve our way of life. Not to conquer any territory, not for any ambitions of our own. But to make sure that Hitler could not destroy freedom in the world.

I think it's just overwhelming. To think of the lives that were given for that principle, paying a terrible price on this beach alone, on that one day, two thousand casualties. But they did it so that the world could be free. It just shows what free men will do rather than be slaves."

*

And, finally, this from my acknowledgments:

General Eisenhower liked to speak of the fury of an aroused democracy. It was in Normandy on June 6, 1944, and in the campaign that followed, that the Western democracies made their fury manifest. The success of this great and noble undertaking was a triumph of democracy over totalitarianism. As president, Eisenhower said he wanted democracy to survive for all ages to come. So do I. It is my fondest hope that this book, which in its essence is a love song to democracy, will make a small contribution to that greatest of all goals.

[1] *D-Day June 6, 1944: The Climactic Battle of World War II* (New York: Simon & Schuster, 1994).

The Greatest Thing We Have Ever Attempted

Hilt of the Sword
D'Ann Campbell

I'd like to talk about two lessons we should have learned and did learn from Normandy. The first concerns the nature of the Allied victory. It really was a team effort, multinational in scope, that won at D-Day and, for that matter, that ultimately brought about the defeat of Germany and Japan. Similarly, research about D-Day has been a team effort. Historians have teamed up with participants to get the story of D-Day, and scholars from many countries have made valuable contributions to obtain information about D-Day and World War II in general. When, for example, I wrote a piece on women in an antiaircraft artillery unit while I was at West Point, I was asked to find roles that women played in World War II other than being nurses. I had to rely on scholars from Britain, Germany, and the Soviet Union to show me what archives I should and could use. With respect to the French resistance movement, I've relied on people like Margaret Rossiter, author of a very good book on the subject titled *Women in the Resistance* (New York: Praeger, 1985). At this conference I've had extensive talks on that subject with Douglas Porch and Martin Blumenson. Michael Foote has provided valuable information on the role of women in the British-run SOEs (Special Operations Executives). I have also learned much from Franz Seidler, who is probably the leading expert on the wartime role of women in Germany.

My second point is that D-Day was an expression of total war, and the Allies got the concept of total war right. They focused on logistics, supplies, and manpower. The date of the Normandy invasion was determined by the buildup of supplies, combat units, and, of course, air power. Overlord was just the tip of the sword, and we need to talk about the entire sword being key to victory on D-Day and beyond.

So I'd like to comment for just a minute on the role of women in World War II, that is, the Anglo-American concept of that role. Total war meant every man, woman, and child working together toward victory. Many women were involved as nurses. Generals Eisenhower and Bradley knew that to keep morale high they had to promise the best medical care for their soldiers, sailors, and airmen. They fulfilled that promise. Nurses were in Normandy on D-plus-four. They were in airvac units and field hospitals, they were all around the battlefield. Some seven months later, in anticipation of the invasion of Japan's home islands, President Roosevelt went to Congress and, in an unprecedented move, asked for permission to draft nurses. Up until then the nursing profession had contributed proportionally more of its members to military service than any other profession; but even so, in the event of an invasion of Japan, military leaders knew they would need at least another ten thousand nurses to provide the sort of medical care they had promised and always provided to the troops.

The British and the French followed suit in using nurses. For that reason I maintained in my book, *Women at War: Private Lives in a Patriotic Era* (Cambridge: Harvard University Press, 1984), that nursing really came of age in World War II. Nurses performed tasks in the military that, on the home front, were reserved only for doctors. The military ran out of doctors in the battle zones, so the women did the doctors' jobs and did them very well.

About sixty-five thousand British women served in antiaircraft artillery units and mixed battery units. The Special Operations Executives employed over fifty women agents. It was found that women were excellent as wireless operators, couriers, and messengers because they tended to be far less conspicuous than men. In this context it is worth noting that at least half of all SOE agents and almost all of the fifty women agents were killed in the line of duty. It should also be noted that the agents went on their missions even though they knew beforehand that the chances for survival were not good.

In occupied France women played a key role in the resistance movement. They helped some five thousand downed Allied airmen, including three thousand Americans, evade capture or escape captivity. According to Margaret Rossiter, about 40 percent of those running the escape lines were women. Moreover, women made up about 18 percent of the intelligence networks, serving mostly as radio operators who parachuted into occupied territory. Almost 50 percent of the women were killed. Women also constituted about 10 percent of the work force on clandestine newspapers.

Unfortunately, there are no reliable statistics for the number of women who served in paramilitary units. But we do know that one of the most important persons in the resistance movement was Marie Madeline Foque, who headed a group known as the Alliance, with over three thousand agents. Foque was captured three times, in 1942, 1943, and 1944. Before D-Day her group drew a fifty-five-foot detailed map of the German defenses at the site of the U.S. landings. She landed behind the lines a few days after D-Day, and her unit was key in getting vital information to the Americans. They also provided information about the V-1 and V-2 missiles.

About 350,000 women served in the armed forces in the United States. In addition, American women were involved in combat service and support roles. In keeping with the total war concept, civilian women were involved in home-front production, working in armaments factories and the like: these were the so-called Rosie the Riveters and the Winnie the Welders. The number of women who served in the armed forces of Britain, Canada, and the Soviet Union was proportionally larger, relative to the populations of their respective countries, than that of the United States.

The Allies' concept of total war differed markedly from the German/Japanese concept. The Germans and the Japanese did employ women as nurses, but basically they believed that women should stay at home to fulfill their traditional roles as wives and mothers or, if they were single, to prepare themselves for marriage and motherhood. For that reason the Germans looked with disdain upon Soviet women. These "gun women," as the Germans called them, were regarded as being lower than vermin and therefore deserving of the worst sort of treatment, which often included rape and murder. Ironically, by 1943 Albert Speer had told Hitler that Germany was losing the war and that he had better employ more of the native work force, especially women, if he wanted to avoid defeat. Then, reluctantly, Hitler did open factory work and military opportunities to women. It should be pointed out that the Germans often depended on slave labor to make ammunition. Nevertheless, German women who worked in the factories were, like Allied women, patriotic volunteers who took their jobs very seriously. As for military service, in antiaircraft artillery alone over one hundred thousand German women served in mixed battery units. By 1945, Hitler had approved and designed an all-female infantry unit, but it never saw action. This was quite a change, a product of necessity. (For a detailed treatment of this topic, see my article "Women in Combat: The World War II Experience in the United States, Great Britain, Germany, and the Soviet Union" in *The Journal of Military History* 57, no. 2 [1993]: 301-23.)

Japan, like Germany, made scant use of its single women in the early stages of the war, even refusing to employ them in factories. Later in the war, however, the invasion threat to the home islands led to a number of women being trained for combat and committed to battle on Okinawa. But their training was inadequate and these "Orange Blossoms," as they were called, were slaughtered.

So what are the correct lessons to draw from Normandy? To repeat, the two I'm proposing are, first, the importance of teamwork—of an allied effort at the time, and the same kind of effort now to record and document the history of the war. The second is the importance of the total war concept as it applies to logistics, supply, and "person power."

The Greatest Thing We Have Ever Attempted

The Lessons to be Learned: Perspectives and Reflections

H. P. Willmott

As a professional historian one is instinctively wary of searching for "the lessons to be learned" from any war, campaign, or battle. The military look at events—study would be too strong a word—to learn their beloved lessons, and we can identify the more important and obvious of these without undue difficulty: the importance of command relationships in both the combined and joint spheres; the importance of force ratios and the balance between the operational and the logistical; the crucial importance of surprise, deception, and intelligence to success; the need to look beyond the shoreline; the critical importance of air power to the conduct and success of amphibious operations—indeed, the fact that the latter may not be conducted without possession of this commodity. Apart from amphibious operations, such lessons are timeless and transcend any individual war, and their identification presents no great intellectual achievement.

There are, however, other matters to which those who claim to be historians should direct their attention, because I would submit that individually and collectively historians, and specifically military historians, must recognize that what is truly important is not what were the lessons to be learned, or the lessons that should have been learned, but whether or not we ask ourselves the right questions in the first place.

As historians our first debt is to Clio and the discipline itself, and I cannot help but conclude that in our treatment of the Second World War our performance has been less than adequate, not least because in the military history field so many members of our profession have been guilty of three offenses: first, of dealing in "panacea history" for a popular market and thus pandering to some of the worst aspects of ignorance and bias; second, of subscribing to narrowly based, parochial, and chauvinistic views of events, in part because the Cold War imposed upon the Second World War an interpretative scheme that was exclusive in its national claims upon victory; and third, of describing events in the belief that they are explaining them.

Let me provide an example of the latter. Ask the question, Why the deadlock of World War I?, and one knows the form of the answer almost down to the last line: the superiority of defensive firepower over the offense; the superiority of strategic and operational movement over tactical mobility; the limitations of the weapons systems—the aircraft and tank—that in another war were to restore mobility to the battlefield; problems of command and control in the timely employment of reserves; the physical condition of the battlefield and the importance of barbed wire; lack of surprise; lack of an open flank. But do these explain the deadlock of World War I? Of course not; they merely describe the overall state of the battlefield. The deadlock of World War I is explicable only in terms of all the parties to the conflict refusing to accept indecisiveness and their willingness to fight on despite the elusiveness of victory.

My point is that after fifty years we should have the distance of time that permits dispassionate reconsiderations—which means asking the right questions—of Normandy in particular and the Second World War in general. The right questions inevitably present themselves at different levels, and perhaps a military historian should first question Normandy's context in the war and the war's context in world history. Normandy's context is one sense very simple, and therefore forgotten or conveniently ignored. June 1944 and Normandy are all but synonymous, but June 1944 also saw the fall of Rome, Finland in effect driven from the war, and the opening of the Soviet summer offensive that destroyed the German front between Minsk and the Black Sea.

At a distance of fifty years we need to develop a new perspective. In that regard, June 1944 was the month that the German era of European history ended; it was the month that spelled the end of European primacy in the world. For one brief period, when for the only time in man's existence it was easier to go around continents than to go across them, Europe had marked out her primacy in the world, and when this imbalance between overland and maritime lines of communication reversed itself European primacy was rendered no more than a convicted man on parole. The review of his case came in June 1944 chiefly in the form of two events, the invasion of Normandy and the Battle of the Philippine Sea (June 19-20).

It is somewhat unfortunate that the landing at Salerno in September 1943 was the first opposed invasion of the European continent by non-Europeans since 1354. It is also unfortunate that Europe's last great love-battle was Alamein in November 1942, in that this was the last battle fought between Europeans without reference to non-Europeans and, appropriately, was fought beyond Europe's shores. The symmetry is not there: how much more appropriate it would have been if all could have come together at once! But history seldom unfolds conveniently, and we have to content ourselves with recognizing that the landings in France and the crushing of the Japanese carrier force in the Battle of the Philippine Sea marked the emergence of the United States as the greatest power in the world, with the Soviet Union, though massively inferior to her in every respect other than military power, the only state that could realistically compare to her.

An awareness of the diversity of June 1944 is key to appreciating the most important lesson of Normandy and of World War II: that there are limits to national power and that these limits must be recognized. In the past it has been all too easy to see the over-arching primacy of one's own national effort in the outcome of World War II, and at this conference we have been subjected to an American perspective, with several speakers referring to the United States as if she had the power and means to win the European war by her own unaided efforts. For instance, we were told by Stephen Ambrose that "the lesson of Normandy is that there is nothing a democracy cannot do once it agrees on what needs to be done. No power in the world can match that of an aroused democracy," i.e., the United States. This statement fails to take into account the achievements of the Soviet Union, which was certainly no advertisement for liberal democracy. It is also an expression of the sort of logic that allows Normandy to be identified as the climactic campaign of World War II, as if any single campaign in a war of six years duration can be climactic, as if any single campaign once the issue of victory and defeat has been decided can be considered decisive.

More to the point raised above, it would seem to give the United States too much credit for the Allied victory. World War II in Europe was won not by the United States, but by an alliance in which she was one member and in which the contribution of other nations was vitally important. To recognize the reality of alliance warfare is to recognize that one nation cannot handle any more than one single part of the alliance effort, just as to recognize that war is total is to recognize that the military cannot handle more than one of its constituent parts. Say it ever so softly, *sotto voce,* but say it: that the Soviet Union was the prime agent of Germany's military defeat, and the Anglo-American contribution to this specific dimension of the war was small.

Nations that come late to a war must take it as

they find it for seldom, if ever, can they impose upon it their own hallmark, at least not immediately or quickly. Wars between great industrialized powers, between powers of great capacity and stamina, cannot be won quickly. There are no shortcuts to victory, and if Normandy has any relevance it must be how long it took after her entry into the war for the United States to make war as she would. Lead-times in warfare are, or at least can and tend to be, very long. It took more than two years for the United States to raise an expeditionary force sufficient for operations in Northwest Europe. It took thirty months, until spring 1944, for the U.S. armed forces to come to grips with the command problems associated with the conduct of a Normandy landing. It took Sicily, Salerno, and Anzio before air power was properly incorporated into a plan for an amphibious operation.

The military will look for "the lessons to be learned" and will no doubt focus upon such matters, particularly in the present climate in which the notion of "jointness" seems to be a substitute for rather than an encouragement to serious thought. But if we look carefully at Normandy we will see the complexity of issues, particularly at the highest level of command, and as historians we should note the perils of the use of such terms as "the high command" with their overtones of unanimity and singleness of purpose.

At the same time, we should be properly objective about the Anglo-American effort and achievement. Even with all the advantages the Allies held in 1944, things came within measurable distance of disaster on June 6. Omaha went wrong, Utah could have gone wrong had the landings taken place as intended, and at day's end two British beaches remained separated by a German armored division that had fought its way to the coast. The emphasis of these proceedings has been placed upon the actions of generals, decisions made at the highest levels of the government and the military, and great impersonal forces shaping history—a sort of strategic determinism or military Marxism. One can take a deterministic view of the events of 6 June 1944 and conclude that the Germans were beaten by the 5th. But this would be wrong. Victory in Normandy was not preordained; it had to be fought for, and, moreover, total victory could not be won in a single campaign.

One views as rather tedious contrary assertions, in particular the line of argument that suggests that the war could have been ended in 1944. The assumption seems to be that the Allies could have taken the war into Germany in autumn 1944 if certain episodes had been arranged to slightly different endings, Falaise being the obvious point in time and place when events might have unfolded to a more helpful end. To counter this argument I would begin with a consideration of the distances involved. It is about 620 miles as the crow flies from Caen to Berlin, and about 740 miles by rail via Rouen, Brussels, Maastricht, Dortmund, and Hanover. In military terms the distance must be nearer a thousand miles, and in the British army, at least, one worked on the basis that for every mile of advance a tank traveled two. So how many railhead movements do such distances involve, how many changes of tank tracks? And when do we bring the campaign to a close? At the end of October or November? Even if we limit the depth of advance to Hanover, and thereby identify the Ruhr rather than Berlin as the German heartland, does one seriously believe that it was within the ability of the two Western Allies to conduct a landing in Normandy and then advance some seven hundred miles into the heart of Germany in four or five months?

The fact that logistically the Allies were unable to reach the Rhine across a broad front in September 1944 is hardly an advertisement of an operational ability to reach into the German heartland by October. We may assess blame for this failure on national or personal levels, but frankly one wearies of such finger-pointing, as it causes us to lose sight of the more obvious and important questions of why, after the breakout from Avranches, Allied forces moved against the ports to the west rather than against the enemy to the east; and why Allied armor was not concentrated in corps in order to conduct encirclement operations en masse.

One notes the contemporaneous Soviet experience. On the Eastern Front between 22 June and 31 July 1944 the Wehrmacht lost 620,000 men in two Soviet offensives, Bagration and Lwów-Sandomiercz; nevertheless, in August the Germans were able to halt the Soviets in East Prussia and on the Vistula, and deny them the Dukla Pass which permitted entry into Czechoslovakia. Could one campaign in the West have done more than the Soviet army achieved in all of its 1944 offensives? Even admitting the proximity of the Ruhr to the Western armies, a positive assertion that such a campaign could have done more is not self-evident.

In any event the British and Americans could only take on and defeat what they faced, and there is certainly no reason to be anything other than properly proud of what we achieved. If one wants to summarize matters one could state the obvious: the Americans could not have conducted D-Day and Normandy without the British and the British could not have conducted Northwest Europe without the Americans. Both had their share of failures, and their generals—not just one of them—managed to get quite a bit wrong. Even so, they won the campaign or rather the campaigns in Normandy, France, and Northwest Europe, and in so doing made a full and proper contribution to the final victory that was won in 1945.

We often sell ourselves short on this score. At such times we would do well compare our record with that of the enemy. In six weeks in the spring of 1940 the Germans conquered the Low Countries and half of France, and did so with a force equal to the sum of the four national armies that opposed them and across a nine hundred-mile border with an intact communications system behind them. In three months in the summer of 1944 the Western Allies conducted an assault landing, established and then stocked a beachhead fifty miles across, and thereafter crushed an enemy that was in terms of numbers of divisions always superior, liberated France and much of Belgium, and did so across a transportation system that had been shattered in the process. I submit that the latter was the more remarkable accomplishment.

It becomes all the more remarkable when we take into account the fact that throughout history opposed river crossings have been the exception rather than the rule (it was not until the advent of mass armies that the exception and the rule reversed themselves); and that in 1944 for the third time in the war the Allies landed an expeditionary army on a hostile continental mainland and thereafter successfully conducted major offensive operations against major enemy field forces. This was no mean achievement, and one not to be written down by assertions that more might have been achieved.

In this context one notes in so many Western histories an uncritical acclaim of military matters German. One has written of one's alternating amusement and irritation at this acclaim, not least when paraded by a German military that after one war declared itself undefeated and after another that it would have won but for Hitler. To borrow and amend a saying: to lose one world war may be regarded as a misfortune; to lose two looks like carelessness. And to have lost two wars in societies so very different from those of Wilhelm and Hitler would suggest a fault line that cannot be explained in terms of individuals. On the subject of Normandy, many histories stress how superbly German ground forces fought in Normandy, such accounts invariably ending in the last week of July when German defeat—for which Hitler is held responsible—took shape. It should be remembered, however, that the Germans suffered this defeat in a region they had occupied for four years, fighting defensively over ground that was tailor-made for defensive warfare, at a time when the defense held the upper hand over the offense, against an Anglo-American enemy that lacked depth and width in the conduct of offensive operations.

But facts must be faced. The Germans divided their formations between those that could stand on the Eastern Front and those that could not; and many of those that could not were in Normandy. The truth is, the greater part of the German divisions in the West would not have made the Wehrmacht's starting lineup: the Western Allies faced the second team, and nothing that either the British or Americans had was as bad as the worst of the enemy's formations.

Were we not very lucky in this respect? Last night we viewed a film that told us how one U.S. infantry company on Omaha Beach incurred 96 percent casualties and how dreadful were such losses. Yes, they were dreadful, and one would not denigrate or belittle the sacrifice: for those involved and their families the cost could hardly have been greater. But in any discussion of Allied casualties in the West one is constrained to offer this statistic from the East: of every one hundred Soviet males born in 1923 and alive on June 21, 1941, only *three* were still alive on May 12, 1945. So, when considering the losses of one American company on Omaha, one can only say: welcome to Continental warfare.

In the Soviet Union we are not talking about the annihilation of a company but of a generation. We hear how hard was the fighting on the Normandy beaches, and in the bocage and in front of Caen—what of the fighting on the Eastern Front? Again, statistics tell the tale. Averaging the figures, between June 22, 1941, and May 11, 1945, the Soviets lost 22,535 dead *every day*. The road between Berlin and Moscow is twelve hundred miles long. If the Soviet dead of World War II were buried along its length, each corpse would be allowed 2.82 inches of ground. Such figures begin to put the question of whether Bradley forged documents, the approach lines of bombers, and Montgomery's conduct of operations into some sort of proper perspective. And a proper perspective is essential for avoiding the errors of the past.

In the discussion following the reading of his paper, Stephen Ambrose disparaged Hitler's belief that in any contest between men raised as Hitler Youth and men brought up as Boy Scouts, the former would prevail. "Man-for-man the American soldier in the campaign in Northwest Europe was far superior to his German counterpart," Dr. Ambrose declared; "the American best, the rangers and the airborne, were much better than the German best. Even National Guard divisions like the 29th were much better than the standard German division. The reason for this was precisely that the junior officers and the noncoms in the American army had been brought up as Boy Scouts. . . ."

At last we know why the Allies took so long to break out of the Normandy beachhead: we made the mistake of sending the Canadian corps against the 12th SS Panzer Division—the *Hitler Jugend*. We should have sent a troop of American Boy Scouts; no doubt they would have opened the front, presumably with their tin-openers. What an insult to Canada. What chauvenistic claptrap.

Make no mistake: this is not on my part a *reductio ad absurdum;* it is the argument itself that plumbs the depth of absurdity. Anyone can beat the patriotic, nationalist drum, and on the subject of Normandy a Britisher can hand out the punishment, of that make no mistake. If American divisions were so good, how was it that the American formations in Normandy incurred greater losses than the British and inflicted fewer casualties? If the British performed so poorly in this campaign how was it that they took Caen against three-quarters of the German armor in Normandy before the Americans took St.-Lô? As for the breakout by Third U.S. Army—was it the cause of a victory that remained to be won or the result of victory that had already been won? And was the British failure to take Caen on the first day deplorable? If so, then one must provide an example of an American division that made an advance of over four miles on the same day it conducted a full assault landing while being subjected to counterattack by an entire armored division. The British failed to take Caen because they picked strawberries and brewed tea? No doubt if they had made some curry they would have run all the way to Caen, if not Paris.

But enough. Because it blinds us to the realities of power—with sometimes tragic consequences—one may best characterize this ethnocentric treatment of the Normandy campaign as not noly being of little value, but positively dangerous as well.

If one looks at postwar American history one sees among the swamps and forests, the valleys and rolling countrysides, the lakes and villages, one mountain ridge, scarred and foreboding: Vietnam. Wherein lies the American tragedy here? In the failure to understand the nature of the war in which the United States involved herself? Perhaps. In the assumption that the United States had the means to ensure that the war would be fought on her terms of reference, in a way of her choice and to an end she desired? I would suggest that herein lies the basis of the American tragedy and failure in Vietnam: that the same impatience and restlessness, the same desire to take the battle to the enemy and destroy him in the shortest possible time that characterized U.S. policy in the European context of a landing in Normandy (note especially Operations Sledgehammer and Roundup) also characterized U.S. policy in Vietnam, with disasterous results.

To repeat: we were told that "the lesson of Normandy is that there is nothing a democracy cannot do once it agrees on what needs to be done. No power in the world can match that of the teamwork of an aroused democracy." So the escape clause is there: the United States failed in Vietnam because she was not agreed and was neither an aroused nor united democracy in the prosecution of this war. Perhaps. But perhaps the real problem lies in the overweening self-confidence that recognized no limits to national capability. How else can we explain "the loss of China," as if China were ever the United States' to lose? What is going to happen in the future when Russia goes rogue? That the United States lost Russia? How do we explain Somalia other than the failure to recognize the limits of national capability born of the over-confidence bred by the 1991 Gulf campaign?

One could go on in this vein. But there's one more issue I think we really need to address, and then we can bring this matter to a halt. At this conference we have, apart from Mr. Rooney in his remarks, been very clinical, very antiseptic in the way we have dealt with the Second World War. Jack Huston talked about bomber operations but didn't mention scraping his buddies—or should I say the bits of his buddies?—out of their turrets. We didn't talk about the tank crews that had to be cleaned out from the inside of their vehicles. We didn't talk about the men who were burned to death, broiled, grilled underneath the decks of ships. How many of the pictures that adorn this room show a body? Where are *les grands mutiles?* Where are the headless corpses, the hopelessly disfigured, the men who lost their sanity amid the insanity of these proceedings? What of the countless number of ordinary people who wished to do nothing more than live out their lives as best they could but who instead found their lives ruined by widowhood, bereavement, or crippling wounds?

We are talking about the greatest war in history. If we think back to the Anglo-Saxon chronicles and the Norse sagas, what sort of work do we remember? Hacking. You read through Shakespeare, what do you read about but bodies being cut to pieces. Yet what do we see in films of the Second World War? Do we ever see a headless American or British corpse? We have a very clean, very proper image of this war. It doesn't do us any good. It wasn't like that.

Let us, as historians, address the realities of this war; let us act upon what Paul Fussell so brilliantly identified in the last chapter of his book *Wartime*, published in 1989. Referring to the antiseptic way we often view the war, he wrote, "As experience, thus, the suffering was wasted. . . . America has not yet understood what the Second World War was like and has thus been unable to use such understanding to re-interpret and re-define the national reality and to arrive at something like public maturity."

In the same chaper, Fussell presents us with images of the the war quite different from those that have been impressed upon the public consciousness by the TV camera and Hollywood. He quotes General Sir John Hackett's recollection of the parachute assault over Arnhem: "I saw an inert mass . . . swinging down in a parachute harness beside me, a man from whose body the entrails hung, swaying in a reciprocal rhythm. As the body moved one way the entrails swung the other." And this from two soldiers in North Africa: "Neil McCallum and his friend 'S.' [came] upon the body of a man who had been lying on his back when a shell, landing at his feet, eviscerated him: 'Good God,' said S., shocked, 'here's one of his fingers.' S. stubbed with his toe on the ground some feet from the corpse. 'Christ,' went on S. in a very low voice, 'look, it's not his finger.'"

We have to get away from the clean-cut image of this war, and we must do so for very obvious reasons, not least because it was anything but "clean." Those who lived through these events are passing from the scene. The demands of Cold War rhetoric have gone: we no longer need exclusive claims upon victory over a monstrous tyranny to provide the basis of legitimacy for our actions. We have opportunity to look afresh at these events, and overwhelming reason to do so. Society at any time stands on the edge of a brave new world, but we stand on the edge of a new world in which national consensus as we have experienced that concept over the last fifty years will be destroyed. The information revolution—in particular the proliferation of cable and satellite television, as well as the growth and use of the Internet and the Worldwide Web—will erode the common basis of societies as developed over the past decades, and one suspects that the effect will be the lowering and degradation of standards, not their raising. The danger that presents itself may already be here: we may well have seen the last book-reading generation. One knows from one's own students the lack of familiarity with these events and, even worse, their lack of knowledge about how to rectify their ignorance. But the information revolution will force historians to make a choice between history and a pandering to a ruthless entertainment industry that feeds upon what people want to believe and cannot question. We owe future generations the right choice. By the year 2000 we will be further in time from Munich than a person in 1938 was from the end of Reconstruction. A hundred years from now people who will be almost as far from World War II as we are from Waterloo will look to what we have written about World War II as the basis of their understanding of this event. How will we describe it? I know not, but I trust that individually and collectively we will make the right choices as we seek to develop new perspectives and a real understanding of World War II.

The Greatest Thing We Have Ever Attempted

Discussion

Geoffrey Perret: It seems to me that Ned has not given sufficient credit for what I think is an intellectual advance. For the first forty years after World War II, the war was indeed written about and discussed more or less in the same terms you find in the journalism of the time. The military guided the journalists, and it said, "These are the important leaders. These are the important events. And this is the way you will understand it." A lot of postwar military history was written more or less along those lines. But a new generation of military historians came along shaped to a large degree by the Vietnam War, and many people became interested in military history who would never have taken an interest in military history had it not been for Vietnam. They would have been scholars in medieval history or American colonial history. But the fact that they were drafted or they had to spend years of their lives worrying about the draft gave them an interest in military history. They wanted to know how we ever got to a point where we were fighting that particular war. They wanted to identify the guilty parties. So everything in modern American military history was looked at again. We now have not just knee jerk revisionist military history, we also have a level of honesty and integrity in the approach to military history that I think is stunning, even though it produces works that I vehemently disagree with. And it seems to me that Ned is talking as though there has been no advance in our approach to World War II. I just don't believe that is true.

H. P. Willmott: I still think that so much of what we have learned and read in our history has been shaped by the biographies and the accounts that were written in the first twenty-odd years. Let's be clear what we're talking about. These biographies and accounts are the building blocks of our understanding of the war. They stress that we should look at the war in terms of national effort. We still conform to that pattern. And when you look at the bottom end of the market, what do you see? Some of the worst historians catering to the junior psychopaths in our midst—to the people who really do want to know how many rivets there were in a PzKw Mark IV. The situation may be changing, it may be improving. But we've still got a long way to go.

Geoffrey Perret: Are there people in this room who write books like that?

H. P. Willmott: We've all written on them.

Geoffrey Perret: Written *on* them. Are there people in this room who have written the kind of works you just disparaged?

H. P. Willmott: I have.

Geoffrey Perret: You have?

H. P. Willmott: Yes. I didn't hold myself up as a paragon of virtue.

Geoffrey Perret: Good. So you have the sackcloth and the ashes, and it seems to fit, but there are a lot of us here who wouldn't feel that it fits us. We have done the best we can.

H. P. Willmott: Indeed, then, sir, as yesterday in terms of being corrected for an argument I didn't make, may I congratulate you on such foresight in the first place.

Lewis Sorley: I can't help observing that not everyone seems to have been paying attention. For example, it was charged that this conference has offered a very antiseptic view of the war. I guess you'd have to say the level of perfection at which you deal with the matters under discussion would dictate that to be pretty much the case. But I remember hearing earlier today a very affecting account of a physician who went below decks on an LST and, as an act of mercy to end the suffering of those who were lost there in the midst of the flame, shut the water-tight hatch to hasten their demise. And it was charged that the images of the war were only of officers and that they were only naval and air force officers, nice and clean. Yet I look around the room, and I see on the walls a poster showing a GI that I'm sure is not an officer, and I see two guys manning machine guns over here who are not officers, and I see other young people at their machines as part of the production effort. I think that the content and the tone, as well as the honesty and the comprehensiveness of this conference is far greater than was implied by those comments.

Thomas Buell: Just a comment on how history is portrayed. I get involved in this because I do quite a few book reviews, so I'm very much aware of the literature. On the whole, I get very discouraged by the quality of the work, at least the work I'm asked to review. The absolute worst has to be documentaries on television. The thing that pains me about the documentaries is that there are so many uninformed people who think that's the way it is. About six months ago I saw a documentary on George C. Marshall which was just the most screwed-up, fouled-up thing I've ever seen. Yet there were people that probably said, "Gee, that's the way it was." That particular documentary said that Marshall did everything and that Marshall ran the war; you wouldn't know there was a Joint Chiefs of Staff. So I really worry about the documentaries.

One other thought about the accuracy of what we write. Any historian when he or she writes has to be very, very humble, because you never know the real story. Eventually you have to start writing, but you write with the knowledge that much of what you're doing could very well be wrong, could very well be inaccurate. You should always encourage others to keep at it. I just started, for example, writing on the Civil War. You would have thought that the Civil War has been written about so many times, what more could possibly be said about it? Yet I find that what has already been written usually can be corrected or updated, or is completely off-base. You have to keep going back and going back. From that I conclude that the final word is never written. And any historian who does claim that what they have written on the subject is the final word and nothing more need be written is absolutely dead wrong.

John Mountcastle: General Talbott, almost fifty years had passed before a definitive history of the 90th Division appeared, and it's made quite an impression on today's generation of military leaders. You had a direct hand in writing that history. To what extent did you and the editors and authors of the manuscript make the difficult choices as to what you included and what you didn't include? I ask this because you were brutally frank in sections of that history.

Orwin Talbott: Let me give just a little bit of background here. One of the people who had gone all the way through the division was a guy named Frank Norris. He commanded the division's Medium Artillery Battalion through most of the war, not just in combat but in training also. He felt there was a unique story here and he kept talking about it and talking it up and finally got things mobilized to the point where he could tackle it in an organized way.

Norris was a professional writer not a professional historian, but he had been in the division, coming in as a second lieutenant and leaving, wounded, as a captain in about February of 1945, when he returned to the States and got out of the service.

Through the organization of veterans called the 90th Division Association, individual stories were solicited. The bulk came from enlisted personnel. I'd say their accounts comprised roughly two-thirds of the book. Most of the choosing of the stories and the first cut at assembling them was done by Norris. The same man recruited two others, yours truly and a man named Ames Yates—who died a year ago—who had come into the division as an eighteen-year-old second lieutenant in December of '42 and stayed with the division all the way through to the end of the war. He had been aide to three different generals during the combat days, including two commanding generals who were relieved. We became the editors. And we spent two years bouncing things back and forth, rewriting and reassembling the sections.

For example, one of the major operations of the division was the crossing of the Moselle River during flood stage. That's really what caught Patton's eye as far as our division was concerned. An account of the crossing had not been included in the manuscript, and I was able to provide an account I had written when I was a student at the Advanced Course at the Infantry School back in '48 and '49. I edited the account to fit it in. We kept editing and re-editing to try to make it a consistent story. It presents the division's history chronologically from the first week ashore; sections including the sinking of the *Susan B. Anthony,* for example, are on the first pages and the operation in Czechoslovakia is on the last pages.

There are two things unique about the account. As I briefly recounted yesterday, the division's record in Normandy had been so poor that General Bradley's staff had seriously recommended that the division be broken up and its people used as individual replacements. General Bradley thought about it but rejected the recommendation. After the relief of the division's second commander in the latter part of July we got a new division commander, a National Guard brigadier named Raymond S. McLain. He had been with the 45th Division in Sicily as artillery commander and had been an extra brigadier in Normandy. At the same time we got out of the hedgerow area. We no longer had all the problems of the bocage and we had a new leadership, including a new assistant division commander, a man familiarly known as Wild Bill Weaver. He later became a division commander himself, and was a little bit crazy and old for the job. But, boy, was he a combat leader! He literally led the combat commands that took off in the race across France. And then we began to think, "Well, maybe we can do something." Weaver began to instill pride and confidence in the division.

When Harry Hopkins came to Paris in February of '45, Ike said he wished he had more divisions like the 90th. He listed five divisions, and the 90th was one of them. At the end of the war General Patton was asked to name a unit for the Presidential Citation. The only division, and there were fifteen in his army, that he recommended for a division-wide Presidential Citation was the 90th Division. So the situation went from black to white. That's one unique aspect of the division's history.

The other unique aspect is the story itself. It's not an author's interpretation, not one viewpoint, but dozens of viewpoints from different levels—but none from men who served in combat in that unit as full colonels or as generals. For example, I have several sections in the account, but I was a captain and then a major at the time of the operations of which I wrote. There were about five articles by lieutenant colonels and all the rest were by lesser ranks, officer and enlisted. I think the name of the history is very apt: *War From the Ground Up.* It has the real foxhole flavor, and not just one person's foxhole flavor, but rather this person and that person, from this unit and that unit and the other unit. I gave a copy to Gordon Sullivan, who is an old friend and current army chief of staff. Shortly thereafter he checked into the hospital for five days, which gave him a chance to read it. He liked it so much that he told the army's chief of military history to buy 250 copies and to give it to all senior personnel in the army with his direct orders to read it. I've just heard from our master of ceremonies today that it became the in-thing among students at Leavenworth to buy it because they thought it was so good. I've been told that the historian at West Point has said it was the best narrative of ground combat in World War II.

Judy Litoff: Geoffrey Perret has questioned whether Ned Willmott has been fair to military historians over the past thirty years as military history has evolved and so forth. I have to question whether Ned Willmott has been fair to this conference in summarizing what I heard discussed over the past two days. When he completed his talk, I was sitting here thinking, "We were not at the same seminar."

Alan Gropman: The ideal is to tell it as it is. You see, Martin Blumenson and Jim Collins and a lot of other people in this room have all worked in official history offices where there is something more involved, because the stakes are very high. We all tend to get captured by the topics we write about; we tend to get captured by the audience for whom we write, by our publishers, by the people we work for. Chauvinistic, partisan, defensive history isn't history. So we're into one of these situations where the glass is either half empty or half full. What Ned is looking at is a glass that's half empty; the rest of us are looking at a glass that's half full.

There have been chauvinistic statements made in this conference, and there have been partisan comments. There were arguments that have gotten to the level of heat and, because of politeness, we've been able to back off. Steve Ambrose spoke eloquently about the powers of democracies, and we got our asses kicked by the North Vietnamese. And they're still not a democracy. The Russians stayed in the Second World War with twenty million losses, and the Japanese fought to the point of self-annihilation. So all generalizations are false; but historians have to make generalizations. Ned's got a point, however: if we don't watch what we're doing, we're in trouble. If we slip into partisanship and chauvinistic writing we're not producing what we need to produce for the future generals and admirals who are going to go out there and do the job. Ned is making a cautionary statement, a warning, and he's taking a lot of heat for it. I think his warning needs to be heeded.

Stephen Ambrose: He has poured a considerable amount of heat on me, and I'd like a shot at this. In the first place everybody in this room, everybody who writes about World War II, is perfectly well aware that more than eight out of every ten Wehrmacht soldiers killed in the war were killed by the Red Army. You are not bringing news to us when you say that. And I must tell you that if you want descriptions of what hot metal and steel-jacketed bullets can do a human body, there's hardly a person in this room who hasn't written a book that doesn't have that in their works.

You're absolutely right on the question of nationhood and what nations cannot do, and I thought that part of your comment was more than on the mark. I thank you for reminding us of that. And I am guilty of stretching, obviously so, when I say there's nothing a democracy can't do. On the other hand, I'll guarantee you that a democracy can do it better than any other system of government.

Now, on this business of chauvinism and nationalism: it's all but impossible to escape. You do your best. I was interested to find out from you that the reason we lost in Vietnam was that we showed impatience and that this was characteristic also of the proposal for Sledgehammer and Roundup. From that I drew the conclusion that we lost in Vietnam because, unlike 1942 and 1943, we didn't have the British there to guide us.

H. P. Willmott: I don't mind being condemned for what I say, but I do object to being condemned for what I didn't say. I said that I would suggest that herein lies the basis of the American tragedy and failure in Vietnam. Certain people seem to be very quick, very sharp to be on me for what I said. But do you think I haven't read Peter Geyl's *History Is An Argument Without End?* Do you think I actually believe that we have set down views of history which haven't changed in fifty years? For God's sake, how many different nations are there, how many different services, how many different unit divisions? It's a changing kaleidoscope. I've never suggested it wasn't.

What I'm suggesting is that, as a profession, many of our members—we've all done it, I have done it—have written some pretty bad books that actually pander to the worst tastes of our society. What I also see is that television particularly is pressing us in a direction which will continue to pander to bad taste. That is the warning I made. I merely suggested something in terms of failure to understand national power. For God's sake, I come from a country that still believes its people are God's chosen and would be made immune from any defeat by divine intervention. Of course I know this attitude is not unique to one nation. The Soviet Union, with its exclusive claim on victory, is equally bad in this respect. You read a Soviet account of the Pacific War and you find that it was won by the Soviets after the Americans had been fumbling around for three and a half years. What crap that is. I'm not blind to this. All I'm pointing out at the end is that we are actually on the threshold of an information revolution that is going to present major challenges to us as historians and to the profession of history. And I'm sorry that at the very end of the conference I gave something other than a summary of other people's papers. I did try to give something that I thought might be of interest.

Martin Blumenson: Ned, I apologize. I'm half deaf, and I didn't understand a word you said throughout, so I cannot respond to you. But may I say this? I question the word "lessons." I don't believe there are any lessons in history. I don't know really what to substitute for that word, but it makes me grind my teeth.

I write history. Forgive me for being personal, it's the only way I can explain what I think history is. I write history for the civilian society in which I live. I do not write for the military. I hope the military will read me, and I hope the military will approve of what I'm doing, but I write for the American public, not for the military. And I believe very strongly in honest history. Historians should be as honest as possible. Somebody back there said it, that historians have to be humble because they understand better than anybody else how many times they guess at the truth. They hope they're right, but they have to be able to admit they're wrong. But "lessons" bug me. I understand what we're talking about, but I just wish we didn't call them lessons.

And I'm sorry, I apologize to you, Ned. I wish you would speak up and get your mouth close to the microphone, because I love listening to you but I just could not hear you.

Steve Dietrich: I don't like the term "lessons learned" because it's misunderstood. I commend the panelists for not using it. You instead used the phrase "lessons *to be* learned." There are indeed lessons from history to be learned. Mr. Blumenson is one of the best writers in pointing out those lessons to us. We as historians do not learn lessons; we discover lessons, we illuminate lessons. The only way a lesson can be learned or not learned is to wait until it's applied and it forces change, such as an institutional change—for example, to army doctrine or organization. In my business, my job is to illuminate the lessons of history to army decision-makers and leaders and hope they implement the correct ones. At that time the lessons we have illuminated will have been learned.

Geoffrey Perret: I would just like to make two small points. First of all, I recognize, Ned, that you are aware that history changes. It just seems to me that you aren't prepared to concede that there has been any progress. The other thing I want to say is this. When Kenneth Clark did that wonderful series called *Civilization,* he pointed to what it is that makes a civilization. He said it's self-confidence. Now admittedly, one side of a nation's self-confidence is bound to be, or appear to be, chauvinistic. But without self-confidence you cannot build anything.

Kenneth Hagan: I'd to comment on Ned's half-filled glass. He mentioned and we have talked about the images of officers, primarily I think the exclusive use of naval officers and aviators and the absence of images of enlisted men. Then the comment was made that when you look around here we'll see images of ground-pounders. However, if we look around this room, I do not see the dead, the wounded, or the mangled, which I think is one of Ned's points. The only direct reference I can see to death is a very sanitized image of a coffin. I'm talking about the actual images of people who have been killed. I want the bodies, that's what I want. I think the absence of them underscores Ned's point.

Stephen Ambrose: Let me jump in for a second here to comment on these broader themes and how nations handle the history of this war. Let's think about some other nations. The Japanese record in World War II was at least as bad as that of the Nazis. You do not find young Japanese historians today digging into World War II and examining their nation's record and trying to figure out why Japanese troops acted the way they did. Germans are doing much better. The new generation of German historians have done a really heroic job of looking at the origins, actions, and consequences of Nazism. We in the United States have a lot to be proud of in this regard. Think of the My Lai incident. I would challenge you to find any army in the world that would examine an atrocity by their own troops with the U.S. Army's thoroughness, and the thoroughness of U.S. historians and journalists as well.

I look at this display of war posters on Chicago, and I see a representation of one of the most important social phenomena of the twentieth century, the movement of black Mississippians to Chicago. The poster makes the treatment those blacks received in Chicago look hunky-dory. Actually, it's an awful story. And American historians are examining that story: they are writing about it and insisting that we deal with it. American historians are doing the same thing with the incarceration of the Japanese-Americans. American historians such as Judy Litoff and D'Ann Campbell are looking at the treatment of women during that war. I'm really proud of my colleagues in American history and what we have done with the history of the Second World War. If we have a long way to go, and if there's a great deal yet to do, then thank God.

Judy Litoff: The last casualty of World War II is going to be a World War II historian, I'm convinced.

John English: I was just going to say something to a beleaguered Brit because I'm a Canadian and I suppose I have some sort of distant loyalty to his country. I agreed with much of what Ned said. I guess from the Canadian point of view, we're still finding inaccuracies in our own history, particularly the regimental histories. For example, the Winnipeg Rifles history explains that in Normandy three companies fell back because they were surrounded by thirty panzers. Then the Army Staff College started running our battlefield tours and we got hold of some German vets. We learned from them that there were no German tanks around the Winnipeg Rifles. There were, in fact, British tanks. So that part of the history, at that low level—and I know you're looking at a higher level—is inaccurate. We're trying to correct these things. But we probably never will totally.

We also get into nasty little things like, we're talking to 12th SS veterans, and our Department of External Affairs refuses to let us talk to them. Because the 12th SS murdered 134 Canadians in Normandy there's still a tremendous amount of bad feeling about the SS overall. But the Germans told us about an artillery colonel named Luxemburger who was captured by Canadians. He was tied spreadeagle to a captured German vehicle, and as they finished tying him up, along came a 12th SS tank, saw the vehicle, and shot poor Colonel Luxemburger. So we're not "safe" from our own atrocities. It all makes what we do very difficult. It has been fifty years since the war ended and I think, from our historiographical perspective, we still have a long way to go on some of the evidence that's been given to us. We certainly weren't all angels over there. I think our 3rd Canadian Division looted and I think there were American divisions that looted.

I'm wondering, can we not be a little more clinical? At Staff College we learn such things as, the first thing you do is move your dead off the roads as quickly as you can. Do we still teach that? You must get your dead off the road and into the trees and hide them from the men that are coming up. I think that's probably a good thing to do because then you won't have tanks rolling over them like Andy Rooney described. So is there not something to the Staff College approach to history, which is to sort of examine war clinically because it is our profession? I'm wondering how far can we carry that approach into what we do as historians, as long as we're truthful about it.

H. P. Willmott: The problem is, there always has to be a balance. When I talk about the realities of war I'm not suggesting that we want photographs of the most gruesome aspects of war produced simply to have them. Clearly, there's a point of balance we must try to strike. And, obviously, if we're talking about a unit history, an army history, or a distinctively national history, we're not after an overall balanced view of the war itself.

We're all guilty of ethnocentric attitudes. We can't help that. We're culturally, ethnically oriented; we all adopt the ethos of the period in which we're brought up and of the society in which we live. We should be more conscious of this. Certainly, our view of history is going to change; as we go farther from events and see things in different ways, it's bound to change.

This morning we did have a presentation on the Soviet front. That was important. I think that Mr. Rooney today corrected certain things that were being said, or not said. What I've tried to do is focus on certain points, raise certain questions. I was born in 1945. Every Empire Day at school we paraded along knowing full well that even if Douglas MacArthur won the war in the Pacific—and no one believed that more than Douglas MacArthur—Bernard Law Montgomery won the war in Europe, or at least he would have if it hadn't been for Eisenhower. That was the national wisdom. I'm not saying my countrymen still believe that. But even today we see ourselves as having a special place in the unfolding of these events.

We all tend to do this. All I'm trying to say is, there's a point where we should be looking beyond enthnocentric views of history and such. Within the various disciplines, the staff college courses, we've got to have different forms of history. God help us if we ever have one, single, common theme of history and one basis of understanding, because that means that there would be no argument.

One can see certain dangers coming on the horizon. What is going to be the impact of the new information technology upon a reading generation? Is it going to be the case that we actually have a power of image that is too strong to be replaced by the spoken word? I don't know.

Bruce Menning: Jack English talked about what we have to do in terms of insights or lessons learned when you're dealing at the staff college level. In that respect, I'm very sympathetic with what Steve Dietrich says. To paraphrase Sir Michael Howard: the job of the military in times of peace is to be the custodians of doctrine so that things don't go too far wrong in the event you actually have to go back into action. Within myself there's always a constant tension between the academic historian who agrees very much with what Martin Blumenson says about not wanting to talk too much about lessons learned, and the person who then goes on to talk about insights and enriching our understanding and all of that. But there are things you have to tell military professionals about, and if you don't do it, the information is going to come from someplace else. We owe it to the military professionals to give them what I call "usable history." There's a certain unity in Professor Willmott's commentary between the ugliness of battlefield reality and wanting to prevent that from happening again. In other words, if we're going to send Americans or coalitions out to die somewhere, what I'm going to do is prepare my officers so as to minimize as much as possible the losses and the ugliness. Therefore, I do enter into lessons learned and I don't make any apologies about it, although I realize the problems that are inherent in that approach.

Second, I don't necessarily disagree with what Professor Ambrose says about the power of democracy at war. I just think it needs perhaps a bit more refinement and examination. I mean, for me, on one level, good infantry is good infantry, whether it belongs to the Russians operating in the 18th century on the steppes of southern Russia or to George Washington at Valley Forge. What I would warn against, and I think Steve is talented enough to avoid this pitfall, is the attitude that, for example, American Minutemen beat the British because we were free men and because their forces were composed of mercenaries and professionals. That's a logical extension of a chauvinistic argument. Remember, a bunch of Black Sea sailors with bags of hand grenades and Tommy guns held off any number of panzer grenadiers. The Russians fought well, for Uncle Joe, for the motherland, for their families, whatever.

One of the things I didn't mention this morning is the problems Stalin thought he might face as the Red Army began to move outside the borders of the motherland. He had to look at what kinds of changes in mentality and preparation would be necessary to get Soviet soldiers to continue fighting. The whole problem with unconditional surrender and so on was part of that.

Finally I would say, in reference to what D'Ann Campbell was talking about, the Soviet side provides ever so much more in terms of what you need for studying the role of women under combat conditions. One of the most wonderful and bravest Russian women I ever met headed a Department of Foreign Language Studies at the university in Rostov-on-the-

Don. I can't remember her family name; her first name and patronymic was Lidia Nikolaevna. I had heard that she was a war veteran, so one day after class I asked her, "Lidia Nikolaevna, what did you do in the war?" She said, "I was a machine gunner at Stalingrad." Yet at the same time, a gentle reminder: a woman machine gunner, that's the really jazzy stuff. There's a whole bunch of women we don't know much about—the Bletchley Park crew, for example, which was greatly responsible for breaking the U-boat offensive in the North Atlantic, and, I think, whose story is probably still classified. So there's a lot that can be done in this area.

Cole Kingseed: I jotted down some comments from the last day and a half, and I will be paraphrasing several of the people here. First, Andy Rooney said that sometimes war is indeed better than peace. I think the men and women of Normandy, the Soviet Army, the Japanese, and the Americans all felt that was true. The other thing I note is, of course, in war men and women die. Perhaps Andy Rooney and others are correct when they say we are never going to be young again. Lastly, I would say that people probably fight and die more for their fellow man than they do for their countries. Going to war, I think, is sometimes different than going into combat. The Germans had a saying that patriotism dies about four or five kilometers from the front. You fight and die for the man or the woman on your right and left. We honor the men and women of Normandy for what they did, and to a degree, perhaps, for what we have become as a result of what they've done. And we should honor them.

I would say, as a final word, you ought to be very proud of what you've done here. Sometimes, I think, you're too hard on yourselves. You've offered many new insights, and I hope that, with the publication of the conference proceedings, they'll find an audience not only in the military community but in the civilian community as a whole. So don't be too hard on yourselves. You did a very good job and I congratulate you. I will take a lot of this back to the Military Academy to help prepare a new generation of leaders for the army and for the challenges ahead.

The Greatest Thing We Have Ever Attempted

Chronology of Events
June–September 1944

Note: In keeping with the themes and issues raised at this conference, the chronology is chiefly concerned with ground operations in Normandy and on the Eastern Front; only limited mention is made of events in Italy, the Asian mainland, and the Pacific, and of air operations in general.

June

1 **England:** BBC transmits coded message informing French resistance that invasion is imminent.

2 **England:** Gen. Eisenhower issues orders for invasion of Normandy.

  Asia: U.S. and Chinese forces begin siege of Myitkyina (north Burma).

3 **England:** Allied assault forces complete loading for Operation Overlord.

  Asia: Japanese forces begin withdrawing from Kohima (India).

4 **England:** Eisenhower postpones Overlord for 24 hours because of bad weather.

  Italy: U.S. Fifth Army enters Rome.

5 **England:** Overlord invasion convoys leave port.

  Asia: Battle of Kohima ends.

6 **France:** D-Day. Preceded by a night airborne assault, Allied seaborne forces invade Normandy. Though Allies fail to reach their first-day objectives, the landings are successful, with over 150,000 troops coming ashore by nightfall.

7 **France:** Allies fight to enlarge and link Normandy beachheads. British 50th Div captures Bayeux. Canadian 3rd Div attacks toward Caen, but is stopped by German 12th SS Pz Div (Hitler Youth).

8 **France:** British Second Army captures Port-en-Bessin and establishes contact with U.S. First Army elements, linking Omaha and Gold beaches. U.S. VII Corps advances into Cotentin Peninsula toward Cherbourg.

9 **France:** British and Canadians engaged in heavy fighting on approaches to Caen. Allied aircraft begin operating from fields in France.

  Finland: Soviet Leningrad Front launches offensive against Finnish Mannerheim Line on Karelian Isthmus, west of Lake Ladoga.

10 **France:** U.S. V and VII Corps make contact at Auville-sur-le-Vey, linking Omaha and Utah beachheads. British renew drive to seize Caen, with 7th Armd Div spearheading attack in Tilly-sur-Seulles area.

11 **France:** British attack in Caen area encounters fierce resistance from Panzer Lehr Div.

  Finland: Soviet forces in Karelia have penetrated Mannerheim Line to a depth of 15 miles.

12 **France:** U.S. forces capture Carentan. By now all Allied beachheads in Normandy are linked.

13 **France:** Caumont falls to U.S. 1st Div. British 7th Armd Div enters Villers-Bocage but is forced out of town by counterattacking German armor, notably elements of 501st SS Heavy Tank Bn, as well as Pz Lehr Div and 2nd Pz Div. Germans begin V-1 attacks against England.

14 **France:** 7th Armd Div withdraws northward to Parfouru-l'Eclin area, terminating offensive against Caen.

15 **Pacific:** U.S. forces invade Saipan in Mariana Islands.

Asia: First B-29 raid on Japanese home islands (Kyushu) launched from bases in China.

17 **France:** U.S. VII Corps reaches west coast of Cotentin near Barneville-sur-Mer, cutting off German forces in peninsula.

18 **Finland:** Leningrad Front breaks through Mannerheim Line.

Asia: Japanese capture Changsha (China).

19-20
Pacific: Battle of the Philippine Sea results in crushing defeat of Japanese carrier force; 3 Japanese carriers are sunk, 4 are damaged, and over 400 aircraft are shot down in "Great Marianas Turkey Shoot."

19-22
France: Great Channel Storm wrecks U.S. Mulberry artificial port at Omaha Beach, impeding buildup of Allied forces. U.S. VII Corps drives on Cherbourg.

20 **Finland:** Leningrad Front captures Vyborg (Viipuri) in Finland.

21 **Finland:** Soviet Karelian Front launches offensive north of Lake Ladoga, on both sides of Lake Onega.

22 **France:** U.S. forces begin final assault on Cherbourg.

Eastern Front: On third anniversary of German invasion of Soviet Union, Soviets launch preliminary attacks of major summer offensive, Operation Bagration, against Minsk salient in Belorussia. Soviets attack with First Baltic Front, and First, Second, and Third Belorussian Fronts; opposing them are forces of German Army Group Center, including Third Panzer, Fourth, and Ninth Armies.

Asia: British forces open Dimapur-Kohima-Imphal road, lifting siege of Imphal; Japanese begin general retreat from India.

23 **France:** U.S. forces attacking Cherbourg penetrate outer defenses of town.

Eastern Front: Operation Bagration unfolds on a 350-mile front between Dvina R. and Pripet Marshes, with main weight of initial attack falling on Vitebsk in the north and Bobruisk in the south.

24 Soviet forces attacking in Orsha-Mogilev area (center sector of Minsk salient) force German Fourth Army to withdraw toward Mogilev.

25 **Eastern Front:** Soviets encircle Vitebsk, trapping LIII Corps (German Third Panzer Army) in vicinity.

26-30
France: Operation Epsom: British attempt breakthrough west of Caen.

26 **Eastern Front:** Soviets capture Vitebsk and Zhlobin.

27 **France:** Germans surrender port of Cherbourg to U.S. forces.

Eastern Front: Soviets capture Orsha; some elements of German Fourth Army trapped in Mogilev area, others retreat toward Minsk. Soviets envelop Bobruisk, trapping most of German Ninth Army. Remnants of German LIII Corps attempt breakout from Vitebsk pocket; in the next few days they will be destroyed by the Red Army and Soviet partisan units.

28 **Eastern Front:** Second Belorussian Front captures Mogilev. Soviets now advancing across Dnieper R. on a 70-mile front.

29 **Germany:** At a conference in Berchtesgaden, Hitler rejects proposal by Field Marshals von Rundstedt (CinC West) and Rommel (CinC Army Group B) to withdraw from Normandy. Field Marshal Ernest Busch is dismissed as CinC Army Group Center (Eastern Front), replaced by Field Marshal Walther Model.

Eastern Front: First Belorussian Front captures Bobruisk, destroying most of German Ninth Army.

30 **France:** British call off Operation Epsom, but fighting continues around Caen and Villers-Bocage.

July

1 **France:** U.S. First Army orders general offensive to begin 3 July. U.S. 9th Div. captures tip of Cap de la Hague, ending organized resistance in Contentin.

Eastern Front: Third Belorussian Front captures Borisov.

2 **Eastern Front:** First and Third Belorussian Fronts close on Minsk; First Belorussian Front cuts Minsk-Baranovichi railroad line.

3 **France:** U.S. First Army opens general offensive, attacking south from Cotentin toward Coutances-St.-Lô area: start of Battle of the Hedgerows. Rundstedt resigns as CinC West and is replaced by Field Marshal Guenther von Kluge.

Eastern Front: First and Third Belorussian Fronts capture Minsk, trapping most of German Fourth Army east of the city.

4 **France:** U.S. First Army encounters tenacious resistance by Germans, who make skillful use of the bocage country's rugged terrain to slow First Army's advance. Canadian 3rd Div captures Carpiquet town but fails to take its airfield.

Eastern Front: First Baltic Front captures Polotsk; First and Second Baltic Fronts advance along Dvina R. toward Kaunas and Riga.

6 **Eastern Front:** First Belorussian Front captures Kovel.

8 **France:** British forces (I British Corps and I Canadian Corps) launch Operation Charnwood against Caen, break into northeast corner of city.

Eastern Front: First Belorussian Front storms Baranovichi.

9 **France:** British and Canadian troops capture Caen north of Orne R.; conclusion of Operation Charnwood. Canadians seize Carpiquet airfield.

Eastern Front: Third Belorussian Front captures Lida.

10 **Eastern Front:** Hitler rejects Model's request to withdraw remnants of Army Group North behind Dvina R.

11 **France:** All four corps of U.S. First Army attack abreast between west coast of Cotentin and Caumont; U.S. 9th Div. repulses counterattack by German armor in Le Désert area.

Eastern Front: Soviets have liquidated Minsk pocket east of city, virtually annihilating German Fourth Army. Third Belorussian Front surrounds Vilnius (Vilno) in Lithuania.

12 **Eastern Front:** Second Baltic Front launches offensive in Latvia's Nevel-Ostrov region; Idritsa captured.

13 **Eastern Front:** Third Belorussian Front captures Vilnius; northern (right) wing of First Belorussian Front captures Pinsk. Soviets launch Lwów-Sandomierz offensive with First Ukrainian Front attacking Army Group North Ukraine in Brody area, east of Lwów.

15 **France:** U.S. First Army halts offensive in sector west or Taute R. to regroup for Operation Cobra, but continues attacking in St.-Lô area.

Eastern Front: Opachka falls to troops of Second Baltic Front; Soviets establish bridgeheads across Niemen R. west and southwest of Vilnius.

16 **Italy:** British forces captures Arezzo, establish bridgehead across Arno R.

Eastern Front: Second and Third Belorussian Fronts capture Grodno.

17 **France:** Returning to his HQ after an inspection trip, Rommel is severely wounded when his car is attacked by RAF fighters; von Kluge replaces him as CinC Army Group B. U.S. forces enter St.-Lô.

18 **France:** Spearheaded by three armd divs, British launch Operation Goodwood in Caen area. Canadians capture remainder of Caen south of Orne. U.S. forces take St.-Lô, ending Battle of the Hedgerows.

Eastern Front: First Ukrainian Front captures Brody, trapping German XIII Corps in vicinity. Start of Lublin-Brest operation as left(southern) wing of First Belorussian Front drives west from Kovel toward Lublin. In north, Soviet forces are halted by German counterattack at Augustów on East Prussian border.

Japan: General Hideki Tojo resigns as Prime Minister.

19 **France:** Operation Goodwood continues: British and German armor engaged in big tank battles east of Caen.

Italy: U.S. Fifth Army captures Leghorn (Livorno).

20 **France:** Operation Goodwood concludes with British forces losing over 400 tanks, but in doing so they draw German armor east from U.S. First Army's sector.

East Prussia: Hitler survives assassination attempt ("Bomb Plot") at his HQ in Rastenburg.

Eastern Front: First Belorussian Front reaches 1939 Polish frontier at Bug R., west of Kovel.

21 **Eastern Front:** Third Baltic Front captures Ostrov; First Belorussian Front crosses Bug.

Pacific: U.S. forces land on Guam.

22 **Eastern Front:** Soviets capture Chelm; surrender of German XIII Corps near Brody. Moscow radio announces formation of Polish Committee for National Liberation, which is established in Chelm later that month and moves to Lublin in August. The committee is denounced by the Polish government-in-exile in London.

Finland: Soviet forces reach 1940 Finnish frontier.

23 **France:** First Canadian Army (Gen. Henry Crerar) becomes operational on the east flank of British sector.

Eastern Front: Third Baltic Front captures Pskov, last major prewar Soviet city occupied by the Germans.

24 **France:** Allied air forces begin bombing German positions in preparation for Operation Cobra.

Eastern Front: First Belorussian Front captures Lublin, liberates Majdanek death camp; First Belorussian Front crosses San R. northwest of Lwów.

Italy: After entering south Pisa the previous day, U.S. Fifth Army begins regrouping along Arno.

Pacific: U.S. forces land on Tinian.

25 **France:** U.S. First Army launches Operation Cobra in St.-Lô area.

Eastern Front: Elements of First Belorussian Front reach Vistula R. east of Radom.

26 **Eastern Front:** Leningrad Front takes Narva (Estonia).

27 **France:** U.S. First Army breaks through German defenses west of St.-Lô, between Lessay and Périers.

Eastern Front: Divinsk (Latvia) falls to Second Baltic Front; Second Belorussian Front captures Bialystok; First Belorussian Front crosses Vistula at Magnuszew; First Ukrainian Front takes Lwów and Stanislav.

28 **France:** U.S. First Army captures Coutances.

Eastern Front: First Belorussian Front storms Brest-Litovsk, First Ukrainian Front takes Jaroslav and Przemyśl.

Pacific: End of organized Japaneses' resistance on Biak (New Guinea).

29-30
Eastern Front: First Ukrainian Front establishes bridgeheads across Vistula south of Sandomierz; First Belorussian Front advances toward Warsaw; Third Belorussian Front crosses Niemen R.

30 **France:** U.S. First Army forces enters Avranches. British Second Army attacks south from Caumont toward Vire.

Eastern Front: Germans counter attack Soviet forces northeast of Warsaw.

31 **France:** U.S. First Army captures Granville.

Eastern Front: First Baltic Front captures Jelgava (Latvia); First Belorussian Front captures Siedlce; Third Belorussian Front enters Kaunus, capital of Lithuania.

August

1 **France:** U.S. Third Army (Lt. Gen. George S. Patton) becomes operational on right flank of Allied line. U.S. First and Third Armies constitute U.S. 12th Army Group, which becomes operational under Lt. Gen. Omar N. Bradley. British Second Army and Canadian First Army constitute 21st Army Group under Field Marshall Bernard L. Montgomery. The breakout from Normandy is underway: U.S. Third Army pours through the Avranches gap, sending two corps (VIII and XX) into Brittany while one corps (XV) advances southeast toward Le Mans. First Army drives toward Mortain and Vire; British Second Army attacks south toward Villers-Bocage; Canadian First Army drives south from Caen.

Eastern Front: Polish Home Army launches uprising in Warsaw. Elements of First Belorussian Front reach outskirts of Praga district on east bank of Vistula. The Red Army's advance in this sector comes to a halt; the Soviets provide little assistance to Home Army, which will fight on for another two months, finally surrendering on 2 October. Kaunus falls to Third Belorussian Front. First Baltic Front reaches Gulf of Riga west of

Riga but is unable to cut off Army Group North.

3 **France:** U.S. First Army overruns Mortain.

Eastern Front: First Ukrainian Front establishes bridgehead across Vistula at Baranov.

Asia: Myitkyina falls to U.S. and Chinese forces.

4 **France:** German forces in Brittany withdraw into ports of St.-Malo, Brest, Lorient, and St.-Nazaire. Despite attempts to capture them, the latter two will hold out until the end of the war. Third Army captures Rennes. British Second Army captures Villers-Bocage and begins pivoting eastward while Canadian First Army drives on Falaise.

Italy: British Eighth Army enters Florence; Allied forces in Italy begin regrouping for assault on German Gothic Line in the north Apennines.

5 **France:** U.S. Third Army takes Mayenne and Vanne, thereby isolating Brittany Peninsula.

6 **France:** U.S. First Army takes Vire. U.S. Third Army advances on Lorient; other elements (XV Corps) cross Mayenne R. and drive on Le Mans. Germans counterattack British Second Army between Vire and Mount Pincon.

7 **France:** German XLVII Pz Corps counterattacks at Mortain (U.S. First Army sector), recapturing the town and advancing toward Avranches. U.S. Third Army reaches Brest and Lorient. Canadian First Army launches Operation Totalize, striking south of Caen toward Falaise to cut off German forces retreating from British Second Army; encounters strong resistance from 12th SS Pz Div.

8 **France:** Driving east from Mayenne R., U.S. Third Army's XV Corps enters Le Mans. Germans still attacking in Avranches-Mortain area.

Eastern Front: Germans launch strong counterattack on Soviet bridgehead at Magnuszew; fighting continues in this area through mid-August.

9 **France:** Heavy fighting in Mortain-Avranches area. Elements of U.S. First Army drive northeast toward Alençon, advancing to meet 21st Army Group forces attacking south in order to trap German forces west of Falaise. In Brittany, fighting continues at Brest, St.-Malo, Dinard, and Lorient. From Le Mans, U.S. XV Corps swings north toward Alençon.

10 **France:** In Mortain-Avranches area, U.S. First Army has contained German counterattack and is pushing enemy back toward Mortain. U.S. Third Army captures Angers, reaches Nantes and Loire R.

Eastern Front: Second Belorussian Front crosses Narew R. near Bialystok. By now, however, the main Soviet summer offensive is all but halted because of stiffening German resistance, Soviet casualties, and Soviet logistical and communications difficulties. To date in the Bagration, Lwów-Sandomierz, and Brest-Lublin operations, the Soviets have advanced over 400 miles from starting points on the Dnieper, reaching the East Prussian Frontier and driving through northern and central Poland across the Vistula and Narew. In the process the Red Army has destroyed more than 30 German divisions, with German Army Group Center losing upwards of 450,000 men, more than half its strength before 22 June.

11 **France:** Hitler agrees to partial withdrawal of panzer forces from Mortain salient to counter threat to Allied threat in Falaise area.

Eastern Front: Third Baltic Front attacks, breaks through enemy lines south of Lake Peipus and advances northward.

12 **France:** U.S. XV Corps captures Alençon, advances to Argentan. U.S. First Army retakes Mortain, completing defeat of German forces in Avranches-Mortain area.

13 **France:** Bradley orders U.S. XV Corps to halt south of Argentan. German forces begin withdrawing from Falaise pocket through Argentan-Falaise gap.

15 **France:** Operation Anvil-Dragoon: U.S. Seventh Army and French forces invade southern France, landing on the coast of Provence between Toulon and Cannes. In Normandy, U.S. Third Army's XV Corps advances northeast toward Dreux. U.S. First Army's V Corps overruns Tinchebray at west end of Falaise pocket, linking up with British Second Army. Allies are now compressing Falaise pocket with attacks from west and north (British and Canadians) and south (U.S. First Army).

16 **France:** Canadian First Army (II Corps) encircles and enters Falaise, British I Corps (part of Canadian First Army) advances east along coast toward Seine R. U.S. Third Army takes Dreux (XV Corps) and Orleans (XII Corps).

17 **France:** Falaise falls to Canadian First Army; U.S. Third Army's XX Corps takes Chartres. In Brittany, St.-Malo surrenders to Third Army forces. Allies exert unrelenting pressing on Falaise pocket while trying to close Argentan-Falaise gap. Without consulting Hitler, von Kluge orders withdrawal of German forces from pocket; he is sacked and replaced as CinC West by Field Marshal Model.

Eastern Front: Germans counterattack in area of Šiauliai (Lithuania) to prevent isolation of Riga by Soviets. Third Belorussian Front reaches East Prussian frontier at Sesupe R.

18 **Eastern Front:** First Ukrainian Front captures Sandomierz.

19 **France:** Von Kluge commits suicide. Canadian and Polish units advancing south from Falaise make contact with elements of U.S. First Army at Chambois, closing Falaise Gap and trapping elements of German Fifth Panzer Army and Seventh Army. French Forces of the Interior (FFI) launch uprising in Paris; Germans arrange armistice with the resistance fighters, lasting until the 23rd, to allow for withdrawal of German forces. Elements of U.S. Third Army's XV Corps crosses Seine at Mantes-Gassicourt, north of Paris.

20 **France:** U.S. Third Army crosses Seine near Mantes-Gassicourt. U.S. First Army captures Argentan; final German attempts to break out of Falaise pocket thwarted by Canadian First Army.

Eastern Front: Soviet Second and Third Ukrainian Fronts start Iasi-Kishinev offensive in Rumania against German Army Group South Ukraine.

21 **France:** Falaise pocket is liquidated; Germans losses amount to about 50,000 captured, 10,000 killed. About 20,000 Germans have escaped across the Seine. Allied armies begin swift advance east and northeast in pursuit of retreating German forces. Third Army's XII Corps, on right flank of Allied line, captures Sens. In south, Allied forces capture Aix-en-Provence.

22 **France:** French 2nd Armd Div and U.S. 4th Inf Div ordered to help FFI liberate Paris. U.S. forces enter Grenoble.

Eastern Front: Second Ukrainian Front captures Iasi.

23 **France:** In Paris, armistice between FFI and Germans expires with the city largely controlled by the French. Third Army's XX Corps takes Fontainebleu, south of Paris, and advances toward Montereau.

Eastern Front: In Rumania, Soviet forces trap large formations of German-Rumanian Sixth Army southwest of Kishinev between Prut and Dniester Rivers; Third Ukrainian Front captures Bendery, encircles Rumanian Third Army along Black Sea coast. Marshal Ion Antonescu, Rumanian dictator, deposed in *coup d'etat* and arrested; King Michael surrenders unconditionally to the Soviets.

24 **France:** Fighting resumes in Paris; French and U.S. forces advance on the city. U.S. Third Army elements cross Seine at Melun and Montereau. U.S. Seventh Army liberates Cannes.

Eastern Front: In Rumania, Soviets take Kishinev; Rumanian Third Army surrenders; elements of German Sixth and Rumanian Eighth Armies flee west and south.

25 **France:** The German governor of Paris, General Dietrich von Choltitz, has been told by Hitler to raze the city, but he disregards the order. French and U.S. troops enter the French capital and von Choltitz surrenders his forces to the French commander, General Jacques Leclerc. All four Allied armies in Northwest France have now reached the Seine, ending the Battle of Normandy eighty days after the D-Day landings. But fighting continues in Brittany, where U.S. Third Army's VIII Corps assaults Brest. British Second Army crosses Seine at Vernon, prepares to cross at Louviers. In southern France, U.S. forces capture Avignon.

Italy: British Eighth Army attacks across Matauro R., beginning main assault on German Gothic Line.

Eastern Front: Rumania declares war on Germany. Third Baltic Front captures Tartu (Estonia).

Finland: Finnish government asks Soviets for peace terms.

26 **France:** Canadian First Army crosses the Seine south of Rouen and advances on Calais; British Second Army expands Vernon bridgehead, advancing toward Belgium; U.S. First Army drives northeast from Paris.

Eastern Europe: In Rumania, Third Ukrainian Front reaches Danube R. east of Gala±i; Second Ukrainian Front advances through Foc§ani-Gala±i Gap; Soviet armored formations reach Siret R., cutting off escape by German and Rumanian forces. Bulgaria declares its neutrality, begins peace negotiations with Allies, orders German troops within its borders to be disarmed.

27 **France:** Canadian First Army reaches mouth of Seine, begins crossing river between Pon-de-l'Arche and Elbeuf. British Second Army crosses Seine at Louviers; U.S. First Army crosses Marne R. near Mieux; U.S. Third Army crosses Marne at Chateau-Thierry.

Eastern Front: Second Ukrainian Front takes Focsani; Third Ukrainian Front captures Galati.

28 **France:** Allied armies continue expanding bridgeheads across Seine and advancing

eastward, but difficulties in keeping the armies supplied are hindering progress. Surrender of German forces in Toulon and Marseilles.

Eastern Front: Second Ukrainian Front advances through Oituz Pass (Carpathian Mountains) into Transylvania. Hungary announces it will seek peace with Soviets.

29 **France:** U.S. First Army captures Soissons, crosses Aisne R.; U.S. Third Army advances toward Meuse R., captures Reims. British Second Army completes crossing Seine, advances toward Somme R. at Amiens.

Eastern Europe: In Rumania, Third Ukrainian Front takes Constanta; destruction of German Sixth Army and Rumanian Eighth Army is completed. Beginning of partisan uprising in Slovakia (suppressed by Germans in early October).

30 **France:** Canadian First Army captures Rouen. Laon falls to U.S. First Army. General Charles de Gaulle establishes Provisional Government in Paris. U.S. Seventh Army captures Nice.

Eastern Front: Second Ukrainian Front captures Ploesti oil fields (Rumania).

31 **France:** British forces capture Amiens, cross Somme R.; U.S. Third Army crosses Meuse at Verdun and Commercy.

Italy: British Eighth Army breaks through Gothic Line.

Eastern Front: Soviets capture Bucharest.

September

On 1 September, General Eisenhower assumed supreme command of Allied ground forces in Northwest Europe. Three days later he issued orders for an advance on a broad front, with General Montgomery's Twenty-First Army Group on the left driving toward the Ruhr and, on the right, General Bradley's Twelfth Army Group advancing toward the Saar. But supply and fuel shortages were reining in the Allied armies, slowing the pace of operations in some sectors and halting it altogether in others. Adding to their difficulties was the Wehrmacht's recovery from the defeat in Normandy, a process not unrelated to the failure to annihilate the totality of German forces at Falaise. The British liberated Brussels on the 3rd and Antwerp the next day, but Antwerp's substantial port facilities remained unusable for supply purposes because the Germans still controlled the seaward approaches to the city along the Scheldt Estuary. On 11 September elements of the U.S. 5th Armored Division crossed into Germany over the Our River at Stalzemberg, and U.S. First Army's assault on the West Wall south of Aachen (12-15 September) resulted in additional incursions into German territory. But the Allies were unable to exploit these penetrations, thus providing the Germans with the breathing room needed to regroup and strengthen their defenses. With autumn approaching, the war in the West had entered a new phase, one that would soon see the defeat of a major Allied offensive, Operation Market-Garden (17-26 September), and with it any realistic hope that the war would be over by the end of the year.

In the East, September found the Red Army halted on the east bank of the Vistula opposite Warsaw while the Germans systematically crushed the Home Army's uprising in the Polish capital. Whether Soviet inaction in this sector was deliberate or not remains open to debate, but the result was the same in either case: the fighting arm of the anti-Communist Polish Home Army was decimated, thus opening the way for the imposition of Communist rule in Poland after the war. Also in September two more members of the Axis deserted the alliance when

Finland and Bulgaria made peace with the Soviet Union; on the 7th Bulgaria, following the example set by Rumania the previous month, switched sides with a formal declaration of war against Germany. In mid-September the Soviets resumed operations against German Army Group North, overrunning Estonia, Latvia and most of Lithuania, and trapping German forces in Lithuania's Courland Peninsula. In the south, the Red Army drove through Bulgaria and Rumania, advancing into Hungary and Yugoslavia at the end of month. With the Soviets poised for a thrust toward Belgrade, the Germans evacuated the Greek islands and prepared to withdraw from the Greek mainland, a movement that was accomplished in October.

Sources

Badsey, Stephen. *Normandy 1944: Allied Landings and Breakout*. Osprey Military Campaign Series, no. 1. London: Osprey Publishing, 1993.

D'Este, Carlo. *Decision in Normandy*. New York: HarperCollins, 1994.

Erickson, John. *The Road to Berlin*. Boulder, Colorado: Westview Press, 1983.

Glantz, David M., and Jonathan M. House. *When Titans Clashed: How the Red Army Stopped Hitler*. Lawrence, Kansas: University Press of Kansas, 1995.

Greenfield, Kent R., ed. *Command Decisions*. Washington, D.C.: U.S. Army Center of Military History, 1994.

Keegan, John, ed. *The Times Atlas of the Second World War*. New York: Harper & Row, 1989.

Messenger, Charles. *The Chronological Atlas of World War Two*. New York: Macmillan, 1989.

Pitt, Barrie, and Frances Pitt. *The Month-by-Month Atlas of World War II*. New York: Summit Books, 1989.

Salmaggi, Cesare, and Afredo Pallavisini, comp. *2194 Days of War: An Illustrated Chronology of the Second World War*. Translated by Hugh Young. New York: Barnes & Noble, 1993.

Sommerville, Donald. *World War II Day By Day*. Greenwich, CT: Brompton Books, 1989.

Williams, Mary H., comp. *Chronology: 1941-1945*. The United States Army in World War II, Special Studies, vol. 4. Washington, D.C.: U.S. Army, Office of the Chief of Military History, 1960.

Zaloga, Steven J. *Bagration 1944: The Destruction of Army Group Centre*. Osprey Military Campaign Series, no. 42. London: Reed International Books, 1996.

Contributors

Stephen E. Ambrose is Director of the Eisenhower Center and Boyd Professor of History at the University of New Orleans, and is president of the national D-Day Museum in New Orleans. He is the author of numerous books on historical subjects and personalities, including *Undaunted Courage: Meriwether Lewis, Thomas Jefferson, and the Opening of the American West* (1996), *D-Day, June 6 1944: The Climactic Battle of World War II* (1994), *Band of Brothers* (1992), and *Eisenhower: Soldier and President* (1985).

Joseph M. Balkoski is the author of *Beyond the Beachhead: The 29th Infantry Division in Normandy* (1989) and a contributor to Simon & Schuster's *D-Day Encyclopedia* (1993). He has also been involved in creating a realistic, computer-driven simulation of modern naval operations.

Clay D. Blair is a writer specializing in military history. After serving on a submarine in the Pacific during World War II, he was national security correspondent for *Time, Life,* and the *Saturday Evening Post*, and editor in chief of the *Saturday Evening Post*. He is the author of twenty-four books of non-fiction and fiction, including *Hitler's U-boat War: The Hunters, 1939-1942* (1997), *The Forgotten War: America in Korea 1950-1953* (1987), *A General's Life* (with Omar N. Bradley, 1983), and *Silent Victory: The U.S. Submarine War Against Japan* (1975).

Martin Blumenson is the author of sixteen books and numerous articles dealing with military history, including *Discovering the Rommel Murder: The Life and Death of the Desert Fox* (with Charles F. Marshall, 1994), *The Battle of the Generals: The Untold Story of the Falaise Gap* (1993), *Patton: The Man Behind the Legend,* 1885-1945 (1984). He has taught at the Naval War College, Acadia, the Citadel, the Army War College, the National War College, and other institutions of higher learning.

Colonel Vitalii N. Bogdanov is an author who writes on Russian military affairs. He is affiliated with the Institute of Military History of the Ministry of Defense, Russian Federation.

Klaus-Richard Böhme is Associate Professor and Director, Department of Military History at the Swedish War College in Stockholm. A prolific writer, he has also served as an archivist at the National Archives of Sweden and as a lecturer at the Universities of Uppsala and Stockholm.

Commander Thomas B. Buell USN (Ret.) is Writer-in-Residence at the University of North Carolina at Chapel Hill, and a guest lecturer at Duke University and the University of North Carolina. He has the author of *The Second World War: Europe and the Mediterranean* (1989), *Master of Sea Power: A Biography of Fleet Admiral Ernest J. King* (1980), and *The Quiet Warrior: A Biography of Admiral Raymond A. Spruance* (1974).

D'Ann Campbell is Dean of the College of Arts and Sciences and Professor of History at Austin-Peay State University. She is the author of *Women at War with America: Private Lives in a Patriotic Era* (1984) and numerous articles on women during World War II, and women in the military.

Brigadier General James L. Collins Jr., USA (Ret.) was coeditor of the *D-Day Encyclopedia*. He graduated from West Point in 1939 and served as an artillery officer in World War II, landing on Utah Beach in Normandy. After retiring from he army in 1969, General Collins was twice called back to active duty, serving as Chief of Military History from 1970 to 1982. He is the author of *Undercover Fighters: The British 22nd SAS Regiment* (1985), *The Marshall Cavendish Illustrated Encyclopedia of World War II* (with Eddy Bauer and Peter Young, 1985), and *Allied Participation in Vietnam* (with Stanley Larsen, 1975).

Lieutenant Colonel Steve E. Dietrich, USA is Chief of the Military Studies Branch in the Research and Analysis Division of the U.S. Army Center for Military History. Since graduating from the U.S. Military Academy in 1976 he has served as an army armor officer and historian. Steve Dietrich was the moderator for Panel 2.

Lieutenant Colonel John A. English retired from the Canadian regular army in 1993 after thirty-five years' service. He is currently Professor of Strategy at the U.S. Naval War College. An editor and contributor to several publications dealing with military affairs, he is the author of *The Canadian Army and the Normandy Campaign: A Study of Failure in High Command* (1991), *On Infantry* (1994), and *Marching Through Chaos: The Descent of Armies in Theory and Practice* (1996).

Alan Gropman is Professor of History at the Industrial College of the Armed Forces. He teaches courses in both the Strategy and Resources Departments and mentors student research. Retiring in 1986 from the Air Force after twenty-seven years of commissioned service, he became a Senior Principle Analyst and Program Manager for SYSCON Corporation. He is the author of *Air Power and Airlift Evacuation of Kham Duc* (1979). Alan Gropman was the moderator for Panel 1.

Kenneth Hagan joined the history faculty at the U.S. Naval Academy in 1973. He recently retired as the Naval Academy Archivist and Museum Director to devote himself to writing books on naval history. His most recent book is *This People's Navy: The Making of American Sea Power* (1991). Kenneth Hagan was the moderator for Panel 4.

John B. Hattendorf is Ernest J. King Professor of Maritime History and director of the Advanced Research Department at the U.S. Naval War College in Newport, Rhode Island. He has earned degrees in history from Kenyon College, Brown University, and the University of Oxford, where he received his Ph.D. in Modern History. He is the author and editor of many works in the field of naval and maritime history; among his most recent volumes are *Maritime History: The Age of Discovery* (1996) ; *Ubi Sumus?: The State of Naval and Maritime History* (1994); and *Doing Naval History* (1995).

Major General John W. Huston USA (Ret.) flew a combat tour with the Eighth Air Force as a nineteen-year-old officer in World War II, including a mission on D-Day. He subsequently earned a Ph.D. from the University of Pittsburgh. He served as Chief Historian of the U.S. Air Force from 1976 to 1981 and has taught at the U.S. Naval Academy and the U.S. Air Force Academy. He has published in journals and has edited the World War II diaries of General Henry H. "Hap" Arnold.

Bruce W. Menning is an instructor of strategy in the Department of Joint and Combined Operations at the U. S. Army Command and General Staff College. He holds a Ph.D. in history from Duke University and is a specialist in Russian and Soviet military affairs. His publications include numerous articles and a book, *Bayonets Before Bullets: The Imperial Russian Army, 1861-1914* (1992).

Brigadier General John W. Mountcastle, USA is chief of Military History and commander, U.S. Army Center of Military History. Other assignments include two combat tours in Vietnam, and teaching at West Point. He has also served as chief of staff of the U.S. Army Combined Arms Command and Fort Leavenworth, and as the director of the Strategic Studies Institute, U.S. Army War College. He holds a Ph.D. in history from Duke University. Brigadier General Mountcastle was the moderator for Panel 5.

Geoffrey Perret served in the U.S. Army from 1958-61. After earning his M.A. from Harvard, he attended a year of law school at the University of California, Berkeley, before deciding to become a writer. He is the author of several books on military history, including *Ulysses S. Grant: Soldier and President* (1997), *Old Soldiers Never Die: The Life of Douglas MacArthur* (1996), *Winged Victory: The Army Air Forces in World War II* (1993), and *There's a War to Be Won: The United States Army in World War II* (1991).

Captain-Dr. Werner Rahn, GN is Commanding Officer of the German Military History Research Office in Potsdam, Germany. He holds a Ph.D. from Hamburg University and has published on the history of naval warfare in World Wars I and II. Capt.-Dr. Rahn is coauthor of volume 6 of the *The Global War*, published in Stuttgart in 1990.

Andy Rooney has been a writer-producer with CBS-TV News since 1959, appearing regularly as a commentator-essayist on *60 Minutes*. He served in the army from 1941-45 as a reporter for *Stars and Stripes* and is the author of several books, including *The Story of Stars and Stripes* (with O.C. Hutton, 1946 and 1970), *Word For Word* (1986), *Not That You Asked* (1989), and, most recently, the autobiographical *My War* (1995).

Paul Stillwell is Director of the History Division at the U.S. Naval Institute in Annapolis. He is the editor of *Assault on Normandy: First-Person Accounts from the Sea Services*. His 1993 book, *The Golden Thirteen: Recollections of the First Black Naval Officers*, was selected by *The New York Times* as one of its notable books for 1993. His most recent book is *Battleship Missouri: An Illustrated History*. Paul Stillwell was the moderator for Panel 3.

H. P. Willmott is Senior Research Fellow, Institute for the Study of War and Society at De Montfort University. A former senior lecturer in the Department of War Studies at the Royal Military Academy Sandhurst, he served six years in the reserve with Special Forces and has taught at other institutions of higher learning. He has written extensively on warfare in general and the Second World War in particular. His books include: *Empires in the Balance: Japanese Allied Pacific Strategies to April 1942* (1982), *The Barrier and the Javelin: Japanese Allied Pacific Strategies, February to June 1942* (1984), and *The Great Crusade: A New Complete History of the Second World War* (1990). He is currently preparing a new book entitled *When Men Lost Faith in Reason: A Study of War, Society and the Twentieth Century, 1945 1968*.

The Greatest Thing We Have Ever Attempted

Conference Sponsors

The First Division Museum is located in Wheaton, Illinois, on the grounds of Cantigny, the estate of the late Colonel Robert R. McCormick. Its state-of-the-art facility features innovative exhibits and presentations on the history of the division, a gallery for temporary exhibits, and the Colonel Robert R. McCormick Research Center. Containing more than forty-five hundred books, periodicals, microfilm, and other research materials, the center provides an environment for the serious study of the division and general military history. The center is open to the scholars, students, veterans, and persons interested in this subject area.

The U.S. Naval Institute traces its origins to 9 October 1873, when a group of fifteen U.S. Navy officers began meeting at the U.S. Naval Academy's Department of Physics and Chemistry to discuss the serious implications of the smaller, post-Civil War Navy and other matters of professional interest. The "proceedings" of those discussions were eventually published and read throughout the fleet. Today, at another crossroads–in the post-Cold War world– *Proceedings* continues to be a forum for the open discussion of issues important to the armed services of the United States. In addition, the Naval Institute's Seminar Program brings the issues alive with an ambitious schedule that includes one of the premier military seminars in the country, the Annual Meeting and Annapolis Seminar each April. A member of the Association of American University Presses, the Naval Institute Press publishes approximately sixty book titles each year. The Naval Institute currently has a worldwide membership of more than one hundred thousand naval professionals and supporters.

The Greatest Thing We Have Ever Attempted

Index

Abrams, Gen. Creighton, 65
Air-ground coordination, 46
Air-sea cooperation, failures of, 46-47
Air superiority, Allied, 14, 17, 35, 55, 57, 99-100, 113, 116-17, 121
Alexander, Field Marshal Harold, 7-8, 15, 57, 103
Allen, Maj. Gen. Terry de la Mesa, 103
Alliance warfare, 178-82
Allied victory, nature of, and reasons for, 173-75, 177-79
Amphibious operations, 22, 25, 28-29, 31, 43-45, 47, 82, 99, 107, 146
Arnold, Gen. Henry H. ("Hap"), 32, 34-36, 43, 115, 119
Atlantic Wall, 14, 17, 143
Atomic bomb, 59, 117

Battle of the Atlantic, 22, 28, 98
Battle of Britain, 114
Battle of the Bulge, 15, 79, 90, 147
Belorussia, Soviet offensive in, 127-28, 137-40, 145, 147, 151
Berlin, 13, 115, 127, 147
Black troops, 38
Bradley, Lt. Gen. Omar N., 8, 13-14, 32, 39-40, 42, 57, 80-82, 87-88, 90, 98, 101-104, 122-23, 187
Brereton, Lt. Gen., Lewis, 114
British-American alliance, 51-58, 60, 82
British policy, Overlord, 51-54, 56, 58; reaction to Eisenhower as leader, 60-61
Brooke, Field Marshal Alan, 7, 30, 53-54, 61
Buchenwald, 159, 161

Caen, 9-11, 90, 97, 157, 181-82
Cairo Conference, 29-30
Canada's contribution to Normandy operation, 66, 73-78
Casablanca Conference, 55, 115
Casualties, civilian, 166-67; Normandy, 37-38, 43, 181-1; Soviet, 181
Cherbourg, 61-62, 65
Churchill, Winston, 13, 29, 57, 60-61, 75, 114-16, 119, 137, 145-46, 153
Clark, Lt. Gen. Mark W., 33, 56, 80
Collins, Maj. Gen. J. Lawton, 103, 120
Combined Chiefs of Staff (CCS), Allied, 27-29
Coningham, Air Vice Marshal Arthur, 114

Deception, 8-9, 26, 97, 108, 117
De Gaulle, Gen. Charles, 13
Democracy vs totalitarianism, 16-17, 165-66, 169-71, 188, 192
Dieppe Raid, 93, 142
Dönitz, Adm. Karl, 141, 149, 152-53
Doolittle, Lt. Gen. James H., 114

Eaker, Lt. Gen. Ira C., 115
Earlier invasion of Normandy, 14-15, 51-57, 59, 61-62, 145
Eisenhower, Gen. Dwight D., 29, 31, 80, 86-87, 102-104, 107, 113-14, 116, 121, 146, 153, 157, 171, 187, 191 ; ability to maintain good relations with British, 7-8, 11, 13-14, pivotal role of in Overlord, 7-8, 11, 13-14, 30, 32, 42, 61

Falaise Gap, Battle of, 63, 66-67, 77, 79-83, 179; failure of victory to knock Germany out of war, 80-83, 88, 90

Finland, 133-34, 152
First Canadian Army, 73, 76-77
1st Infantry Division, U.S., 1, 65, 69, 85
4th Infantry Division, U.S., 10, 16, 25, 38, 87-88
Fredendall, Maj. Gen. Lloyd, 14, 22, 103

Germany, ineffectual response to Normandy invasion, 15-17, inferior production, 152; leadership strategy, 150-51; military, nature of, 88-90

Halsey, Adm. William, 41, 44
Harris, Air Chief Marshal Arthur, 114-16, 119
Hedgerows, 9-11, 15, 65, 82, 157
Hitler, Adolf, 16-17, 38, 47, 90, 128, 132-33, 141-42, 144-45, 147-53, 166, 169, 171, 174, 180-81
Hodges, Lt. Gen. Courtney H., 32, 40, 104
Huebner, Maj. Gen. Clarence R., 33, 85

Images of war, 182-83, 186, 188, 190-91
Intelligence, Allied, 9
Italian campaign, 28, 55-57, 60, 62, 76, 80, 144

Joint Chiefs of Staff, U.S., 8, 27-28, 60, 104

King, Adm. Ernest J., 7, 21-22, 41-42, 44, 54, 59-60, 75-76; attitude toward Russia, 27-28; contribution to Overlord, 27-30; relations with British, 28
Kirk, Rear Adm. Alan, 107, 120
Knox, Frank, 29

Leaders, Overlord, choice, of army, 8, 11, 13-15, 30, 42-44, 60, 80-81, 86-87; of naval, 107; of air forces, 114-17, 119; quality of, 22, 32-33, 44, 61, 74, 80-81, 98
Leigh-Mallory, Air Vice Marshal Trafford, 114, 116
Luftwaffe, 14, 35, 99-100, 113, 115, 117, 120, 142

MacArthur, Gen. Douglas, 7, 31, 33, 104, 191
McNair, Lt. Gen. Lesley J., 69, 86, 92
Marshall, Gen. George C., 7, 21, 27-29, 31, 35, 42-44, 53-55, 59-60, 62, 69, 86-87, 102-103, 186
Matériel for Overlord, importance of, 33-36, 47
Media and the military, 161
Military historians, role and nature of, 185-193
Montgomery, Field Marshal Bernard L., 7-11, 13, 15, 75, 80, 82, 103, 122, 146, 149, 191
Moon, Rear Adm. Donald, 120
Morgan, Lt. Gen. Frederick, 116
Moscow, 127, 131-32

National Guard roundout brigades, 65-66, 69-72, 85-86, 103, 181
Naval gunfire support, 44-47, 110, 123
Naval operations, Allied, 98-99, 106-110
Naval production, 28, 34, 41
Nimitz, Adm. Chester, 37, 44
Normandy landings, concepts, critical factor in Germany's defeat, 129, 141-44; importance of to Europe, 127-35
Normandy, lessons learned from, 167-68, 177-78, 189-90
North Africa landings, 27-28, 56-57, 103-104, 142
Nurses, 38

Index

Omaha Beach, 10, 16-17, 35, 38, 46, 65, 72, 85, 90-91, 98, 121-23, 171, 181
Operation Tiger, Slapton Sands, 13, 21, 25-26, 38, 85, 98, 120, 122

P-47 Thunderbolt, 157-58
Patton, Lt. Gen. George S., 8, 13-14, 45, 80-81, 86-87, 98, 102-104, 187
Prisoners of war, 127

Quebec Conference, 28, 75
Quesada, Maj. Gen. Elwood R. ("Pete"), 32, 46, 92

Ramsay, Adm. Bertram H., 107-108, 110
Red Army, 14, 127-29, 137, 146, 148-49, 151-52, 188, 192
Roosevelt, Franklin D., 7, 13, 29-30, 42, 75, 122, 137, 146, 170, 173
Royal Canadian Air Force, 76
Royal Canadian Navy, 75-76

Saipan, 29, 44
Sea power, supremacy, Allied, 27, 29, 55, 57
Sicily, 14, 22, 57, 76, 80-81, 83, 86, 103, 107, 142
Slapton Sands (see Operation Tiger)
Smith, Lt. Gen. Walter Bedell, 35, 103
Soviet Union, 28, 59, 129-35, 137-38, 141, 147, 150-51, 154, 166, 178, 189
Soviet view of Normandy landings, 145-46
Spaatz, Lt. Gen. Carl ("Tooey"), 114-16, 121, 153
Speer, Albert, 152, 174
Stalin, Josef, 28-29, 59, 129, 137-38, 145-46, 148-49, 151-52, 192
Stalingrad, 128, 152
Stark, Adm. Harold, 42
Stars and Stripes, 157

Stilwell, Lt. Gen. Joseph, 30, 102
Strategic bombing, 82, 90, 114-20, 122-23, 128, 152-53; cause of collapse of German war economy, 120-21
Surprise, importance of, 8-9
Sweden, view of Red Army dangers, 152; view of World War II outcome, 131-35

Tedder, Air Chief Marshal Arthur, 114-16, 133
Teheran Conference, Nov. 1943, 145-46
Total war concept, Allied, 167, 173-75; German, 166-67
Training (U.S. Army), failures in, 39-40, 42; importance of education, 22-23, 32-33, 37, 41, 47; quality of, 14, 21, 25, 45-46
Transportation of ground forces, 21-22, 114, 153
29th Infantry Division, U.S., 38, 40, 42, 65, 69-72, 85-86, 181
Two fronts, military effects of, 147-48

U-boats, 22, 141-42, 149, 151-53
Unconditional surrender, 148, 192
Utah Beach, 15, 17, 25, 38, 120, 157

Vandenberg, Maj. Gen. Hoyt, 114, 116
Vian, Rear Adm. Philip, 107
V-weapons, 153

War equipment, 22-23, 33-35
Warsaw Uprising, 149-50
Women in WW II, 173-74, 192-93

Zhukov, Marshal Georgii, 146, 151
Zuckerman, Solly, 114, 116, 153

The Greatest Thing We Have Ever Attempted